The War Game

The War Game

A Critique of Military Problem Solving

Garry D. Brewer
and
Martin Shubik

HARVARD UNIVERSITY PRESS
Cambridge, Massachusetts
and London, England
1979

066313

Library of Congress Cataloging in Publication Data

Brewer, Garry D
  The war game.

  Includes bibliographical references and index.
  1. War games. I. Shubik, Martin, joint author.
II. Title.
U310.B73   355.4'8   78-16411
ISBN 0-674-94600-6

Foreword

GARRY D. BREWER AND MARTIN SHUBIK conducted a broad-gauge study of models, simulations, and games; their investigation resulted in a series of reports for the Defense Advanced Research Projects Agency of the United States Department of Defense. Over the past five years, the authors have built on this information base and have produced a book of general appeal, one that includes new material, new insights, and well-considered recommendations for improvement in gaming. Thus eight years of hard professional effort and activity have produced a soundly researched, lavishly documented, and comprehensive book on war games. It is the most advanced and sophisticated book on gaming available in the English language. It is also the most critical and honest book in the field.

This book was written primarily for serious, responsible practitioners interested in improving the profession and expanding its usefulness, but it provides an instructive account of war gaming as well. It is organized so that different audiences may read it selectively, concentrating on the specific aspects of the field that are of greatest interest before considering related areas; to this end, the authors have provided a guide to direct attention and reading.

The authors' overriding objective in writing this book has been to help raise the professional standards of modeling and gaming in the United States, particularly as carried out by the Department of Defense and in defense-research organizations.

Although they stress the need to perfect methods and raise standards in this field, Brewer and Shubik show an awareness of the difficulties involved in applying new techniques and methods in organizations that function within a bureaucratic and political context, such as those in the Department of Defense, or within other analytic, research, and operational communities. They take into account the constraints imposed by economics and by the administrative necessities of these real-world settings.

What distinguishes this book from others in the field is the responsible manner in which Brewer and Shubik have advanced proposals to improve professional standards, methodologies, analytic processes, and institutional settings related to war gaming. While their main focus has been on the Department of Defense, the biggest spender in the field, they have also examined other groups that carry out modeling and gaming for research, instructional, and other purposes. Because of the importance they attach to the improvement of modeling and gaming within the Department of Defense, the authors advance many positive, detailed recommendations for reform, based on painstaking research and a sophisticated understanding of the field as a whole. Staff officers, the only group that could conceivably put the suggested reforms into practice in the Department of Defense, will find these recommendations particularly useful. Although far less money is spent on models and games by other funders in the public sector than by the Defense Department, some of the authors' recommendations—particularly their suggestions regarding greater professionalism—might profitably be considered by nonmilitary managers and administrators.

The authors call attention to a number of questionable practices in the field. Certain defense-research institutions, for instance, permit staff members to participate as experts in modeling and gaming, and other activities, in fields in which they have no professional training or qualifications. Brewer and Shubik believe that "questionable or even counterproductive results" may flow from this practice. They do not condemn the inclination of some defense researchers trained in economics to assume the roles of area experts, military historians, international-relations experts, and strategists, but they call attention to the problems created by this practice. The authors are also concerned about the tendency to deal with incredibly complex political and military problems by the use of numbers. They share the concerns expressed by Sir Solly Zuckerman in *Scientists and War: The Impact of Science on Military and Civil Affairs* (London: Hamish Hamilton, 1966):

> The total situation with which the theorists deal also contains extremely broad parameters of so qualitative a nature that no one could attribute numerical values to them. Some of these parameters are among the most important issues with which the new school of strategists pretend to deal—if not the most important. For example, they include such matters as the enemy's intentions, as well as his strength and capacity; the resolution of the people; the capacity of a country to restore itself economically when it has suffered a degree of devastation well beyond anything that lies within human comprehension—let alone experience—and other matters equally vague. These are vitally important issues. But they are not numerical issues, and probably could never be made so, even if they were ever to come within our experience. (pp.118–119)

The War Game will force other scholars, analysts, and practitioners to be aware of the dangers in this area and to be responsible for the results of the uncritical application of mathematics to the solution of defense problems in the complex world of nuclear weapons.

One of the consequences of the rush toward quantification and mathematics in gaming to which Brewer and Shubik call attention is the neglect of the role of the scenario in manual and free-form games. This neglect stems from the assumption that, if numbers count, it makes little difference who writes the scenario or what it contains. The authors present convincing reasons why this unhealthy attitude should be opposed and argue that it would be profitable to fund research on these matters in the future.

Part of the difficulty in raising the standards of the professional, a major theme of the book, results from the relatively small number of professionals involved in gaming in the United States; in the authors' words, "attacks on the priesthood . . . are made only at serious personal peril." This caveat applies to an examination of the professionalism of model builders and game directors as well as to the review of the professional standards in the areas of design, scenario construction, documentation, and attendant analyses. Brewer and Shubik remind readers that "judgment enters and colors the gaming process at several points. The factors selected to structure a war game are based on judgments, as are the assumptions and estimates used to assign input values when verifiable data are not available; the selection of game strategies is also largely a matter of judgment. Any results produced by a game must, therefore, be subjected to other scientific and experimental testing to verify their validity and worth." Judgmental factors can also be introduced by a colorful or charismatic game director whose virtuosity in leading players along the paths he wants the game to follow is often concealed by the skill with which he accomplishes it. No individual game directors of this type are mentioned by the authors, but nearly everyone familiar with gaming can remember several. They were a major factor in selling free-form games to the largest users in the 1960s.

Other, more recent problems, particularly those related to all-machine simulations, are openly and powerfully characterized by the authors. The cumulative effect of these factors has been to cause some people to question the value of modeling and gaming and to stimulate Brewer and Shubik to outline the reforms necessary for the survival, recovery, and further development of these techniques.

The authors see hope for improvements in war gaming in the possibility of increased professionalism and higher standards. They are optimistic about the future. Despite all of their reservations about past gaming activities associated with the Department of Defense, they consider them to be "remarkably rational when compared with activities in other organizations like the Departments of Energy or Health, Education, and Welfare." Brewer and Shubik feel that reforms will come about when the decision-making system and the nature of modeling and gaming problems are better understood. Their book makes a substantial contribution to the understanding of these problems, as well as a number of practical proposals for their solution.

HARVEY A. DE WEERD

Preface

THE MILITARY ANALYSIS SYSTEM is fragmented, large, and even inchoate; it considers topics that are often highly technical, if not esoteric. The institutions active in the field vary greatly; they are public, private, profit-making, nonprofit, military, civilian, and intricate hybrids and combinations of these types. The individuals responsible for the system represent a broad spectrum of academic and professional specialties and range from physicists who worry about the effects of modern weapons of war to historians who try to make sense of past conflicts. The difficulties we experienced in observing, analyzing, and understanding the military analysis system as a result of this complexity were overcome, when they were, only because of the assistance we received from numerous dedicated professionals in the field.

The War Game began in August 1970 as a broad inquiry into the state of operational modeling and gaming in the United States. Our initial investigation, which resulted in three technical research reports, was sponsored by the Defense Advanced Research Projects Agency, a research arm of the Department of Defense, and was conducted under the auspices of The Rand Corporation.

In writing this book we incurred many professional and personal debts. We are grateful to the people mentioned here; without them, the project would never have been possible.

They are in no way implicated in its form, execution, or results; for these matters we are solely responsible.

Throughout the preparation of the book and the research on which it was based, we benefited from the comments and suggestions of many professional gamers and simulators. They helped us shape our research, brought us up to date on who was currently doing what kind of work, and served as valuable sounding boards for ideas on a variety of technical topics. At the earliest stages, Jack Lind, Francis McHugh, M. G. Weiner, William Jones, Edwin Paxson, and Harold Guetzkow made important contributions. Later in the project, Norman Dalkey, Francis Kapper, Lincoln Bloomfield, Herbert Goldhamer, Maxine Rockoff, and Alice Rivlin provided useful assistance. Lieutenant Colonel Austin Kibler did yeoman service on behalf of the Defense Advanced Research Projects Agency. Throughout the course of our work, Harvey A. De Weerd, senior staff member and consultant at The Rand Corporation for the past quarter-century, was steadfast in his encouragement and support.

Members of the United States General Accounting Office were able and industrious collaborators and colleagues during the survey and questionnaire phase of our study. Among the many auditors and analysts involved at one time or another, Jerome Stolarow and John Potochney deserve special thanks for their careful attention to essential details and for their overall interest in our joint endeavors.

The final manuscript was read by and improved through the efforts of Ronald D. Brunner, J. P. Crecine, Harvey A. De Weerd, Michael Inbar, Harold D. Lasswell, Arthur Pasteris, Henry S. Rowen, and Robert Specht. Nothing else in professional work is so valuable as a thorough and critical appraisal, and we are grateful for the efforts of all our reviewers.

Our work extended over several years and found us at a variety of institutions. We appreciate the many resources and facilities afforded by The Rand Corporation. At later stages, the Center for Advanced Study in the Behavioral Sciences at Stanford, California, Yale University, and the Office of Naval Research offered support.

Typing and research assistance have been provided in ample measure and with rare good humor and patience by Eve

Savage, Twylah Lawson, Marjorie Roach, Jane Tarlow, Elizabeth Walker, Joan Pederson, and Joyce Levy. Special thanks are reserved for Janet De Land, a highly skilled and always enthusiastic editor, who somehow, albeit gently, brought order, consistency, and a modicum of style to the manuscript. At Harvard University Press, both Barbara Gale and Aida Donald provided sensitive and sensible counsel and guidance in bringing this project to a conclusion.

The epigraphs to chapters 7 and 19 are drawn from Jacques Stella, *Games and Pastimes of Children*, trans. Stanley Applebaum (New York: Dover Publications, 1969); figure 6-2 is from the Research Analysis Corporation brochure "Gaming and Simulations: A Department of the Research Analysis Corporation" (McLean, Va., n.d.). They are reprinted by permission.

GARRY D. BREWER
MARTIN SHUBIK

Contents

Illustrations

Tables

PART ONE

General Background

1 | Models, Simulations, and Games

> Well, Prince, so Genoa and Lucca are now just family es-
> tates of the Buonapartes. But I warn you, if you don't tell
> me that this means war, . . . I see that I have frightened
> you—sit down and tell me all the news.
>
> Tolstoy, War and Peace

THIS IS A BOOK about war. More precisely, it presents a critique of war-related activities broadly characterized as modeling, gaming, and simulation. We are concerned with the applications of these activities to military problems, especially those for which the United States Department of Defense is responsible. Yet our inquiry, like our subject matter, is often wide-ranging and technical. To provide the context in which these new methods of investigating military questions and those who employ them can be properly understood, we must at least sketch their implications for other types of problem solving as well.

Because this book is intended to be comprehensive in its scope and treatment of war gaming, not all parts of it will be of equal interest to all readers. While we encourage readers to try to view the field and the profession broadly, we are also aware that their interests are apt to be specialized. The following general description may help readers to choose the parts of the book on which they wish to focus their attention.

The first three parts of the book (chapters 1–10) provide a general background, history, and typology of model, simulation, and game (MSG) activities;[1] part four (chapters 11–14) presents the findings of a detailed survey of the status of operational MSGs in the Department of Defense inventory. Part five (chapters 15–16) presents our assessment of the methods of game playing that are responsible for the many problems and deficiencies discovered in our survey; attention is focused there on the context, the participants, the institutions, the processes underlying practice, and many other aspects of the professional environment. Part six (chapters 17–19) recommends changes that we believe would begin to improve current practice in the short run and to stimulate necessary longer-term professional development; what should be done, who should be doing it, when it should be done, and how much time and effort are needed to effect necessary and desirable change are topics treated at length in this part. Two technical appendixes describe the criteria used for evaluation and summarize survey questions posed.

Those who sponsor, fund, and use operational MSGs for military purposes, to cite one key group of specialists for whom this book was written, should be particularly interested in parts four, five, and six, where we report on items pertinent to their areas of managerial responsibility. Professional modelers and gamers, who are mainly responsible for design and execution, will probably concentrate on parts two, four, and six. Analysts who are interested in the historical background of the methods and who wish to consider broader applications of gaming and modeling are advised to read parts one, two, and three. Other scholars, such as those who concentrate on the bureaucratic and political aspects of knowledge and action, will be most at home with materials presented in parts one and five and, to a lesser extent, part six and appendixes A and B. Informed and concerned citizens reading the book may wish to focus their attention on parts one, five, and six, where the general background and specific institutional aspects of the system that sponsors and produces military MSGs are considered and recommendations for improvement are made.

Although we accept the fact that many readers will not approach all parts of this book with equal care or interest, we believe that this very fragmentation of knowledge and compartmentalization of responsibility have contributed in no small measure to the unsatisfactory professional practices, to the intellectually questionable methods, to the dubious results, and to the inefficient bureaucratic and political processes that are treated in this book. The ability to understand a phenomenon is closely related to the ability to describe it. An art expert's description of a painting or a physician's diagnosis of a disease differ considerably from those made by laymen. The same is true with any other complex process. Although it may be relatively easy to present an intelligible overview of gaming, simulation, or the application of analytic models, developing a useful technical description is an exceedingly difficult, professional task. Part four of this study deals with many aspects of describing a game or simulation. The busy decision maker may be willing to take the counsel of his advisers on faith. Yet without a reasonably good understanding of how to describe a game or simulation, he remains at the mercy of their judgments. He will not know many of the right questions, nor will he have a language in which to ask them.

Certain questions are popular: How much did it cost? What did we buy for the money we spent? Did it come within our budget? Did it work? All of these appear to be sensible and reasonable. They are the questions a skilled accountant, trial lawyer, or politician knows how to ask even though he has little technical background or understanding of the subject. The technique of questioning is in itself an art, but the nature of any large democratic and bureaucratic system precludes an individual's becoming expert in more than a few areas. Without either knowledge or expert assistance, the questioners may not understand the answers they receive. Baffling with science has for centuries been a potent defense against debating techniques and the trial lawyer's skill in cross-examination.

In the subject areas we investigate, the cost figures that can be obtained by means of standard accounting measures are virtually meaningless. They tell a tale of the bureaucratic allocation of dollars, but, because of problems with joint cost measurements, hidden costs, and capacity considerations, they may or may not provide information concerning the allocation of resources. Furthermore, they do not indicate the value obtained for money expended. Because there is no well-defined market mechanism to indicate these values, an investigator without a profound and sensitive technical knowledge or without the appropriate technical staff is at the mercy of bureaucratic myth making. Charts, diagrams, briefing films, and flip-chart presentations abound. What they mean is another matter, one that is properly considered from as broad a perspective and as general an understanding as can reasonably be brought to bear on it.

Activities in the Defense Department

Models, simulations, man-machine games, manual games, and analyses are employed widely by the Department of Defense. The problems and questions they are used to investigate vary considerably; their aims, specificity of purpose, and size cover a broad spectrum; and their costs range from a few thousand to many millions of dollars. The major applications of games, models, and simulations in the military area include the following:

- Technical evaluation
- Doctrinal evaluation
- Force-structure evaluation
- Analysis of military and diplomatic factors and international relations
- Analysis of military, political, and economic factors, including domestic relations
- Training and education
- Development of research methology

Technical evaluation is the evaluation of the performance of a specific weapon or device in a situation in which doctrine and force structure are given. For instance, one might be interested in determining the operational characteristics and implications of an enhanced-radiation weapon within the current NATO and Warsaw Pact context. Taking the weapons and force structure of the weapons as given, doctrinal evaluation concentrates on the study of different methods for employing given resources. One might, in this case, want to understand the interactive effects of different deployment patterns and schedules for the main elements of the strategic force, including bombers, submarine-launched missiles, and intercontinental ballistic missiles. How many of what kinds of weapons should be expended under various alert and attack conditions would be a typical question for doctrinal evaluation. Force structure evaluation is concerned primarily with problems of "product mix." It cannot be completely disassociated from doctrinal evaluation because large changes in force structure may necessitate a certain amount of modification in doctrine. All of these purposes assume that the overall military, diplomatic, and economic environment is given. Between 90 and 95 percent of Defense Department modeling and gaming is used for purposes of evaluation.

Military and diplomatic and international problems are also amenable to investigation by means of simulations and games. The expenditures of the Defense Department and other agencies for this purpose are relatively slight, although the amount of publicity and public awareness of this sort of war game and diplomatic and military exercise is far higher. There appears to be little or no integrated military, political, and economic gaming, although combining these types—as "economic warfare," for instance—has occasionally been considered and discussed within the professional gaming community. Gaming is used widely for training and educational purposes by the Department of Defense and to some extent in private industry and in universities. Expenditures for these purposes are more modest than those for the three types of evaluation. In addition, a relatively small amount of money is spent directly on developing research methodology. A percentage of the expenditures in all of the other categories, however, should be regarded as supporting research methodology.

Definitions and Questions

The use of large-scale models, computers, games, and simulations is relatively new. Professional researchers, military war gamers, social psychologists, and academic business teachers use many of the same terms, but the words convey quite different meanings to each group. Before discussing the applications of gaming and simulation in military and more general activities, we shall present some basic definitions.

Gaming. A gaming exercise employs human beings acting as themselves or playing roles in an environment that is either actual or simulated. The players may be experimental subjects or participants in an exercise being run for teaching, operational, training, planning, or other purposes.

War gaming. One of the major applications of simulation is war gaming. A war game is defined by the Department of Defense as a simulated military operation involving two or more opposing forces and using rules, data, and procedures designed to depict an actual or hypothetical real-life situation. It is used primarily to study problems of military planning, organization, tactics, and strategy. A war game can be designed to cover the entire spectrum of war—politicomilitary crises, general war, or limited war. The game may be based on hypothetical situations, real-world crises, or current operational and contingency plans. Some games are designed for joint use by two or more military services; some, for use by a single service. Others may be used by individual field commanders or even by division or battalion commanders. The level of command at which the game is to be played influences the type of units represented and the scope of operations conducted.

Three types of war games are in common use today: the training game, the operational game, and the research game. The training game is the least complex and is designed to provide the participants with decision-making opportunities similar to those they might experience in combat. The operational game deals with current organizations, equipment, tactics, and strategy; it is more complex than the training game, uses input based on known quantities, and is employed to test operational plans. The research game, the most complex of the three types, requires careful preparation to achieve maximum objectivity and is usually designed to study future tactical or strategic problems.

A war game may be accomplished manually, may be computer-assisted, or may be wholly computerized. Manual games, often called free-form games, are played using symbols, pins, or pieces to represent forces, weapons, and targets on maps, map boards, and terrain models. A computer-assisted game is a manual game using computerized models that free the control group from many repetitive and time-consuming computations. In computer, or all-machine, games, all simulation of conflict is performed by the computer in accordance with the detailed instructions contained in its program. The primary advantage of computer gaming is that the same situation can be simulated many times under differing conditions; thus the variability of results can be observed. A computer war game requires the use of a model, that is, computer program, that contains all the rules, procedure, and logic required to conduct the game.

Simulation. Simulation is the representation of a system or organism by another system or model designed to have a relevant behavioral similarity to the original. Games utilize a simulated environment, simulated roles for the players, or both. Generally speaking, all games are simulations; the reverse categorization, however, may not apply. In other words, not all simulations are usefully regarded as games. In the questionnaire we developed to survey the current status of MSGs (see appendix A), we categorized computer simulations representing conflict or cooperation, such as completely computerized battle models, as games. Some logistics or resource-allocation models in which the single, automated or live, player or team may be regarded as struggling against a statistical or strategic opponent called Nature may also be considered as games. On the other hand, simulations of machine-production scheduling or inventory control would not fit into this category.

Computer simulation is an analytic technique using mathematical and logical models to represent and study the behavior of actual or hypothetical events, processes, or systems over extended periods of time. It provides a means of gaining experience and of making and correcting errors without incurring the costs or risks of actual application. It offers opportunities to test theories and proposed modifications in systems or processes; to study organizations and structures; to examine past, present, and future events; and to use forces that are difficult or impractical to mobilize. Simulation is valuable both as an educational device and as a means of discovering and devising improved methods. It should be used when (1) it is either impossible or extremely costly to observe certain processes in the real world, (2) the observed system is too complex to be described by a set of mathematical equations, (3) no straightforward analytic technique exists for solution of appropriate mathematical equations, or (4) it is either impossible or very costly to obtain data for the more complicated mathematical models describing a system. On the other hand, simulation should not be used when (1) simpler techniques exist, (2) data are inadequate, (3) objectives are not clear, (4) short-term deadlines must be met, or (5) the problems are minor.

Model. A model is a representation of an entity or situation by something else that has the relevant features or properties of the original. The five basic types are verbal models, analytic or mathematical models, diagrammatic representations or pictures, analog simulations, and digital simulations. In practice, the words *model* and *simulation* are frequently used interchangeably; this usage confuses more than it clarifies the issues. Nearly all forms of gaming and analytic study use a simulated environment; conducting a computer or computer-assisted war game or related simulation requires the use of a computerized, that is, an analog or digital, model. As used in this context, a model is a document or program containing all the rules, methodology, techniques, procedures, and logic required to simulate or approximate reality. A computerized model is a computer program or series of programs designed to simulate the logic of actions or interactions of an environment or a context and to provide the results to player personnel for subsequent analysis.

Contract studies and analyses. Contract studies and analyses, performed under a contract or grant, examine various subjects systematically and critically. Their purpose is to provide greater understanding of alternative organizations, tactics, doctrine, policies, strategies, procedures, systems, and programs. Studies and analyses often require advanced analytic techniques to integrate a variety of factors and to evaluate data.

A number of questions remain to be answered about current uses of models, games, and simulations. Are the activities in gaming, simulation, and model building important? Is a large amount of money expended in a serious way for these activities? What has been bought for the money spent so far? Who are the instigators of the work, who are its builders, and who uses it? Who evaluates what has been bought? Is gaming purely an art form, or is there a scientific basis to the work being done? Is it used for scientific purposes or merely to support arguments in an adversary process? Have the applications and costs of these activities changed much over the last few years? Will they change in the next few years? Is it possible that the errors committed when large military models were first constructed might be committed again, as fashions and funding change, by individuals who claim to use these tools to answer questions like "What ails the central city?" and "What will our energy policy be?"

Our study represents an attempt to investigate these issues. It is not concerned only with scientific methods. It also aims at understanding the application of new techniques and methods in a decision-making system set within a bureaucratic and political context, and it deals with the economics and the alternatives as they are limited by the realities of the context. Up to now, the military services have been by far the largest users of these new techniques. This fact alone is a sufficient reason for investigating their use in war gaming, the evaluation of weapons and doctrine, gaming in a military political context, gaming with attention to international affairs, and military gaming for teaching and training purposes.

Frequently learning spills over from one application to another. Already the applications of business games have grown considerably. The development of socioeconomic simulations is not completely independent of the development of techniques for military simulation. Will expenditures grow in other areas? Will such growth, if it occurs, result from success in applying this work elsewhere? What are the dangers of misapplication in other fields? Are there lessons to be learned from the military experience in gaming and simulation that go beyond the context of military applications? With these questions in mind, we will attempt to describe the state of the art; to understand the criteria for judging quality; to view clearly actual and ideal applications and their costs; and to grasp the relationship between stated purposes and the processes by which those purposes are attained.

2 | The Scope of Operational Gaming and Simulation

> The computer has quantitatively enlarged the sort of calculations and experiments an individual scientist can take on in his lifetime, but, as far as I can tell, it has, on its own, created nothing.
>
> Jeremy Bernstein, "When the Computer Procreates"

THE MANY FORMS of gaming and simulation stretch from complex mathematical models to free-form verbal interchanges. Individuals whose world views and professional backgrounds are quite different may still regard themselves as being involved in gaming.[1] Figure 2-1 shows the four most important purposes for which MSGs are used in both military and nonmilitary activities. In this chapter, we are concerned with the first of these: operations. At least in the domain of field exercises, operational and teaching and training games overlap somewhat. It is difficult to say where the dress-rehearsal and coordination aspects of an exercise cease and where planning, testing of strategy, and exploration begin.

Operational MSGs are used almost exclusively in military, governmental, and corporate organizations. Military applications are by far the most extensive; in comparison, operational gaming by businesses is insignificant. The use of operational gaming for social planning is still in its infancy but may eventually be important. Because a great deal of money is allocated to operational gaming, and because it is such a broad area, the goals of users—for instance, a consulting firm that wants to build a large game, a general who wishes to advocate a weapons system, and a colonel assigned to play in or operate the MSG—can be extremely diverse (see fig. 2-2 for the different goals of operational gaming and simulation).

A commonly overlooked use of operational games—the

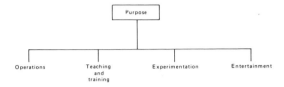

Figure 2-1. The primary purposes of models, simulations, and games.

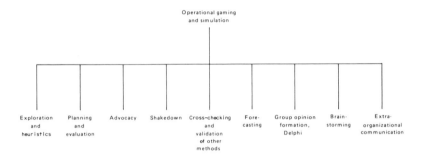

Figure 2-2. The goals of operational gaming and simulation.

heuristic—is associated with their capacity to stimulate play-ful, albeit constructive, explorations of problems that are either not well understood or misunderstood. Especially in free-form and scenario-based MSGs, the discovery or realiza-tion of unimagined difficulties and opportunities is a standard outcome. Using games in this manner may help to inform em-pirical inquiry, but it is by itself insufficient to achieve scien-tific understanding; follow-up investigations and studies must ascertain the validity and reliability of the heuristic insight.

The most prevalent and important military uses of MSGs are in technical evaluation, doctrinal evaluation, force-struc-ture evaluation, and planning. These games and simulations deal primarily with present and future weapons systems, dif-ferent ways to employ them, and logistical and economic as-pects of the weapons used for different purposes. They generally involve machine simulation, analytical models, and man-machine simulations and games.

The operational uses of games outside the military have

been extremely limited. Occasionally claims are made at meetings of professional societies such as the Operations Research Society of America (ORSA) or The Institute of Management Science (TIMS) that some gaming exercise has been put to operational use; on investigation, however, it usually turns out that the game was built by professionals more as a device for persuading managers to use gaming than as an operational tool.

Industry has used simulations and analytical models for operational purposes. A vast literature exists on production scheduling and other problems involving queues. Simulation studies have been used in the construction of hydroelectric dams and in irrigation programs, as well as in inventory control. In general, however, operational gaming involving individuals has been mainly a military activity and—judging by expenditures—operational simulation, while not purely military in content, has been predominantly military in application.

Operational MSGs are often used for advocacy. A competent designer can build a bias of almost any kind and degree into a game or simulation. Advocates of specific policies or weapons systems can load the dice so that the MSG is most likely to produce the results they want to see. Modeling and gaming are enjoyable; they are also effective as propaganda devices. Gaming has even been used to announce a basic change in policy by asking noncommitted or opposed decision makers to participate in an exercise whose outcome is a foregone conclusion. Japanese war gaming prior to Pearl Harbor appears to have been an example of such a situation.[2]

In the context of bureaucratic decision making, the confusion between the scientific roles of the construction and operation of MSGs and their use in a political, resource-claiming process is profound and critical. When the construction of large models depends on the evaluation of an environment with many characteristics that are hard to measure, the use of large-scale MSGs can easily give a false impression of scientific precision. A one-sided case can be presented, even unintentionally, by a decision maker in support of a partisan policy or position. The general and his model-building, analysis-and-study staff are frequently more than a match for a congressman and his lawyers and accountants. In spite of the great sophistication, political sensitivity, and pragmatism of members of the United States Congress, a curious naiveté, bordering on irresponsibility, pervades their half of the adversary discussion when it comes to technical matters. The one-sidedness of the struggle seems to result from a basic lack of understanding and appreciation on the part of congressmen and their staffs of the importance of expert scientific advice in the decision-making process. In addition, we may be entering an era in which, partly because of the vigorous overselling of the virtues of modeling, the use of MSGs for advocacy will spill over into nonmilitary applications as well.

An MSG may be used as a backup procedure to provide additional insight into a process investigated by another means. For example, a recommendation based on expert opinion or other empirical evidence may be presented in report form. A model-based study of the same problem might produce information or raise questions overlooked in the report. Because operational MSGs tend to be expensive in both time and money, however, the problem studied must be sufficiently important to merit the extra effort and expense.

Behavioral scientists and practitioners trying to evaluate aspects of the present situation and to forecast the future have very few hard data to go on. Unlike the natural sciences, in which experiments are performed and replicated frequently, the behavioral sciences must rely heavily on expert opinion. Until recently, little systematic thought had been given to the ways expert opinion is used in the behavioral sciences and policy professions; even less was known about techniques that might make its use optimally effective. Furthermore, little was known about the relative worth of pooled or multiple expert opinions and those of individuals. When do diminishing returns set in? What sort of controls are needed on expert interactions?

An operational MSG may be regarded, in one important guise, as a formal structure for eliciting group planning—a process involving both evaluation and prediction of the likelihood of contingencies. Olaf Helmer and Norman C. Dalkey have advocated the use of Delphi techniques, which consist of having a group of experts who are anonymous to one another

respond to questionnaires, after which the results are processed and returned so that individuals can adjust their estimates in light of the new information generated by the
collectivity.[3] Many thorny methodological and philosophical
issues are yet to be resolved in the application of Delphi techniques; Dalkey has conducted experiments to resolve some of
them.[4] Formal operational MSGs differ from Delphi techniques in the nature of the participants' motivation and its relationship to performance. So far little has been done to blend
these two approaches, but the potential for doing so in a
worthwhile way appears to be great.

Formal models, simulations, and completely computerized
games are normally used when someone is convinced that the
phenomena under study can be accurately described. When
this conviction is lacking, free-form or loosely structured
games tend to be used; in these, the information base and the
rules of procedure are modified by a control team or other expert participants as the game unfolds. Such games stress explorations into the unknown as a means of clarifying and
correcting misperceptions about the aspects of the actual
world replicated by the game. Free-form activities are, in effect, formalized brainstorming sessions. In this case, as with
Delphi, it is important to distinguish the results of pooling
knowledge from those of pooling ignorance. There is little evidence indicating that a consensus obtained by pooling nonexpert opinions about technical subjects is any better than that
obtained from individual nonexperts. Furthermore, some evidence suggests that even with experts, brainstorming sessions
favor the loudest talkers and best debaters over others who
may be better informed. This is yet another example of the
clash between science and advocacy, a major theme of this
book.

In general, an MSG is not a forecasting device, although a
good operational MSG may make use of reputable forecasting
procedures. That they are not in themselves aimed at making
predictions in no way affects the value of MSGs in indicating
new alternatives and in helping to evaluate future possibilities.[5] Forecasting and contingency planning are related but different activities. In particular, a good forecaster may not be at

all interested in the importance or usefulness of his forecast. Rather, accuracy in and of itself, not relevance to the planning phase of the policy process, may be his goal. Because an MSG may aid the coordination of forecasting activities with the policy process, however, it may be important to involve forecasters in the design and operation of MSGs intended for policy use.

Simulation, econometrics, and analytic models are occasionally used for forecasting, but this practice is fraught with dangers. Users must know clearly what they want to forecast, they should be able to judge the value to be gained from additional forecasting accuracy, and they should have confidence that the builders of the forecasting device possess a good abstraction of the system being studied. Operational uses of large-scale forecasting models are probably more common in economic and industrial than in military settings. Many economic and business applications make use of the law of large numbers—that is, the systems being modeled are stable and repetitive; in addition, in the absence of deadly conflict, there are fewer intangibles, hence more certainty, involving policy changes by one's competitors. Although economic and business forecasting with computer models is far from an exact science, expenditures on these methods are growing.[6]

There may be a game outside of the game being played. With operational MSGs it is crucial to understand both the stated and the unstated goals of the individuals involved in the exercise. In a professional seminar, for example, a free-form game could be used to establish informal means of communication. A modest game could, in this instance, be a stunning success merely by trapping two or three ranking individuals together on neutral ground for a period of time. Participants in diplomatic and military war games frequently comment on the value of being able to compare the decision-making styles of high-ranking individuals. Success in establishing communication often depends on the style and location of play. If the enterprise is held in an isolated locale for an intense period of play—three, four, or more days—the effect may be quite striking, as participants begin to live the games and identify personally with the shared experience. If, however, the exercise is played either in or near places of normal employment or intermittently over several weeks or months, most participants tend to minimize the disturbance in their set patterns.

Just as one is able to identify and classify MSGs according to the diverse purposes they serve, so, too, may one characterize them according to their dominant intellectual and methodological bases. Individuals representing many disciplines—some as disparate as theoretical mathematics and history—have made important contributions to the general corpus of modeling and gaming methods. Knowing the nature and impact of these diverse intellectual sources goes far toward understanding today's modeling and gaming environment.

3 | Methods of Modeling and Simulation

It seems to me that the very fact of our limited capacity for processing information has made it necessary for us to discover clever ways to abstract the essential features of our universe.

George A. Miller, *The Psychology of Communication*

IN THIS CHAPTER we will briefly describe the methods available and the resources needed to construct various types of models, simulations, and games. Comments made here apply to all model-building, gaming, or simulation activity, although we are primarily concerned with national-security applications.

Verbal Models

A verbal description may be a model of the phenomenon it describes. It is certainly not the same as the original; rather, it is an abstraction. In many games, verbal scenarios are used to provide background information. The best military scenarios have been written by people trained in history and the behavioral sciences. Public speakers, historians, and lawyers are generally good builders of verbal models, although neither public speakers nor lawyers think of themselves as such. When phenomena that are hard to quantify and that arise from a complex and subtle environment are modeled, a verbal description is invariably called for. Numbers alone seldom provide the necessary insight or "feel" for the situation.

A verbal abstraction is much like a representation by means of mathematics, physical devices, or computer programs, although many people who are skilled at building verbal models do not like to admit the similarity between their work and that of mathematicians or other specialists in formal representation. The relationship between verbal and more formal models

19

is obscured by the radical differences in the world views and the training of individuals involved in the two sorts of enterprise. These factors similarly impede a full, productive blending of both groups' skills and knowledge—to the detriment of many modeling enterprises. In general, mathematics tends to be poor in adjectives and limited in its descriptive power; its strength lies in its precision, logic, and parsimony. Verbal models tend to be looser, ambiguous, and prolix; they are most useful in treating nuance, subtlety, and rich detail. When a problem is complex, ill defined, and not easily quantified, as is often the case in martial matters, a verbal description may be both more natural and more valuable than a mathematical description of the same phenomenon. When the situation can be relatively well described numerically, however, the advantages of using mathematics can be enormous.

Analytic and Mathematical Models

People acquainted with formal model building, especially engineers, are most likely to think in terms of analytic, or mathematical, models that describe a situation or phenomenon in a set of equations. Mathematicians frequently employ logical models, in which the entities being described are not necessarily numerical and the model provides a set of logical relationships that can be manipulated according to formal rules.

An important requirement for the construction of a mathematical model with numerically defined variables is that the variables should be easy to describe and their units of measurement known. The firepower of a machine gun, for example, may be reasonably well defined and the unit of measurement is known (an individual bullet or the number of clips or belts fired per unit of time). "National morale," on the other hand, is not an equally well defined variable; we do not know the appropriate unit of measure, and we have very little hard knowledge about how well it can be measured. This factor may be important in analysis, however; if so, it would be extremely difficult to treat mathematically. Of course, ad hoc surrogates can easily be invented for morale or for our faith or lack of faith in our allies or an index to represent "officerlike qualities," for instance. Anyone who knows how to write an equation can combine a few of them and claim to have captured or reflected these imponderables. It is therefore necessary to guard against spurious specificity, accuracy, and precision. With a complex phenomenon, a premature mathematical model may be far worse than a verbal description that contains clear warnings about its own limitations.

Mathematical models easily become straitjackets, encompassing complicated qualitative situations in a prematurely formalized symbol system. When the model builder is not sure of the structure being modeled, premature use of mathematical representation may provide a formal model for analysis—but a model of the wrong phenomenon. A good model in general, and a good mathematical model in particular, is unrealistic. That is, it is as parsimonious as possible in its representation of the relevant features of the actual situation. In analyzing a weapons system, an uban-development program, or a war plan using a specific doctrine, some questions are always more pertinent than others. No single research method, no game or simulation is an all-purpose tool. The better and clearer the questions posed, the greater is the likelihood that a good and clear model—even a "correct" one—can be designed to answer them.

The two types of mathematical model commonly utilized in gaming and simulation activities lead to somewhat different forms of analysis. One is the sequential or dynamic model, in which relationships may be formulated in terms of difference or differential equations; description is focused on the behavior of an analytic unit, but no explicit assumptions about human motivations or rationality are made. For example, a simulation of the behavior of a group of drunks building up to a brawl in a bar may contain equations representing the behavior patterns of the individual drunk as a function of the amount of money he has, the amount of alcohol he has already consumed, the number of people in the bar, and other factors. These equations do not generally explain why the drunk does what he does; they merely describe what he will do under various circumstances. A goal-directed model, in contrast, concentrates on the behavior of each individual, which is determined by specifying his goals, applying some form of operator (for instance, all individuals will maximize or minimize their expected gains or utilities) to his and others' goals, and then solving the resultant mathematical system simultaneously in order to determine the outcome. For example, a game-theory model might be used to analyze a duel. There is a large body of literature on dueling games, games of search, and games of allocation; most of these forms have been applied to the large array of tactical and weapons-evaluation problems.

Diagrams and Maps

For many purposes, the blackboard-and-chalk talk is still among the most effective forms of briefing and description known. The materials are cheap; together they provide a flexible display device. The descriptive flexibility of a chalk diagram is generally not as great as that provided by a verbal representation, although it may be so in specific situations—try giving travel instructions without a map.

Although a map is, of course, not a country or environment itself, it may serve as an appropriate abstraction for many gaming and simulation purposes. A grid placed over a map facilitates the identification of locations; a hexagonal marker enables movement in six rather than four directions to be considered for any operational unit being modeled. Rules prescribe kinds and rates of motion—a tank may not move through deep water or at more than 40 miles per hour—and a set of markers—colored flags, blocks, or miniature tanks and other equipment—may be used to represent the resources available to each side. From this point of view, chess is a map war game, albeit a highly abstract one. Board games used for entertainment are frequently related to or, in some cases, are map war games. The board game Gettysburg, for example, stresses the railroad and logistical systems that existed in the American Civil War.

Other diagrammatic models are also important. The flow chart—most commonly found in computer programming—is a special type of diagram that stresses the sequential, logical, and dynamic aspects of a system. It is especially useful in descriptions of the planning process. Flow charts are valuable both in the structure of computer programs and as part of the analytic tools of planning. A sample flow chart is shown in figure 3-1. In this simple example, the word *start* indicates that

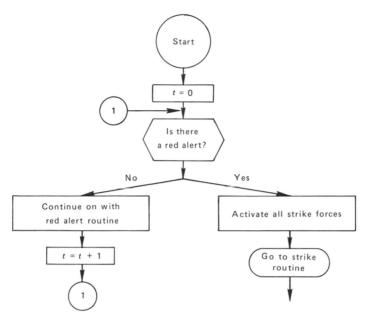

Figure 3-1. *A sample flow chart.*

the program commences with time set equal to zero. The question "Is there a red alert?" leads to two possible answers. If the answer is no, the instructions specify, "Continue on with red alert routine." This procedure is followed for the length of the period under consideration, after which an update occurs, as indicated in the instructions $t = t + 1$. On the right-hand side of this relationship, the current value of t is substituted; in this case, it equals zero. After substituting the value of t, we can calculate the new current value: $t = 0 + 1 = 1$. Having updated the system, we are now instructed by the next symbol (a circle containing the numeral 1) to reenter the program and check for the existence of a red alert. This pattern produces a looping effect; as long as a red alert does not appear, the no-attack-warning routine continues indefinitely. If, however, a red alert is finally observed, the program instructs us to "Activate all strike forces" and then proceed to another routine dealing with further procedures for the possible strike. Many simulations are built up from flow diagrams like this one, which describes the behavior of a part of a system through time. In this flow chart, the program branches after a question has been asked. Only two branches are indicated in figure 3-1; in other instances, many more branches may be used. For example, a "not certain" answer might be added to yes and no and would call for another procedure.

The use of this sort of logical switch makes it easy to ask a question in the middle of a process and then, depending on the answer, to do one of two or more things. In gaming with human players, as well as in all computer simulations, this flexibility may be valuable. Games are sometimes run in a branching mode; depending on how the situation unfolds, the play or flow of the game may go in one of several directions at certain points. Often more than one branch will interest the gamer. The game may be designed so that first one branch and then another can be explored. In other words, the players return to the decision point, which may be in the middle of the whole game, and play out another, different branch or logical sequence.

Analog Models

Systems can also be represented by analog models, that is, by a physical device that reproduces, in three dimensions, the relevant aspects of the actual system. Aircraft performance, for example, may be tested in wind tunnels with detailed, realistic representations of the exterior of the aircraft. Flood-control and harbor-design problems have been solved with the help of detailed scale models, such as the one of the San Francisco Bay area built and used by the United States Army Corps of Engineers. Realistic machine representations of an operational environment can be used to familiarize and train individuals when the costs or dangers of actual operation are excessive. Analog-digital hybrids are also used, especially in training airline pilots and crews. In the Boeing 747 simulator, flight routines and other essential elements of the in-flight environment are controlled by means of digital programs and displays and test pilot and crew performance and proficiency in response to many logical possibilities.

Analog models also include real situations that may be regarded as analogs for a whole set of other environments. The Vietnam War, for instance, provided simulations of jungle warfare in other Southeast Asian environments. Similarly, the

Germans, Russians, and Italians used the Spanish Civil War as a gaming exercise to check out future tactical and strategic operations.

Computer Simulations

Much current model building, especially in the Department of Defense, consists of the construction of computer-simulation programs. Computer simulations present both great advantages and grave dangers; in the promotional activities that have been conducted for this type of modeling, the advantages have received nearly all the attention.

The almost incredible speed and capacity of the modern, high-speed digital computer are such that systems of untold complexity may be represented and manipulated. Only twenty years ago it would have been impossible to conceive of investigating the behavior of systems that are now looked at routinely. Although the potential dangers are less well known, they are no less significant. The complicated program and the large computing machine have taken on quasi-religious overtones. Offerings are put into the black box by acolytes who are never sure what is going to come out; those who come to worship are often not sure what has happened either. Large computer programs, like large cathedrals, may be built by generations of unnamed workmen using rudimentary plans and developing technologies, subject to the vagaries of changing doctrines and leadership. With large simulations, unfortunately, unlike large cathedrals—where divine guidance was available and fairly simple empirical tests could be performed to find out whether the arches held—the whole structure may collapse or become meaningless without anyone's realizing it until many years later. New computer technology has vastly increased our ability to model human affairs, but the abuse of simulation will continue so long as confusion remains between the ability to build large models and the ability to build, understand, and control large models appropriate to the questions being studied.

Modelers and Modeling

Modeling remains, to a great extent, an art form. It can be taught, but only up to a point. After certain basic techniques have been mastered, good modeling depends upon a combination of substantive knowledge, insight, the ability to abstract, flexibility, and willingness to build and rebuild many representations of the same phenomenon in order to portray subtle nuances correctly. The five types of models described here are all important, but the problems to which they can appropriately be applied vary considerably. For example, the free-form, political and military exercise depends completely on verbal models; an all-machine analysis of a tank duel does not. Scenario writing, that is, verbal model building, is important for many types of MSGs, but it has been overlooked in the general rush toward quantification and the use of mathematical systems.

Despite large overall expenditures on modeling and simulations, almost no money has been spent on research into the methods of writing scenarios and their validity. Do two or three highly skilled writers produce approximately the same scenario, given identical background research? Are the differences that result so great that professional diplomats or generals could draw contradictory inferences from them? Painting a different backdrop for a play or an opera makes very little difference in the performance, since the actors or singers are given little or no strategic freedom; they may move their positions or vary their pitch or tone somewhat, but they do not have the option of making major changes in the dialogue or the unfolding of the action. The verbal backdrop to a free-form game, however, is far more important. We are not suggesting that free-form gaming is invalid because of possible variations in the scenario; if it is to be used for serious purposes, however, research is needed to find out what makes a good scenario, how much scenarios vary, and how much influence they have.

Drawing maps, diagrams, and pictures is also an art. Diagrams have probably contributed most in the area of economics, a field in which mere words are not sufficiently precise for description, yet problems are often far too complex and subtle for analysts to proceed immediately to formal mathematical models. The diagrammatic model provides a halfway house. Furthermore, the use of the blackboard or pencil and paper allows models to be tried out inexpensively, explained to those concerned, and discarded if they are faulty. It is much easier to throw away an essentially costless model with substantive flaws than an expensive, large-scale computer program that even professionals may not understand—either because the model is not comprehensible or because of the time involved in trying to communicate the model's content and results. The two models may be equally useless, but the blackboard version is easily destroyed and replaced, while the computer program is not.

Map and board games and table exercises are likewise relatively cheap. Important problems related to abstraction and detail exist even in the construction of maps for simple wargaming exercises, however. How important, for example, is the presence of plowed fields or swamps to the progress of the troops and units being represented? If details like these are omitted, inaccurate conclusions can easily be drawn from exercises based on the map. Diagrams and mathematical models are closely related. In economics and mathematics, simple diagrams may be used as preliminaries to the construction of a mathematical model. The Edgeworth Box, developed for use in economics studies, is a simple, ingenious, and adequate representation of a four-dimensional phenomenon in two dimensions.[1] In essence, it is a diagrammatic explanation of the existence of a price system in an economy and requires far less skill and sophistication than the mathematical formulation and representation of the same problem.

The flow chart has greatly simplified the portrayal and explanation of decision-making activity, and the use of the tree diagram in game theory provides a clear way of describing information conditions in certain situations of conflict.[2] Mathematical descriptions of these factors require more sophistication than is needed to understand the diagram. Most good economists, computer scientists, senior programmers, and mathematicians are also good diagrammatic modelers: they have to be. Economics is an area in which models can often be applied fairly directly to real-world problems; building models requires an understanding of both the methodology and the economic relevance of the situation. Mathematicians and programmers, on the contrary, often lack a substantive reality check. When required to model "softer" or "squishy" problems, such as war games, methods specialists may not have detailed substantive knowledge and, indeed, may resist learning the critical details in an attempt to keep their representations parsimonious or "clean."[3]

Mathematical modeling is probably the most abstract kind, and mathematicians strive to achieve parsimony and elegance, sometimes to the exclusion of the reality of the situation or environment. That applied mathematics as an enterprise differs from pure mathematics is not always appreciated. The applied mathematician knows that most real-world phenomena do not lend themselves to elegant and simple representation. Although underlying principles may be simple, the models needed to investigate operational details are usually not. In applying game theory to war gaming and simulation, the difference between underlying principles and actual operations is critical. Work in the pure mathematics of war is intellectually exciting and is worthwhile in building up a body of much-needed basic knowledge. The best models are usually built by the smallest groups of people. Abstract models built by skilled game theorists who have little interest in substantive details may be appropriated by an equally skilled group of programmers who work together with an experienced group of military officers. The latter two groups may appreciate the power of the initial mathematical work and may enlarge and computerize the original model to make it realistic and applicable to specific problems, but the result can easily be a large and expensive computer model worth less than any of its components.

Being able to write a computer program is not the same as being able to model substantive problems. Computer programming is a middle-level professional skill that can be taught relatively easily. A good computer programmer may have no more interest in the content of the program he is writing than a mathematician has in his work's eventual applications; however, the dangers associated with large computer models are much greater than those associated with pure mathematical models. The mathematician strives for brevity; his finished work is easily visible to anyone interested in it. Anyone unable to understand the few pieces of paper containing the mathematical model will not use them. If users do understand, their task is to translate the mathematician's results into an operational model. Misuse of analytic work is less likely than misuse of large computer models. Large flow charts can be constructed and programmed so easily that large-scale programs can readily be made operational—at least in the sense that they can be put on a computer and will produce reams of tabular, graphic, or other material. While impressive to the unwary, this output may in fact be incomprehensible in a way that is qualitatively different from the incomprehensibility of a technical or mathematical paper. In the former case, the mystique of the computer, combined with secrecy, may encourage people to accept the work even though they do not understand it and even though it may not be appropriate to the questions being asked. In the latter case, most people feel free to say, "This may be a fascinating piece of work for the pure mathematician, but it is incomprehensible or irrelevant to me and to the problem."

Throughout this book, we stress the need to define the purpose of a model or game clearly and simply before beginning to build and use one. In addition to deciding whether the model or game is to be used primarily for training, research, planning, technical or doctrinal evaluation, or some other purpose, it is necessary to state specifically the particular purpose of a particular game. Many situations are not amenable to treatment by gaming; a precise statement of purpose may clarify the appropriateness of the method to the circumstances.

A great deal of background information is usually required to create an MSG. Not only must data be identified and collected; they must also be organized so that they can be readily used. The development of scenarios, in either verbal or more abstract form, is a key way of organizing data and structuring games.[4] Documentation, that is, detailed information about a particular MSG, is essential in order to reconstruct moves and decisions, to allow careful examination of rejected alternatives and of research questions unearthed in the course of play, and to measure the extent of knowledge before, during, and after an MSG is used.

Adequate staff and facilities are also important. Serious operational war games cannot be played on a shoestring budget with inexperienced participants. Because the situations being considered are important, the time and resources invested in studying them should be adequate. Experienced and qualified talent is also crucial, but good modelers are hard to find. In the construction of MSGs, the best results can be expected from an individual who knows both the necessary modeling techniques and the substantive features of the problem—a rare combination. The next best situation is one in which meaningful and frequent communication exists between different, talented individuals in the same organization, that is, where technical and substantive specialists have established a common language and *modus vivendi*. In the third best, but far less desirable, situation, those who know the techniques reside in one organization and those who know the problem, in another; communication between the two is not particularly extensive or clear. This is, unfortunately, the most common pattern.

4 | Trends and Expenditures

> Trends are extrapolated into the future, and the plausibility
> of the extrapolation is estimated in the light of all available
> knowledge of trends and factors.
>
> Harold D. Lasswell, "The Policy Orientation"

IN 1974 THE GROSS NATIONAL PRODUCT of the
United States was approximately $1.3 trillion. The
total budget of the federal government was $274.7
billion, of which $93.9 billion was allocated to the Department
of Defense. In the same year, $96.3 billion was spent on edu-
cation by all levels of government in the United States, while
about 9 percent of the total defense budget, or $8.4 billion, was
spent on defense research and development.[1] Approximately
65,000 computers, representing a total investment of $25.6
billion, were in use in the United States during 1970.[2] The same
year, between 400 and 500 MSGs were in the active inventory
of the Department of Defense. The average cost of building
one of these systems was probably around $375,000; the aver-
age annual cost of running one was $45,000. In 1975, according
to a survey sponsored by the National Science Foundation,
there were approximately 1,200 nonmilitary MSGs in the
United States, each with an average development cost of $140,-
000; together they represented a total development cost of
about $100 million.[3]

These cost estimates are extremely crude, to be sure, and
may be off by as much as a factor of two in either direction. In
any event, the cost is small compared with the costs of choosing an incorrect policy in the absence of responsible analysis.
Problems with overhead conventions and unreported, hidden,
and incorrectly counted factors of MSG production, however,
make any more precise account of costs impossible—particu-

larly when these models have been built piecemeal over a length of time. Our best guess is that our estimates are conservative.

At least in terms of total expenditures, reliance on large-scale simulations and games is probably on the decline in the military; without systematic longitudinal assessments, however, we can only speculate on this point. The highest level of activity was apparently in the early to mid-1960s, probably roughly from 1962 through 1964. At that time, total expenditures may have been twice what they are now—largely because of analytic activities related to the war in Vietnam; the number of active MSGs may have ranged from 500 to 700, although we know of no effort to assess the full range and scope of such activity during that period. These numbers may be misleading, however, since computers and computer languages were less powerful and the techniques of gaming and simulation were less advanced than today.

We will attempt here to provide crude cost estimates and to describe the extent of modeling and gaming activities devoted to operations, training and teaching, research, and entertainment. Summary information presented in this chapter has been drawn from a variety of sources, including reference books such as the *Statistical Abstract of the United States,* interviews with gaming and modeling professionals, historical accounts of specific MSGs, and two surveys conducted specifically to determine the nature and extent of military and nonmilitary MSG activities under federal auspices. Our own military survey was made first, and more detailed results are presented in part four. The nonmilitary survey, by Fromm and his associates, as previously noted, was based to a large extent on our work; its results are discussed here and throughout the book, wherever appropriate.

Operational Gaming

The primary application of operational MSGs in the United States in 1974 was military. The vast majority of the 400 to 500 MSGs found in the military survey were operational MSGs devoted to the investigation of doctrine, the composition of forces, or problems of allocation. This work was sponsored by all branches of the Department of Defense, including the Office of the Secretary. The Air Force was probably responsible for about 25 percent of the total activity; the Army, for about 40 percent; and the Navy and Marine Corps together, for about 25 percent; the remaining 10 percent could be traced to the Joint Chiefs of Staff and the Office of the Secretary. About 60 to 70 percent of the MSGs were developed by contractors, but we note a trend toward increasing reliance on in-house staffs to develop and operate them. The major contractors included the Research Analysis Corporation, The Rand Corporation, the Center for Naval Analyses, Stanford Research Institute, Battelle Memorial Institute, Tech Ops, Raytheon, General Electric, and Booz-Allen Hamilton.

Judging from the membership of the Military Operations Research Society and the authorship of the various MSGs we surveyed, we estimate that in the United States several hundred professionals are actively involved in the construction of MSGs. This number does not reflect part-time and specialized participation, however, which probably brings the total somewhere into the low thousands. The type of person involved in the construction of MSGs differs according to the type and purpose of the activity in question. Purely mathematical models that can be computed analytically or built for operation with a computer, for example, may require mathematicians who are specialists in game theory applied to military problems. Builders of other kinds of models include professionals trained in mathematics, engineering, operations research, economics, and a wide range of other disciplines. A few behavioral scientists have participated in the development of human-factors MSGs, such as those produced by the Army's Behavioral Sciences Research Laboratories or the System Development Corporation in earlier years.

The Rand Corporation played an important role in the development of large-scale operational MSGs. Various mathematicians and logicians contributed to early prototypes that ranged from strictly mathematical exercises to large computer models, man-machine exercises, and sand-table and token-on-board games. These MSGs were used for operational, research, and training purposes.[4] Because the scenarios, or settings, for these large-scale simulations were particularly important, they required more interaction with the military user—interaction concerning data gathering, computer usage, and MSG specification—than the more purely mathematical modeling. Surprisingly, however, very little has been done to develop the writing of scenarios into a real profession. There is little or no literature on scenario writing for simulation and games and no organized professional effort in the form of courses of study, certification, and professional associations.[5]

Building operational computer simulations and man-machine simulations and games can be reasonably profitable, and any firm with computer capacity and a staff of programmers, engineers, and applied mathematicians with some modeling experience can try its hand. Unfortunately, building a model and building a good model are not the same, and one of the major problems in the area has been quality control. The factors that define a good model cannot be separated from the questions the model is intended to answer. Thus the administrative and political aims and application of a model cannot easily be separated from the scientific aspects of model building. Given a division of labor between sponsors and model builders, it is easy for the latter to claim that it would be "unscientific" for them to interfere with posing the questions and specifying the environment of the model, two factors that may in reality be the most important in an operational MSG.

Man-machine games may be used in preference to all-machine games or simulations for reasons of economy, because involving individuals themselves makes it unnecessary to model the behavior of human actors, because the exercise is intended to examine alternatives by means of immediate feedback from live, involved decision makers, or because critical factors cannot be modeled and thus require human input. Man-machine games are used primarily for teaching and training and for experimentation; however, some of these uses may be classified as operational. Possibly the most important example of the continuing use of man-machine simulation for operational purposes is the Navy Electronic Warfare Simulator (NEWS). The work of the Rand Logistics Systems Laboratory is another important example, although it belongs in the category of research as well as that of operations. Other examples of large man-machine games are discussed in chapter 9. Although many of them have cost several million dollars, they still appear to account for only 5 to 8 percent of the total expenditure for all operational MSGs.

At the furthest extreme from purely mathematical models are free-form games played in the Political/Military Division of the Studies, Analysis, and Gaming Agency (SAGA) of the Joint Chiefs of Staff and occasionally in the North Atlantic Treaty Organization (NATO) and elsewhere. The political and military, free-form MSG was designed primarily as a method for investigating substantive questions in political science rather than as a gaming methodology. Such games are usually played with a red team, a blue team, and control team. Players may include ambassadors, high-ranking generals, and other high officials—either represented as roles within the game or playing themselves directly. This type of gaming probably achieved its peak, both in the publicity it received and in the frequency with which it was used, during John F. Kennedy's administration, around the time of the Cuban missile crisis in 1962 (see chapter 8). There appears to be an inverse relationship between the amount spent on various types of gaming and simulation and the amount of publicity and public attention they receive. The commonly known, free-form political and military exercise is by far the least expensive form of gaming. It is unlikely that as much as $2 million has been spent in any one year on this activity. In contrast, expenditures for the less well known, all-machine simulations have been larger by orders of magnitude.

Because they account for the major expenditures, we have mentioned only military uses for operational MSGs so far. Operational gaming has also been applied in city and national planning, transportation and ecological studies, and economic forecasting and planning.[6] Nonmilitary operational gaming includes the work done in city planning by Arthur D. Little and CONSAD Research Corporation for San Francisco and Pittsburgh respectively, and the efforts of Simulmatics Corporation to build a planning model for the Venezuelan government.[7] Models have also been used in private business, and here the literature is voluminous. As in the cases of the applications of Jay Forrester's early work, described in *Industrial Dynamics*, to the Sprague Electric Company and to several other firms and of other business-oriented modeling enterprises, it is often difficult to determine whether the actual applications are primarily research and teaching exercises or are in fact operational.[8] In the late 1960s and early 1970s there was a flurry of activity in the construction of urban-development games. These games, such as CLUG (Community Land Use Game) and METRO (Michigan Effectuation Training, Research, and Operations game), are primarily designed for teaching and research; to the extent that city planners and officials are urged to use them, however, they may be considered to be operational activities.[9]

Accounting for nonmilitary gaming activities is extremely difficult. What funds have paid for these activities? Which activities should be counted? Forrester's work and the Pittsburgh and San Francisco projects are in the twilight zone between simulations that should be counted as nonmilitary games and those that cannot usefully be considered to be games. The distinction lies in whether or not more than one set of decision makers is considered as players whose free will is capable of influencing outcomes. A simple hydroelectric simulation, for example, is probably not worth considering a game. Yet if government, private industry, and local inhabitants were all considered as players in the model of a hydroelectric project, it would be reasonable to think of it as a game. Urban-development simulations usually fall into this category.

The total cost of developing the San Francisco MSG was approximately $1.2 million; of the Pittsburgh MSG, about $1.1 million. The costs of constructing and running CLUG are minimal by comparison. Expenditures for nonmilitary gaming activities have been small relative to expenditures by the armed forces, but, as the National Science Foundation survey indicates, this gap may be decreasing.

Gaming for Teaching and Training

The armed forces have made extensive use of gaming for teaching and training. Aircraft simulators, shakedown cruises, and field exercises are common throughout the services, and sand-table and map exercises have been employed as teaching and training devices for centuries. Large-scale maneuvers and field and fleet exercises are expensive, and it is probably even more difficult to account for their costs than for those of a computer simulation. It is easy, for example, to overestimate the expense of a large field exercise by attributing the wages of the participants to the exercise and hence overvaluing what they might otherwise have been doing during the period. By the same token, attributing zero costs to the personnel may cause the economic cost of the exercise to be underestimated. One of the most important considerations in the use of gaming has been the fact that machine, man-machine, and free-form MSGs are all considerably cheaper than field exercises and, to a great extent, can perform the same tasks.

Military applications have not dominated the growth and absolute size of teaching uses, as they have those of operational gaming. Jean Piaget and others have argued that a vast amount of preschool and elementary-school teaching and training involves the use of games.[10] Whether most of the preschool and elementary-school budgets should be formally considered to be expenditures for gaming activities depends to a great extent on the questions we are addressing. Thirty years ago, the formal use of games and gaming in education was limited; in the last ten years, however, it has been growing by leaps and bounds. This change is indicated by the growth of educational-gaming companies, by the increasing number of courses on gaming, and by the recent concern for the relationship between games and other educational techniques.[11]

While military gaming for teaching and training appears to have remained constant or decreased over the last ten years, activity in preschool and elementary education has increased considerably. At the graduate-school level, business games scarcely existed fifteen years ago. The first formal business game was used by the American Management Association in the early 1950s. Between 500 and 1,000 such games are currently in use.[12] Although the increased use of gaming for teaching and training has been confined primarily to schools and universities, simple training games, such as inventory and production-scheduling games, are used within corporations. Furthermore, at the interfaces of entertainment, operations, and teaching, new games have been developed and used to inform and entertain the adult public. For example, a host of board games now covers different environmental issues. Games, for instance, are being designed and run for adult groups to illustrate the problems in developing a tourist industry, to explore the difficulties in the location of power plants, and to examine city-planning problems.

Gaming for Research

Few Department of Defense MSGs are explicitly labeled as having been built and used for research purposes; nevertheless, a research component can be identified in many of them. Only 1.5 percent of the MSGs discovered in our survey were identified as intended primarily for research, but approximately 10 percent had some research applications. Although war gaming is a relatively old activity and computer applications have realized enormous growth, surprisingly little money is being spent on necessary research.

In sharp contrast with this pattern within the military, non-military research making use of MSGs has been growing rapidly. Except for the work of a handful of social psychologists and psychologists, no nonmilitary experimental gaming was carried on twenty years ago. Today hundreds of journal articles report on such work. In several important centers and laboratories, a great deal of experimentation is under way. Among them are the laboratories at the University of Michigan's Mental Health Research Center, at the University of California at Berkeley and Los Angeles, and at Purdue University. In the aerospace industry, however, the day of the independent gaming laboratory seems to have passed; well-equipped, well-staffed, and productive laboratories have been converted into cafeterias or office space.

We estimate that the dissertations of between twenty and thirty doctoral candidates annually are concerned primarily with experimental gaming. Assuming that it is not possible to conduct a gaming experiment for less than $1,000 (counting unimputed costs as well as the costs usually recorded) and that between 800 and 1,500 experiments are performed annually in the United States, we estimate that over $1 million is being spent each year on experimental gaming. In our view, both the scope and the absolute magnitude of experimental gaming are increasing. Part of this upward trend results from the growing variety of disciplines involved—among them, social psychology, psychology, political science, economics, and business administration.

Gaming for Entertainment

We have included gaming for entertainment in this discussion in order to provide a broader context in which to assess the expenditures and the extent of participation in different gaming activities. The most important contrast between games for entertainment and those for operational, teaching, or experimental purposes is the balance sheet. The costs of entertainment gaming are offset by revenue; both can be measured in money. For other types of gaming, costs are generally measured in terms of money but revenue is measured primarily without clear monetary value, in terms of services rendered. The four major expenditures for entertainment gaming are those for spectator sports such as football, participant sports such as bowling, gambling, and home games. In 1969 alone, entry fees to spectator sports were estimated at about $487 million; in 1972, expenditures for toys and sporting goods were $3.58 billion, up from $2.21 billion five years earlier.[13] Attendance at college football games doubled between 1950 and 1973, and attendance at professional football games increased fivefold during the same period.[14]

We include amateur war gaming in the category of participant sports. The subscription list for *The General,* the house publication of the Avalon Hill Company of Baltimore, is somewhere around 20,000. Simulations Publications of New York lists about 30,000 subscribers to its general magazine, *Strategy and Tactics,* and some 7,000 subscribers to its more detailed, game-oriented *Moves.* Thus, even assuming some overlap, the number of serious amateur war gamers in the United States in 1976 was about 40,000. This population is considerably larger than that of professional war gamers. Some of the planning factors used in amateur war gaming may even be more accurate than those used by the professionals; at least the data are more openly available and are actively challenged by this large and active group of amateurs. SINAI and MECH-WAR '77, two recent, innovative Simulations Publications games, indicate just how realistic an amateur war game can be.[15]

It is difficult to estimate the number of nonwar games played at home; nor are such numbers particularly relevant to this inquiry. Over 70 million Monopoly sets have been sold in a variety of languages and editions, however, and around 70 million decks of playing cards are sold annually. These numbers suggest that more money has been spent on cards and Monopoly games alone than on all operational and experimental nonmilitary MSGs. Expenditures for gambling appear to be considerably larger than those for other entertainment gaming activities. In New York City alone, revenues from illegal gambling were estimated at $1.8 billion in 1971. Revenues from Nevada's legalized gaming were reported to be about $600 million in 1971.[16] Pari-mutuel turnover from horse racing in 1973 topped $1.8 billion, but no one has ventured a guess at the comparable illegal revenue from either horses or sports betting.[17]

Overall Trends

A broad, comparative summary of expenditures for all types of gaming activity in 1973 is presented in figure 4-1; it is a crude estimate based on extremely shaky data about costs, the number of MSGs being built, the number of papers published, and the number of MSGs in existence. Nevertheless, the information in this figure, along with data presented by Gary Fromm and his associates[18] and our best judgment about the issue, suggests an interesting story. In spite of the difficulty of obtaining hard cost figures, we discern growth in all areas of MSG development up until about 1965. Since that time, some areas, especially manual and man-machine operational MSGs, have trailed off. As of 1973, however, somewhere between $70 and $150 million was being spent each year for operational MSGs. Although this is not a great deal of money compared with the costs of new weapon systems or of running major field or fleet exercises, we must ask whether the product being bought merits this level of expenditure.

Except for a few million dollars spent on urban-development, environmental, energy, and transportation MSGs (and perhaps an additional sum for planning models), comparatively little appears to have been spent on operational MSGs for nonmilitary purposes. Work in the area of simulation and

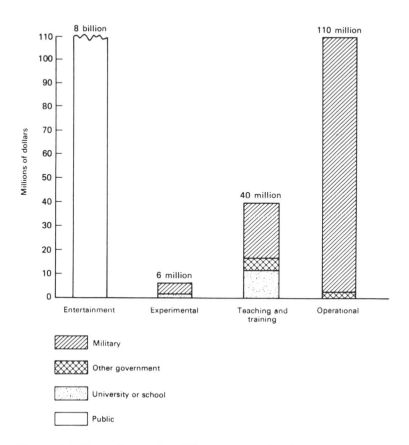

Figure 4-1. *Expenditures for different types of MSG, 1973.*

econometric MSGs for planning has increased, especially since public and policy-level attention has been focused so strongly on unemployment and other concerns related to recession and inflation; such MSGs do not, of course, consider adversaries or explicit conflict situations. With the growing interest in environmental and energy problems and the redevelopment of urban areas, there is likely to be an upsurge in the production of operational MSGs for these sorts of planning.[19] Unfortunately, there is no guarantee that these MSGs will be any better than their predecessors, nor is it clear that the errors and mistakes made in the conduct of operational, military modeling and gaming will not be repeated. In a related area, as better and cheaper data-processing systems become available, some growth may occur in nonmilitary operational gaming in the private, corporate sector. It will probably be relatively small in terms of dollars, however, and it is unlikely to amount to even as much as a few million dollars per annum within the next five to ten years.

In contrast, military MSGs can conceivably go in either direction in the future. Military gaming is beginning to emerge as a profession, but many serious weaknesses remain. In particular, the quality of the product depends to a great extent on the relationship between sponsors and builders. If responsible judgments can be made about the appropriateness of any given model to the issue being studied, sponsors will probably get what they pay for. If these conditions are not met, the money will generally be wasted. If some internal reorganization takes place within the military and if standards are established for MSGs, the military use of operational gaming and simulation should grow in an orderly and efficient manner over the next decade. If a constructive path is to be taken, however, much more attention will have to be paid to the issues of institutionalization and professionalization. An ongoing survey and assessment mechanism outside of the routine process of building and using models, for instance, should be established (see chapter 19). This and other initiatives, undertaken in the same spirit, would facilitate an increase in the productive use of operational MSGs.

PART TWO

War Games
in the Past

5 | A History of War Games

It's not a *game* at all, it's a training for war; I shall recommend it most emphatically to the whole army.

Von Mueffling, Chief of Staff of the Prussian Army in 1824

WAR AND GAMES representing war predate recorded history. Game boards and symbolic representations of soldiers and military equipment have been unearthed in archeological explorations in Greece, Egypt, Persia, China, and India. Chesslike games, thought to have been games of war, were played by the ancient Indians, Iraqis, Chinese, Japanese, and others.[1] Since war is one of humanity's oldest activities, and one that involves great costs, it is not surprising that substitutes have always existed.

Without attempting to compile a detailed history of war gaming through the ages, a task far beyond the scope and purpose of this book, we shall describe several of the more prominent game forms to show some of the main purposes for which these war surrogates have been used.[2] We shall also summarize the limitations confronting early gamers and some general issues that continue to arise today.

There is some debate about the earliest origins of games related to war. Karl Groos has made at least one plausible guess:

The primitive races, who find it difficult to convey their thoughts in speech, naturally take to marking on the sand, and hence the figures (i.e., game boards) might arise. If [a] leader . . . wished to instruct them concerning some past or future combat, it would be a simple method of illustrating his meaning to draw an outline on

45

the ground and represent the position of the hostile forces by small stones or similar objects, whose movements would symbolize the manoeuvres of the forces . . . This would, no doubt, be exceedingly interesting to those conducting it, and also to the spectators, and might easily be repeated for the sake of the amusement afforded until some inventive genius turned it into a veritable play with board and men.[3]

War games, minimally defined as replicas of two-sided human adversary situations involving a contrived conflict and a few procedural rules, probably originated as tools for planning military operations. If this assumption is correct, some commander, who could have been Chinese, Indian, or of any of several other nationalities, planned an operation by representing his forces and his opponent's by marks on the ground or on a crude version of a map. It was then easy for him to try out various tactical moves on the part of the opposing forces to see whether and how a battle might be joined. This crude game was thus a model of the projected course of events; a variety of moves and countermoves could be assessed by the commander to help him select what he thought would be the most effective course of action. Experience from past wars and constraints in the situation at hand would play a role in these games and in the deliberations resulting from play. The two-sidedness of the anticipated conflict was probably even represented, in more sophisticated versions of the basic game, by an opposing player—a feature that would add one more point of view and would help the commander not to overlook something of importance. Reduced to its basic elements, even the most sophisticated computer representation of a conflict situation has the same key ingredients: two sides, a context, rules and constraints, and a variety of scenarios that might be played out when the time comes to wage war in earnest.

War games could also have originated as educational or instructional devices. According to this interpretation, troops were shown "pictures," in the form of modeled representations in sand, of some impending conflict, and were then instructed in what they should do in various situations. Contingency plans were probably formulated by the more sophisticated gamers in time to prepare the troops for eventualities beyond the control of one side or the other. The modern equivalents of this type of gaming are the fleet exercise and the maneuver. A more ancient speculation about war gaming's origins holds that chess and its antecedents were used as symbolic equivalents of war, in particular as a means to reduce aggressive tendencies among Hindu princes.[4] A fourth reason for the development of war games was probably what we have referred to as entertainment. Games have always had a social component, and the use of games as socially acceptable competition must have contributed to the development and use of games in general and of war games in particular.[5]

Despite debate about the original purposes of games, it is clear that very early in their evolution they became both formal and abstract.[6] The formal aspect involved the creation of rules that would guide play and also indicate various outcomes; the abstract aspect stemmed from the fact that the rules, the board or map, and the related instruments used in the game were not exact replicas of their real-world counterparts.

Early Applications

TRAINING

In the earliest days, little, if any, distinction was probably made between games for training and for the evaluation of plans.[7] A game was played to test a plan of operations; simultaneously, troops and troop commanders were getting some idea of what lay in store for them. Ultimate validation often followed the next day, and the quality of the game could be determined by counting up the bodies and deciding who had won and who had lost.

Chesslike games were probably used for military training purposes as early as the 1500s; the tactical maneuvers of foot soldiers were replicated on game boards with several types of piece—to represent a coarse specialization of function among pikemen, halberdiers, and horsemen—and an ever increasing number of squares intended, in all probability, to capture the reality of increasing numbers of combat participants. Given the military capabilities of that century, chess was probably a good abstract form for the maneuvering principles of combat and the clash of arms.

By the mid-1600s, the so-called King's Game (the invention of which is attributed to Christopher Weikhmann of Ulm) had come into vogue.[8] It had thirty pieces to a side, thirteen finely differentiated functional specialties, and fourteen different movement strategies or rules. The use of the game as a training device was effective because it was more realistic than chess or its derivatives.[9] In the next century, two French card games dealing with fortifications and actual engagement situations were used extensively to train military students.[10] Prussia also contributed significantly to modern war gaming. Prussians had long considered war to be an exact science, "particularly as a branch of applied mathematics resembling geometry."[11] Their ideological fascination with exact representation led to their eager adoption of increasingly complex games.[12]

War games not tied to a chess format were invented, according to most accounts, by a Prussian lieutenant, von Reisswitz, in 1811.[13] They used a map, pieces representing troops, two players and an umpire, and a book of increasingly detailed rules and are generally considered to be the first "true war games."[14] A key feature of von Reisswitz's games was the addition of realism. Rules were based on actual operations, and the map format allowed the players to locate themselves in terrain and in situations that did not overly tax their powers of imagination and abstraction. The quest for realism became the game's undoing, however. The rules became so numerous and so complex that, in time, more effort was spent in learning how to play than in actually playing.

The "rigid" *Kriegsspiel*, or war game, was complemented by "free" Kriegsspiel in 1876, when Colonel von Verdy du Vernois developed a version of the game that allowed greater freedom of play and movement and greatly simplified the rules.[15] These two distinct forms of the war game remain to this day: the rigid game, which emphasizes rules and detail, and the free game, which emphasizes tactical freedom and the use of experienced controlling elements or umpires.

By the late 1800s and early 1900s, nearly all the major powers included some form of war game in their training curricula. Although gaming was initially developed and used for training, the experience it provided was quickly transferred to planning and the evaluation of plans. The 1918 spring offensive of World War I was tested and rehearsed by the Germans, who, after finding that it would probably not have a decisive impact on the conduct of the war, carried it out nonetheless.[16] During the hiatus between the two world wars, war games became standard devices for practicing military operations and for training troops, especially in environments constrained by treaties and economic shortages.[17]

PLANNING

The Germans used Kriegsspiel to evaluate a host of plans from the Franco-Prussian War through World War II, as has been well reported elsewhere.[18] Gaming was instrumental in planning the use of railroads in the Prussian campaign against France in 1870; the Schlieffen plan in World War I; the invasion of Poland in World War II; the invasion of France through the Ardennes; a test of the proposed and then discarded invasion of England in 1940; the invasion of Russia in 1941;[19] and the defense of the Ardennes in 1944.

The Japanese also relied heavily on war gaming to test plans, and Pearl Harbor was worked out through games months before the attack. The Japanese even created a Total War Research Institute for the basic purpose of testing operational plans by means of games and other analytic techniques.[20] Gaming did not lead to the misfortunes of the Japanese, however; rather, their games suffered from overaggressive umpiring, and politics outside of the games forced real choices not indicated in the play itself.

Francis J. McHugh relates several details of the Japanese experience in evaluating plans for World War II that indicate the general style of Japanese planners and their heavy reliance on war games:

> War games conducted in the fall of 1941 at the War College in Tokyo were employed to analyze the effectiveness of a surprise attack of Pearl Harbor, and to rehearse such an operation . . . In early 1942 tentative naval plans including the capture of Ceylon, the destruction of the British fleet, and the gaining of air control over the

Indian Ocean were tested by means of war games. These plans, which had as their ultimate goal the joining of German and Japanese forces in the Near East, called for the use of army troops in amphibious operations against Ceylon.

Naval planners . . . prepared ambitious plans for the capture of Midway and the western Aleutians in early June, the seizures of strategic points in New Caledonia and the Fiji Islands in July, air strikes on southwestern Australia, and operations against Johnson Islands and Hawaii in August. These proposed operations were tested in a series of war games in the spring of 1942. During the play the Nagumo Force was attacked by land-based air while its own planes were attacking Midway. Following the rules of the game, an umpire determined that the carriers received nine hits and that two of them, the Akagi and Kaga, were sunk. Rear Admiral Ugaki, the director of the game, arbitrarily reduced the number of hits to three, and the number of sinkings to one, and then permitted the sunken carrier to participate in the next part of the play dealing with the New Caledonia and Fiji Islands invasions.[21]

RESEARCH

The use of war games to suggest or test weapons, strategies, tactics, organizations, and procedures is probably more recent than their use for training or the evaluation of plans, but it can be traced clearly back to the second half of the nineteenth century in Germany. Data generated during the Austro-Prussian War of 1866 were used to compare rifle and musket performance. In conjunction with field tests, games determined the usefulness of the breech-loading rifle and were employed to work out tactical procedures to take better advantage of this innovation.[22] Empirical data generated by the American Civil War, especially on the use of railroads in logistical support of ground forces, were used by the Germans in war games to research and redefine operational procedures later used in their successful war against France in the 1870s.[23]

Research using naval war gaming was developed in the United States, Great Britain, and Japan, in approximately that order.[24] The British Royal Navy researched the characteristics of World War I's *Queen Elizabeth* class of battleship and found, by gaming, that a speed advantage of 5 knots would be critically important—a fact borne out in actual operations in both world wars. Research has become a major purpose of modern war gaming; as such, it occupies the bulk of our attention throughout this book.

ENTERTAINMENT

The use of war gaming for entertainment throughout history should not be lightly dismissed. As already noted, board games have ancient origins as war surrogates.[25] One modern interpretation of historical events based on the old Chinese game Wei-ch'i (in Japanese, Go), discusses the Communists' takeover of China in terms of a global Go game played on a map of the country.[26] In this case at least, the accuracy of the analogy is fascinating. The concepts of encirclement and tenuous control over vast spatial areas are stressed, both in the game and in its real-world analog.

Card games, many of which suggest two-sided conflict situations constrained by rules and providing payoffs, have been popular through the ages. Poker, for example, has generalized, war game-like attributes.[27] Some poker players are highly skilled; others are not. By playing the game many times and learning to calculate probabilities, a player can learn enough to win more often than not. Yet the ability to calculate is insufficient by itself to explain consistently successful performance—a key lesson, though one that is not always appreciated, for many other games and conflict situations as well. The opponent's actions must be accounted for, especially the possibility of bluffing. Although much can be learned about real situations through simplified and even formalized games, game and reality are still not identical.

The distinction between game and reality was easy enough to maintain in ancient times, in highly simplified board, table, card, map, and other war-gaming exercises. With the advent of models of more complicated real-world military situations, which demand intellectual and abstractive powers beyond a single individual's capabilities, and the evolution of scientific and technological methods to cope with these newer and more complex systems and situations, this distinction has become increasingly blurred.

The Reasons for Gaming

War games, developed in antiquity, are equally important in modern settings that are too complex to understand or too terrifying to be tested realistically. Present-day weapons, strategies, and tactics are often future-oriented (games may involve systems that will not even exist for a decade or more) and are therefore impossible to test or evaluate realistically. Military organizations responsible for complex systems and operations—early warning; communication, command and control; weapons design, development, and delivery; and logistical support—must evaluate their plans, procedures, and tools in a gamed or simulated environment. As recently as World War II, planners played a war game and then tested their results on the field of battle, with minimal problems of validation. Contemporary war gamers may have equal opportunities to test their results in the field, but the costs for doing so even partly have risen hideously. As a result, planners rely increasingly on completely computerized simulations as a basis for their decisions.

One of the current real, but basically unrealized, penalties of relying on all-machine abstractions of war situations to the relative exclusion of manual and man-machine representations is that the innovative or creative aspect of game design and play has been diminished or lost. Reliance on gaming by humans, which has been developed most fully in the context of war, forces participants to think hard about a problem—hard enough, in many cases, to make the elements of the problem explicit and logically consistent. By summarizing and integrating what is known about a complex problem, by drawing attention to inconsistencies of perspective and formulation, and by highlighting areas of dubious or faulty knowledge, both game design and play stimulate the creative human impulse.[28] This component of war gaming has always been critical, as Alfred H. Hausrath reminds us:

> Games or map exercises have been used extensively to train officers in military forces throughout the world.

Gaming challenges the competitive spirit and spurs the contenders to do their best in a given situation. It stimulates the search for new and more effective ways of meeting situations and encourages innovation. In these respects, motivations aroused in war gaming serve as incentives which, though less intense than those in real warfare, may have carryover values that will pay off in the ultimate test of actual combat.

Each opponent is impelled to seek out and recognize essential and critical elements of the situation and the limitations of resources. More importantly, each opposing participant is spurred, not only to employ the best of known experiences, but to originate, invent, and employ a still better or newer concept or innovation. Thus gaming is a seed bed for the germination of new ideas and a nursery in which to develop and nurture those ideas.[29]

In principle, participants in war games feel the same environmental and institutional pressures as they themselves or others feel in the real world; this human dimension tends to decrease in importance, however, as gaming becomes depersonalized, grander in scale, and more formalized. What most gaming professionals fail to acknowledge is that the most common and most important war games are highly informal and personalized. Such games are played continuously by individuals and groups as they consciously try to predict and take into account an enemy's reactions in varying circumstances and situations.[30]

Overall, then, war games have been and continue to be played for several general reasons: to attain a better balanced understanding of likely enemy reactions and actions; to determine beforehand how war plans, procedures, and processes could fail; to pool expert knowledge from various areas of competence; to help make the abstract more concrete; to generate alternative courses of action and new information (actually recombinations of old information and data); and to test alternatives in a simplified and well understood setting before trying to use them in a complex, poorly understood, and uncontrolled one.

Problems and Constraints

The actual result of using war games for these reasons has not been an unqualified success. In a recent, provocative exposition, Paul Bracken reviews the experiences of the British in analyzing threats of strategic air attack in 1922–1939, of the French in constructing defenses in the interwar period, and of the Russians in preparing for a German assault on their western border.[31] Even allowing for the limitations of historical analogy, the many unintended consequences and the lessons learned in these cases appear to have contemporary relevance.

In the British case, a small group of statistical specialists within the Air Staff assessed the likelihood of a serious German threat to Great Britain. Only summary results and no documentation were presented to highest-level decision makers. Unfortunately, these results were never subjected to detailed, external evaluation, and the longer-term implications for British decision making were stunning. Because they relied on highly selective "mythical numbers," decision makers' choices emphasized the construction of day bombers to the virtual exclusion of night bombers, fighters, and other components of a total defense system. General fear and popular distrust were generated by later studies based on the results of the Air Staff's original work, which led Lloyds of London, for example, to determine that it would not issue any kind of war insurance, the Home Office to decide that the civilian losses from German bombing would be greater than the country's capacity to build coffins and to give orders for mass graves, and the Health Ministry to issue over a million extra death certificates.[32] While most of these studies were classified and not subjected to outside technical scrutiny, the strong acts they stimulated rapidly became known to the general populace. Several general lessons were learned from this experience:

1. No one ever questioned the assumptions behind the basic analyses, on which so many other studies and decisions were based. Such inquiry must be unrelenting.
2. No one bothered to look carefully at the basic data. Anyone who did would have determined easily that the numbers were carefully selected to support the worst possible case.

3. No one ever looked carefully at the structure of the models generated by the Air Staff analytic team to determine just what kind of output they were capable of generating. Someone should have done so.
4. The need for careful, external professional review is pressing.
5. The methodology of selective omission can prove just about anything.
6. One must question the decisions of political strategists who use the detailed, usually highly quantitative, analyses produced by others but who are themselves incapable of understanding exactly what is included and omitted from the analysis, what the limitations of the analyses are, and where the basic data come from.

These points are nicely summarized by Bracken, who observes, "It is one thing not to have proper clearance to receive certain answers, but it is another not to even ask the questions in the first place."[33]

The French case is parallel in many ways but raises several other critical points as well. Once the strategic decision to build the Maginot line had been made, most subsequent analyses were focused on technical aspects of that single strategic system. Calculations of ranges, concrete thicknesses, firing angles, and the like became a substitute for more comprehensive thought and an anesthetic for decision makers who refused to confront the real problems posed by a mobile, flexible enemy. In this case, analyses served to divert attention from the real problems facing the French military planners and strategists. The general lesson here is that analyses can be used to suppress certain facts and contingencies from view and scrutiny, either by omission or by commission.

This is a lesson that the Soviets learned the hard way in their preparations for World War II. In a series of remarkable strategic games conducted in the 1930s, any and all gaming that did not adhere strictly to the strategic doctrine espoused by Stalin was quickly and brutally snuffed out. In fact, one of the more brilliant gamers among the Soviet generals was purged, in no small measure because of his repeated contradictions of the orthodoxy in the ways that he played these games. At some point, other Soviet military men learned that disputing the basic and nearly fatal strategic assumptions would lead to harsh personal reprisal; dissent ended and the games were played increasingly by the foreordained rules.[34] Similar organizational self-delusion on the part of the Japanese, already mentioned, crept into the prewar planning, through games, of both the Pearl Harbor attack and the Battle of Midway.[35]

The skeptical reader may be willing to dismiss these illustrations with the assertion that we have, in fact, learned our lesson and that we now make truly scientific analyses that can stand up to examination. Our findings consistently contradict this view

It is easy to forget that war games are abstractions, not reality. They stress the items selected for inclusion and deemphasize or ignore items left out by the designers. Thus the connections between war gaming and actual field exercises, maneuvers, and combat are not as clear as they may appear on the basis of enthusiastic historical accounts.[36] Maneuvers and field exercises have always been carried out to teach tactical commanders how to operate their units. The use of judges and referees, in conjunction with routine maneuvers, serves mainly to limit movement—and very little else. Strategic planning has historically involved map exercises to check out the deployment, including disposition and movement schedules, of large forces. The connection between these routine and prosaic military activities and war gaming—Kriegsspiel or "Computerspiel"—is not clear in practice.[37]

Another, more specific lesson provided by a historical survey of war gaming is that the complicating impact of technology has been overlooked in many gamed accounts of conflict. Before World War I, an infantryman and a cavalry trooper were somewhat comparable as fighting elements; symmetrical assumptions about opposing forces and their capabilities could be made.[38] With the advent of technological specialization and increasing differentiation among weapons and systems for their deployment, simply counting men, horses, and cannon no longer sufficed. The question became how diverse and noncomparable weapons systems could be aggregated to determine overall combat effectiveness. It is a challenging intellectual and practical problem that cannot be resolved easily either by reference to tables of firepower scores or by traditional assumptions. In addition, the human element is frequently left out of games, although real experience has forcefully and repeatedly proven that it is a critical feature of actual operations. A war game can provide at best only a hint of the actual fighting capabilities of the individuals.[39]

Great care must be exercised, especially in complex or all-machine games, to keep the players or sponsors from succumbing to the illusion that a real test of presumptions or ideas has occurred. The investment in computer programming, professional time, and emotional energy required to design and operate a war game may be sufficiently great to create a false sense of the validity of its results. In fact, a single game cannot establish any result with great confidence; at best, it may produce limited statements about processes, procedures, and possible outcomes. Judgment enters and colors the gaming process at several points. The factors selected to structure a war game are based on judgments, as are the assumptions and estimates used to assign input values when hard, verifiable data are not available; the selection of game strategies is also largely a matter of judgment. Any results produced by a game must, therefore, be subjected to other scientific and experimental testing to verify their validity and worth.[40]

War games continue to be constrained by a number of factors. First, because a game is an unrealistic abstraction of a complex reality, the use of game results must be augmented by judgment, common sense, and more conventional research. Second, the degree to which all-machine models are reasonable, logically consistent, and structurally relevant depends on the skill and good fortune of their designers. Third, both manual and man-machine games depend on the skill of players and on the judgment of umpires or referees. Finally, war games, like any other enterprise designed to generate or clarify ideas, require experimental testing to establish their appropriateness, effectiveness, utility, and worth.

6 | The Recent Development of War Gaming

> Like Chinese medicine, the military profession is most successful if the client does not become a patient.
>
> E. W. Paxson, *War Gaming*

T HE USE OF gaming to study contemporary warfare has evolved rapidly in recent years. Particularly important strides were taken during the 1960s and early 1970s with the development of more powerful methods and of tools encompassing broader ranges of subject matter. In this chapter, we shall review the major contributions to war gaming that emanated from The Rand Corporation and the Research Analysis Corporation. In order to present the situation from the perspective of the in-house analytic institutions, we shall also attempt to piece together an account of activities in the Department of Defense in the early 1970s.[1]

Organizations and institutions charged with war-gaming responsibilities have proliferated impressively; this growth seems to have occurred, however, without much consideration of its likely consequences. We do not share the view of Edward Girard, who believes, along with many other gaming professionals, that most of the hard work has already been done.

> It is my opinion that the 15 years of hard work of some of the most creative individuals and teams in the field of Operations Research have attained a plateau in the degree of return for effort expended in developing and applying games and simulations to the problems of land, sea, and air combat as defined under scenarios of nuclear

and large-scale non-nuclear operations . . . When the available techniques in a field have so matured, it is time for the research professional to move on and let the users, with the assistance of the required technicians, exploit the discoveries that are his monument.[2]

Rather, we feel that most of the really creative, difficult work in this field has only begun. Later in this chapter we shall consider some of the possibilities and problems awaiting those concerned about various war-gaming topics, techniques, and methods.

The Rand Corporation

The Rand Corporation has been a leader in the combined fields of gaming, game theory, and simulation since the late 1940s. To this day, the Rand staff includes a large number of experts in gaming and game-theory applications. Many of the basic gaming exercises conducted at Rand have initiated extramural programs that eventually consumed resources several times the total annual Rand budget. For instance, Rand's original political and military exercises, performed under the direction of Herbert Goldhamer and Hans Speier in the mid-1950s, resulted in various transmutations, some of which were carried out at the Massachusetts Institute of Technology, Northwestern University, and elsewhere. Rand work in the political and military and strategic areas led more or less directly to the creation of the Joint War Gaming Agency (now the Studies, Analysis and Gaming Agency, or SAGA) in the Office of the Joint Chiefs of Staff. The Air Battle Model (ABM) originated at Rand and became the Air Battle Division of the Air Force. The original logistical MSGs of John Kennedy and others led to the formation of the System Development Corporation. Other examples could also be cited.

Even though the amount of gaming activity has declined at Rand, the investment in modeling and gaming methods and the number and diversity of professionals there are probably greater than anywhere else in the United States. The only other institution that approached Rand in this respect was the Research Analysis Corporation. An overall view of Rand's gaming activity, based on information compiled over a period of months from interviews with most of the key participants, is presented in figure 6-1.

Examples of each type of MSG, discussed below, give some indication of their form and content. A complete compilation has never been made; the history and extent of activity at Rand are so rich and broad that it would undoubtedly fill several volumes. (Rand's involvement in logistical MSGs will be discussed in chapter 9.)

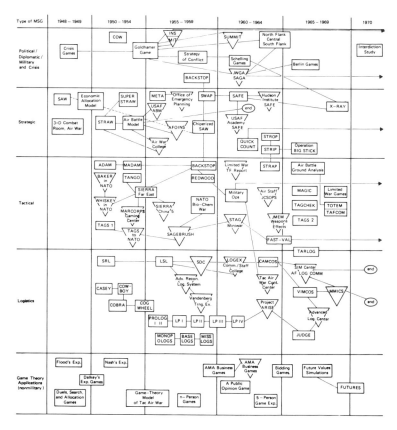

Figure 6-1. *The major contributions of The Rand Corporation to gaming and simulation, 1948–1970.*

POLITICAL, MILITARY, AND CRISIS MSGS

The seminal work of Goldhamer and Speier has rightly been recognized as "one of the earliest post–World War II games conducted in the United States."[3] Its place in the development of manual or free-form gaming, both within Rand and in the larger gaming community, is central.[4] Between February 1955 and April 1956, four separate plays of Goldhamer and Speier's "political exercise" were conducted. Its basic purposes have been retained, in various forms, in other applications of this type of game. Some of the questions for which answers evolved in the course of playing out the four separate cycles of the exercise are listed below.[5]

Would a political game be a useful technique for generating forecasts of political developments and for sharpening estimates of the probable consequences of policies pursued by various governments in international affairs? Is gaming a useful way to test the comparative worth of political strategies and tactics?

Would the partial simulation of reality in the game, with participants trying to play the role of responsible government officials, stimulate political inventiveness? Would a game significantly surpass the quality of political analysis that might be achieved by the more conventional techniques of research and analysis?

Would the game serve to call attention to problems of international politics that need special research and further study? Would these problems be identified in a clearer and more useful way than might otherwise be the case if one looked for worthwhile research projects outside of the context of action imposed by the game?

Would the game train and educate personnel in useful ways? Would it help researchers acquire a heightened sensitivity to problems of political strategy and the consequences of policy decisions? Would it be useful in giving policymakers a means of analyzing more deeply the implications of events in the context of an unfolding political process?

The political exercises were played by teams representing various governments; a referee control team ruled on the plausibility and feasibility of moves proposed by the teams. The games focused on the United States, the Soviet Union, and Western Europe. Written moves were made in response to a scenario describing the world and the decision environment that existed at the start of play. The game itself developed as moves unfolded and the control team introduced external events. In successive plays of the game, eight, eighteen, thirteen, and twenty professionals were involved for two- and, eventually, three-week periods. (The total investment of manpower approximated three man-years.) In the fourth game, three senior members of the State Department's Foreign Service also participated.

In the aftermath of these experiences, a consensus was reached on recommendations about Rand's continuing reliance on the operational use of such games. The first recommendation was that no full-time program of political exercises should be undertaken. Doubts about the amount of time required and the quality of the research results were felt to outweigh the gains from this type of gaming. Second, a major contextual shift in the world situation might provide justification for replaying broad-scale exercises in order to assess the coarse meaning of such change. Third, exercises that were focused on problems, rather than geographically based, should be conducted from time to time in order to test substantive assumptions and to examine broad technical and procedural issues. The consensus was also that the political exercises had succeeded in attaining some of their original purposes; on balance and from a practical standpoint, however, their usefulness in the comparison and testing of broad political strategies was judged to be less than that of other, more conventional techniques. It was agreed, nonetheless, that gaming of this type was a useful complement to other techniques and that it could have great value as an educational and training device.

Although crisis decision making has served as a focal point for historians and students of politics and diplomacy for years, research directed to improving decision making in crisis situations has been relatively rare.[6] In the mid-1960s, three crisis games, the North Flank, Central Front, and South Flank Exercises, were conducted at Rand. These manual games were designed to explore problems of national decision making in political and military crises; they focused on Europe in a period of crisis some five years in the future.[7] Among the options explored were the escalation of political and military confrontations to limited war, using conventional or tactical nuclear weapons, between the United States and the Soviet Union in Europe and escalation to general war, should that be warranted in terms of national objectives and the play of the game. The following questions were singled out for special consideration in these three crisis exercises:

What are the effects of game structures on decision making? What is the nature of these decisions compared with decisions in real, historical crises?

How does the escalation of violence in gamed exercises compare with that in reality?

What is the impact of the internal and external flow of information in the game setting?

What unanticipated research and operational questions developed in the course of the three exercises?

Among other findings, it was determined that the structure of a game affects the conduct of hypothetical crises in many important ways. These three exercises took into account the learning or wisdom generated by the earlier Goldhamer-Speier experiences; specific substantive issues were permitted to be examined from time to time with manual games, and their results were subjected to scrutiny by other research and analytic methods. The game structure, for instance, proved to have a strong impact on the nature of diplomatic threats and moves made during the game. Structure dictated the pace of escalation and interfered with perceptions of the opposing teams; in addition, the role and functions of the control team—a structural matter—were shown to be difficult to define and regulate, even though they had important implications for the play and outcome.

Although the exercises suggested that this form of manual gaming was unable to predict crises or to prescribe optimal decision-making behavior in crises, they showed that such games could identify many factors likely to enter into general crisis situations in the future (several of these topics are discussed later in this chapter).

> In our crisis gaming the political decisions did not produce consistent military actions nor were the military sections able to adapt promptly to political constraints. Moreover, the political leaders were often deficient in adapting policies to the command-control constraints that emerged during interactions with the subordinate military sections . . . these failures did not arise simply from lack of transmission media, or of timely information, but rather from differences in responsibilities, in perceptions, and in operational styles among the different agencies.[8]

STRATEGIC MSGs

In the late 1950s, SWAP, Strategic War-Planning game, was developed to study procurement strategies for an all-out war. The game was played by two opposing teams located in separate rooms but using identical maps of the northern hemisphere; each was made up of at least two players. Military units were represented by tokens placed on a map. The game itself had complete rules; at each stage, all strategic options available to the players were clearly shown, and the outcome of the play was entirely determined by the rules. A team of at least two umpires functioned solely to coordinate the play and filter the information between sides. Detailed considerations of the strategic air war setting were suppressed in order to stress the main problems of long-range planning and preparation for war.

The game modeled a five-year procurement phase, during which the actual number and configuration of strategic forces in 1959 were replicated as a starting point and yearly adjustments to these forces were made according to the teams' decisions. Decisions considered and made included changes in the number, level of resources, or status of aircraft, missiles, bases and base improvements, alert status for aircraft, active and passive defenses, intelligence, and research and development. After the procurement phase, the game was reset to an earlier period selected at random by the umpires, and a detailed test war was carried out. During this phase, measured in terms of hours of play, various problems were presented to the competing teams: scheduling takeoffs, refueling in the air or on the ground, penetrating the enemy perimeter, allocating bombers and missiles to targets, using decoys, and so forth. Play was ended when the first wave of major strikes had been carried out. Winners and losers were roughly determined by calculating military and civilian losses. In actual play, no winner was determined; rather, a detailed postmortem examined why particular decisions were made and what their actual results were likely to have been.

Like other games of this sort, SWAP was meant to increase awareness of the multiple factors interacting in long-range planning for a strategic air war. It is a fair example of a manual strategic game with rigid rules, one that could serve as a teaching device for planners, a generator of strategic ideas, or a preanalysis tool for researchers. Other MSGs with more complex representations that depend more heavily on computational backups evolved later from this game (SAFE, Strategy and Force Evaluation game, a prime example, is described in chapter 8).

TACTICAL MSGs

An extensive gaming facility dealing with questions related to limited war and the tactical use of air power had been developed and was operating at Rand as early as 1954. The SIERRA and REDWOOD series of tactical models and games were used, among other purposes, to maintain up-to-date information on hardware developments, operations, and threats; they also provided a nucleus of expert talent to work on specific tactical research and operational questions.

In the mid-1960s, several MSGs concerned with the structure of future tactical air forces in the 1970s were produced.

They included TOTEM (Theater Operations Tactical Evaluation Model), a highly aggregated computer model of air-land combat; TAFCOM (Tactical Fighter Combat Operation), a game that concentrated on tactical fighter operations; and STRAP (Strategic Actions Planner), one of a family of models that generated war plans down to the tactical level.[9] Tactical modeling and analysis continues at Rand in the form of the Military Operations group, which treats a variety of operational matters, including air-superiority operations, missile defense and suppression, penetration, command and control, and air-ground interactions.

GAME THEORY AND MILITARY APPLICATIONS

One of the most famous works to come from The Rand Corporation was John D. Williams's *Compleat Strategyst*.[10] Although many copies were sold and the book was translated into several languages, however, its impact on actual military applications is not clear. Work by L. D. Berkovitz and Melvin Dresher produced a formal solution to the problem of air-power allocation, but the results thus obtained had several drawbacks for actual application.[11] Solutions tend to be extreme and payoffs rather forced; a player may have to concentrate his entire effort against the opposing air force, for instance, and must then shift to concentrating on close support of his ground troops.[12]

The Research Analysis Corporation

The Research Analysis Corporation (RAC) was one of the major gaming and modeling centers in the United States; its major contributions have been detailed in Alfred H. Hausrath's *Venture Simulation in War, Business, and Politics*.[13] From 1951 through September 1972, RAC provided the United States Army with consultative and technical assistance in many fields; gaming was a major form relied on for much of this work (summarized in figure 6-2 for the period up to 1970).

In 1972, the trustees of RAC reached a decision to become a profit-making institution and to withdraw from the Federal Contract Research Center (FCRC) status under which it had until then been operating. This special status, shared by

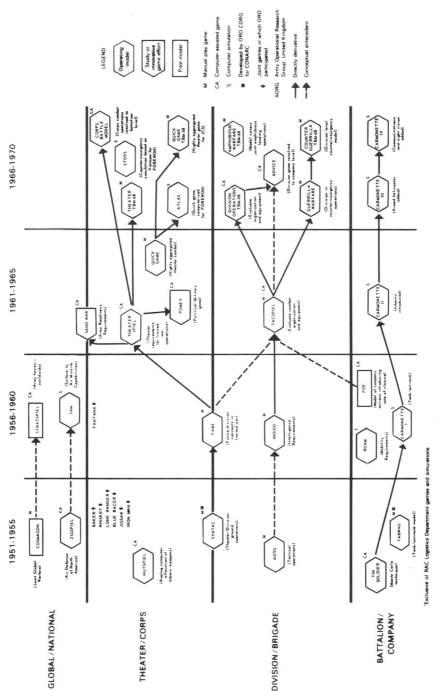

Figure 6-2. *The contributions of the Research Analysis Corporation to gaming and simulation, 1951–1970.*

several other analytic firms, bound RAC contractually to its Army client; in return, the corporation operated as a non-profit entity the budget of which was guaranteed in large measure by the Army, subject to congressional review and approval. Because the corporation needed financial and administrative assistance as a result of its decision, the General Research Corporation (GRC) assumed responsibility for the remainder of RAC's final-year obligation to the Army; GRC also acquired many of RAC's assets and personnel. In a subsequent corporate restructuring, Flow General Corporation, a firm engaged in medical research and development, assumed overall control of GRC, which became a subsidiary. Throughout the 1972–1978 period, a core group of eight to ten of the RAC gaming and simulation staff was retained and continues to operate, albeit at a sharply reduced level of activity. (A version of CARMONETTE, discussed in this section, and the Division Battle Model, or DBM, are presently being exercised by this group under contract to the United States Marine Corps.)

Lawrence J. Dondero, leader of that core group, has been a constant source of information about RAC and GRC activities. As author of an informative brochure published by RAC's gaming and simulations department, he identified RAC's objective during this period as the modeling of a wide spectrum of war situations with a family of MSGs, in order to "develop a capability of providing a rapid response and flexibility in meeting user requirements. [The department] has for some time had as its primary objective the development of a family of mutually supporting war games/simulations."[14] In meeting this objective, RAC gamers produced an impressive inventory of MSGs for conflict situations falling between the extremes of global strategic interaction and guerrilla or counterinsurgency warfare. The Corps Battle Model (CBM), for instance, was a two-sided, closed war game simulating corps-sized operations down to the level of the individual battalion. The Theater Battle Model (TBM-68) was in fact a family of MSGs, including the Theater War Game, the Theater Quick Game Model, the Division Operations Model, the Counterguerrilla Warfare Model, and the Amphibious Warfare Model.[15] CARMONETTE, which encompasses several generations of MSGs dating back to about 1958, is the most highly detailed and complicated model developed and used at RAC. It is a computerized Monte Carlo simulation of battalions or smaller units in ground combat operations (as a Monte Carlo simulation, it contains random elements the impact of which is assessed through repeated plays while all nonrandom components are held constant); in one version or another, it explicitly simulates the acquisition of targets, direction of fire, deployment of weapons, movement of forces, effects of terrain, and outcome of combat involving small-unit operations. Tactical decisions are preselected and stored in the model's input. CARMON-ETTE involves as many as twelve company-sized units on each side and counts single shots in the interaction. It has been used for a variety of purposes over the years, including the evaluation of alternative equipment mixes and new weapons, such as fixed- versus rotary-wing aircraft.[16]

While these and other RAC games were valuable and extensively used, some general criticism can be made about both the games and their use. Large games such as TBM-68 used between ten and thirty professionals and required several months to prepare and play. The game and its variants were used to study questions about ground-force size and mix, tactics, doctrine, organization, and operations; because of the sheer size of the operation, the resources required to run through even one play of the game precluded the necessary analysis of its sensitivity. Furthermore, the outcome of such games at the level of the theater or corps is ordinarily determined as a simple relation of force ratios between opposing sides; calculations are a function of gross rates of movement and losses of men and material. The RAC games, and all others focused at the same ambitious levels of detail and specificity, suffer from severe data problems. The capability of large units must be determined in terms of a single index from which a force ratio can be calculated, and such aggregated indexes must be developed or presumed from fragmentary experiences in World War II and Korea.[17]

In effect, there is no such thing as a validated, large-scale land-combat model. The historical and statistical analyses that would enable such land-warfare MSGs to be used with confidence have not been made. Indeed, questions about the monumental changes that have occurred in the weapons of land warfare, including the development of precision-guided munitions and other electronic advances, render many of the analyses that do exist suspect. In the aftermath of the acquisition and restructuring of RAC, the Army's Concepts Analysis Agency assumed responsibility for CARMONETTE and continues to use versions of it. Although we have not had an opportunity to review the current incarnation, we seriously doubt that the conceptual, specification, and data problems of its antecedent have been surmounted.

The Status of Military Modeling

Although the numbers are somewhat dated, the institutional breakdown generated by the United States General Accounting Office in its survey of modeling in 1970–1971 is still instructive. As already noted, the GAO was able to find 450 operational MSGs in actual use in the various agencies and institutions of the Department of Defense in May 1971. The following list shows the agencies involved and the number of active, operational MSGs for which each was responsible:[18]

Studies, Analysis and Gaming Agency	14
National Military Command System Control Center	49
Deputy Chief of Staff for Military Operations, Strategy and Tactical Analysis Group	41
Army Combat Development Command	115
Other Army activities	23
Navy Department, Assistant for War Gaming Matters	22
Other Navy activities	31
Center for Naval Analysis	34
Marine Corps	2
Air Force Chief of Staff, Studies and Analysis, Chief Operations Analysis	36
Other Air Force activities	10
Other Defense Department activities	11
Research Analysis Corporation	31
Other contractor activities	18
Unknown agency	13
Total	450

Today the field of military modeling and gaming appears to have reached a plateau. A great deal of development has occurred over the last decade, and much money and professonal talent have been expended in the construction and use of MSGs, but many problems remain. In addition, many tempting possibilities deserve increased attention.

Thus far, none of the attempts to create truly realistic representations of full-scale conflict has been successful. Piling detail on detail and complexity on complexity in an effort to capture reality has simply not resulted in anything useful or productive. Furthermore, many families of MSGs contain added-on or grafted portions that reflect changes in the operational requirements of the users and a desire on the part of builders to extend or reuse work originally intended for other purposes. This mismatching occurs for at least two general reasons. First, attempts are made to integrate MSGs with basically different functional and spatial levels of detail and consideration. The Army's Strategic and Tactical Analysis Group (STAG), for instance, tried to integrate an air-operations simulation, CASCADE, with TARTARUS 4, a land-combat MSG. After considerable effort, the structures of the MSGs proved to be incompatible and the results from the combined MSGs to be highly suspect. The second major cause of mismatching is the joint treatment of political, social, and organizational factors, in either single or combined MSGs; because the military criteria and factors are more solid in the computational sense, they tend to predominate; the political and social factors, which are less tractable and more difficult to mainipulate, are slighted. GUEVARA and the ARPA/COIN, or counterinsurgency, games of the late 1960s are prime examples of this situation.[19]

Other problems arise from the fact that several of the larger and more frequently used MSGs appear to have a data base that is partial and fragmentary at best. Difficulties in the validation, archiving, and review of data severely limit the usefulness of many key operational MSGs. As a result, it is necessary to resort to best guesses and conventional planning factors, such as test results obtained under ideal controlled conditions, intelligence estimates, and expert judgments, to structure and assign values to parameters. An equally important problem, which has failed to receive adequate attention, results from the use of even the best historical information about conflict. In the case of data generated by tank and anti-tank encounters in the Russian steppes in the dead of winter during World War II, for instance, using the data in other situations without first establishing their contextual similarity would certainly lead to erroneous and misleading conclusions. Reliance on a single planning factor, we believe, is very poor practice. In order to solve this sort of problem, hundreds of contextual profiles need to be created that could be used to build composites to fit the planned or contingent combat situation. This method would guard against planning for a past war through inappropriate use of historical data and planning factors.

As we have noted, there are grave limitations to the manageability of huge models, several of which can be compensated for by performing sensitivity analyses. If time and resources limit the use of a large model to a single play, the scientific issue of which factors in the MSG are most important remains unsolved, as does the question of whether the single play of the model is indicative of anything more than a unique confluence of chance and judgmental events. Resorting to simple indexes to describe the aggregate outcome of hundreds or thousands of individual interactions (all or most of which have been modeled) merely glosses over these unresolved issues.

Several even more fundamental issues appear to be making the appropriate use of operational military MSGs more difficult. It is necessary to step back from the details of particular MSGs to examine these issues with more care. The following discussion does not exhaust the list of basic problems, but it does call attention to areas that require scrutiny and professional attention.

No distinct theory of gaming, for instance, exists—at least as distinguished from game theory, decision theory, small-group theory, or any one of a number of other theoretical paradigms. (Any theory of gaming will be primarily a coherent body of wisdom, characterized by judgment rather than analysis—in the narrowest sense of that term.) Little scholarship has been devoted to the exploration of the limits and validity of knowledge generated by modeling, simulating, or gaming—that is, of its epistemology. How, for instance, might implicit theories embedded within military MSGs be identified and compared? Everyone in the field works with grossly oversimplified representations of complex contextual settings; questioning underlying theories focuses on the need for systematic ways to expose and compare the simplifications actually being used.[20] In the current state of knowledge, games are more likely to yield insights than to solve problems directly; however, no one is certain about what game players, builders, and users are actually getting out of the play, construction, or use of these devices. The problem is an empirical one; its resolution would improve game construction and play for many potential operational purposes and uses.

Little attention has been given to data validation; the data sets commonly used by operational modelers are seldom tested for their appropriateness to the intended application. The absence of efforts at validation is frequently explained away by statements that a data source is the only one known to exist, that others have used it in similar ways, that collecting data is too time-consuming and expensive, or that the data have become "standards" for the generation of planning factors or estimates.

The perspectives and assumptions used to structure a problem, even as embodied in highly technical all-machine MSGs, are often more important than the subsequent formal analysis itself. It should be possible, for instance, to expose the scenarios built into the typical "engineering" representation of strategic or command-and-control MSGs, but this is seldom done. Moreover, because of the multiple problems of documentation and secrecy, it is usually not possible to recreate the images and simplifications that underlie most quantitative MSGs.[21] As a result, the user is faced with a take-it-or-leave-it situation that makes intelligent questioning of the results of a given MSG difficult at best.

The size of MSGs is another general issue that has yet to receive the attention it warrants. What are the effects of MSG size on construction, operation, and ultimate use? Is it better, for instance, to build simple, small, and easily understood

MSGs, knowing that they are not truly realistic? Or is it better to opt for large, highly detailed, complicated MSGs that purport to capture reality? The latter have been prevalent in the operational modeling community.

It is our view that most of the real problems confronting operational decision makers are far less technical than the preponderance of technical evaluation MSGs would indicate. The assessment of weapons technologies, like the assessment of any other technology, almost invariably turns out to be an institutional and political issue. Comparatively little work is going on, however, in areas related to political, diplomatic, and military gaming. If the repeated political experiences of the last twenty years have taught the military modeling and analytic community nothing else, it should be clear by now that for complex conflict situations, narrow technical analyses, no matter how elegant, are probably as bad as or worse than no analyses at all.[22]

PART THREE

Intellectual
Foundations

7 | Mathematical and Game-Theory Models

MATHEMATICAL REPRESENTATIONS of combat have long fascinated analysts and practitioners. Many individual approaches and techniques have been developed and used over the years; several archetypical forms are described in this chapter in order to give the reader a fundamental grasp of what each form entails.

Lanchester's Equations

Since 1916, when the English mathematician Frederick W. Lanchester published his *Aircraft in Warfare*, a considerable literature has sprung up on variations of the equations Lanchester devised to calculate casualties of war.[1]

The basic Lanchester equations may be represented as two differential equations of the following form:

$$\frac{dr}{dt} = -\beta_1 b \qquad \frac{db}{dt} = -\beta_2 r . \qquad (7.1)$$

These equations can be interpreted as follows: r and b represent the number of red and blue units in an engagement. It is assumed that any element of any force can fire at opposition elements without hindrance. The parameters β_1 and β_2 are the unit operational combat-effectiveness coefficients for the two sides. Equations 7.1 can be stated in words, as "The rate of attrition of the red or blue force is equal to the combat-effective-

77

ness coefficient times the size of its opposing force, all other things being equal." In solving the equation, we can show that the probability of either blue or red winning is given by the following expressions:

$$\frac{\beta_1 r^2}{\beta_1 r^2 + \beta_2 b^2} \qquad \frac{\beta_2 b^2}{\beta_1 r^2 + \beta_2 b^2} . \qquad (7.2)$$

Here we have Lanchester's N-Square law in its most elementary form: "The fighting strength of a force may be broadly defined as proportional to the square of its numerical strength multiplied by the fighting value of its individual units."[2] The N-Square law thus provides a qualification to Napoleon's well-known dictum on war: God is on the side of the stronger force in proportion to the squares of their respective sizes, all other things being equal.

Unfortunately, all other things are rarely equal in warfare. In applying mathematics to human affairs, including warfare, the ability to solve models must not be confused with the ability to formulate the correct or appropriate model. Lanchester's equations were an intellectual breakthrough in the analysis of warfare insofar as they provided a deep insight into the possibilities inherent in simple models of combat. This is not the same as providing operational information or explicit guidance in setting policy for complicated situations in actual warfare.[3]

Several simplifying assumptions underlie the models represented in equations 7.1. Each individual can fire on anyone in the opposing forces, and the war will be over in one brief engagement. Thus, it is not necessary to account for the operational losses on both sides as they accumulate over time. If we wish to consider a lengthy set of engagements, we may replace the simplest representation by this more complex one:

$$\frac{dr}{dt} = P_1 - \alpha_1 r - \beta_1 b \qquad \frac{db}{dt} = P_2 - \alpha_2 b - \beta_2 r . \qquad (7.3)$$

This model includes two new terms. The terms P_1 and P_2 stand for the production rates or the speed at which new forces are added to the battle for the red and blue fighting units. The parameters α_1 and α_2 are the unit operational losses expressed as a coefficient for each side.

Equations of this general form have been used to analyze the outcomes of specific battles.[4] In his study of the battle of Iwo Jima in World War II, for instance, J. H. Engel used the following representations:[5]

$$\frac{dr}{dt} = -\beta_1 b \quad \text{and} \quad \frac{db}{dt} = P_2 - \beta_2 r . \qquad (7.4)$$

The Japanese began with a fixed force and did not introduce extra forces as the combat continued. On the other hand, Allied forces landed 54,000 troops on the first day; none on the second; 6,000 on the third; none on the fourth and fifth; 13,000 on the sixth; and none thereafter. The battle ended in thirty-six days. Engel was able to show that, given the values of $\beta_1 = .0106$ and $\beta_2 = .0544$, the Lanchester equations produced results that fit the data extremely closely.

Differences in combat effectiveness between opposing troops must be explained to a great extent in terms of the extreme aggregation in this model. Obviously, an individual who knows warfare would demand a much more realistic model than Engel's to represent the known and complex details of combat. Such a model might separate out factors such as differences in training and morale on each side, the difficulties encountered in making the landing, the number of targets on opposing sides that could realistically be fired on by an individual, and a host of other factors. It is usually impossible, however, to obtain usable data on these other key factors; it is hard enough even to get accurate casualty information, as the generally unreliable reporting of Viet Cong and People's Army of Viet Nam casualties in the Vietnamese War strongly suggests.[6] An impressive feature of the Lanchester equations is that they apparently explain so much so parsimoniously.

Simple forms of the models may yield important insights. When they are elaborated to any extent, however, they become difficult or impossible to solve mathematically. It becomes necessary to rely on the computer, which can manage complex algorithms, numerical approximations, and simulations, to carry out the needed calculations. Once the computer is introduced, however, there is a considerable danger that the model builder will feed his uncertainties into the black box.

The results are far less susceptible to challenge and modification than are the simpler model and its parameters, which can be easily explained and understood.[7]

Ivan Driggs has suggested a simple dice game that helps teach operational personnel some of the implications of Lanchester's N-Square law.[8] Each side rolls a set of dice with some red and some black faces. The number of red faces gives the measure of unit combat effectiveness. For each red face rolled, one of the opposing player's dice is removed. This game shows plainly that the Lanchester equations are a mechanistic representation of combat in which free will does not operate. Differences in roles and in the effects of morale, intelligence, strategy, and so forth are overlooked in analyses based upon these highly aggregated models. Equations could be modified to take into account breaking-point phenomena—that is, behavioral changes that occur when casualties become large enough to destroy or significantly change the morale and fighting effectiveness of a unit—but the difficult choice must still be made between simple but understandable models of complex phenomena and complicated, often incomprehensible, representations in the interest of capturing detail. A more basic question addresses the usefulness of highly complex models when there is no reason to believe that they are adequate representations of the phenomenon studied or when the important additional factors cannot be evaluated. Furthermore, it is extremely difficult to apply any sort of mathematical model to human affairs because assumptions—that morale can be ignored as a factor in combat, for instance—frequently turn out not to be justified. Mathematicians are generally interested in solving differential equations, not in arguing about the subtle empirical meaning of their models.[9]

Work related to Lanchester's, initially concentrating on the two arms races of 1908–1914 and 1929–1939, was done by another Englishman, Lewis Richardson. In capturing reaction processes—in which the actions of one party stimulate the responses of an opponent, which, in turn, cause a reaction from the first, and so on in an upward spiral—Richardson was able to capture the essence of a variety of complex behavioral situations, including arms races, price wars, and labor negotiations, to name only a few, in a set of relatively simple differential equations.[10]

It is easy for the skilled model builder to write down differential equations and explain that they stand for an international bargaining process, an arms race, the spread of disease, or some other complex process. It is less easy to show that they are actually good representations of the situation or that the equations square with even some aspects of reality.[11]

Articles on Lanchester equations number in the hundreds and are produced primarily by mathematicians, operations researchers, and people with military backgrounds. We do not have a good estimate of the resources expended in studying models of this type. That activity in this area continued in 1975, however, is evidenced by the work of the Vector Research, Incorporated (VRI) consulting group, mainly for the Department of the Army. This group has developed extremely detailed and elaborate models for fire support and other related analyses. The models include DIVOPS (Division Operations) at the division level of analysis and VECTOR-0, -1, and -2 at the theater level.[12] We have been unable to uncover evidence of the successful operational use of the more elaborate Lanchester models.

Game-Theory Models

A specific set of mathematical models, essentially based on the early work of John von Neumann and Oskar Morgenstern, has evolved over the last thirty-five years and is known as game theory or game-theory models. The theory and its models treat competitive or cooperative situations involving two or more players whose interests are pursued through a variety of strategies and whose gains and losses can often be calculated in terms of outcome or payoff matrixes.[13]

Most of the specialized literature applied to evaluation of weapons, problems of force structure, allocation of resources, duels, and search problems (such as determining how best to deploy a submarine so as to maximize chances of contacting an enemy's shipping) has used game-theory models and representations of the two-person, zero-sum variety (zero-sum games are those in which one side's losses count directly as gains for the other side).[14] Analysts have stressed the "maxmin solution" concept associated with that type of game. Its major assumption is that the enemy is rational and utterly opposed to his opponent's interests; he is expected to take advantage of

all opportunities and acts accordingly. Thus the concept of individual rationality is extended to a situation of conflict.[15] Like
most other models, game-theory models may provide insight
into one process at the expense of losing clarity elsewhere.
Unlike the models based on the Lanchester equations, in
which the players are modeled as mechanisms, the game-theory model treats human players as efficient, rational actors
lacking personal and social qualities beyond their ability to
compute advantages, choose strategy, and aim at maximal
gains.[16] In the following pages we shall describe, as a specific
example, the application of a particular game-theory model to
tactical air war. This model is based on the work of L. D. Berkovitz and Melvin Dresher.[17]

The process of deciding on the best ways to employ tactical
air forces for different tasks in the theater can be analyzed as a
multistage game between opposing forces (a multistage game
proceeds in steps, and the outcome of previous interactions
helps structure and determine later ones). In the course of the
campaign, the commanders make decisions like what type of
weapons to use for a particular mission, what targets to attack,
and what tactics to use for delivery. An abstract game-theory
model may provide qualitative insights about such policy
matters even though precise quantitative results would be impossible without a much more complicated and detailed model
of conflict.

Berkovitz and Dresher list the usual tasks involved in tactical air war as follows:

Counter-air—operations against the enemy's airbases and
    organization to destroy aircraft, personnel, and facilities
Air defense—operations against the enemy's attempts to de-
    stroy one's own air forces
Close air support—operations against concentrations of
    enemy troops or fortified positions, intended to help the
    ground forces in the battle area; firepower delivered from
    the air
Interdiction—operations to reduce the enemy's military po-
    tential by attacking his transportation facilities
Reconnaissance—operations carried out to obtain informa-
    tion about targets
Airlift—aerial transport of troops and equipment

For the purposes of their model, these six tasks are grouped into counter-air, air-defense, and close-support operations. Berkovitz and Dresher's model consists of a series of strikes or moves made simultaneously and involving all three operational tasks. Each side moves to maximize the gains from a given theater mission or payoff.

At the start, blue has p planes, and red has q planes. A strike involves splitting them up into three groups according to the operational task possibilities. For example, blue allocates x planes to counter-air operations, u planes to air defense, and the remaining planes, $m = p - x - u$, to ground support. Red allocates y planes to counter-air operations; w, to air defense; and the remaining number, $m = q - y - w$, to support of ground forces. Each side is assumed to be ignorant of the opponent's allocations until battle commences; however, each is assumed to know the total number of enemy planes.

The number of blue planes that get through to counter-air targets depends on the number of planes that red has allocated to air defense. It is assumed that the number of interceptions by red will be proportional to the number of planes allocated to this task. If w stands for the number of planes, then there will be a proportionality constant c such that the term cw approximates the number of interceptions by red. This constant obviously depends on the planes' characteristics, flying altitudes, weapons characteristics, and similar factors. The number of attacking blue planes that penetrate red's defenses is $x - cw$, as long as cw is not greater than x. If it is, no blue aircraft will penetrate red defenses. The number of planes that successfully reach their targets can be expressed mathematically as

$$\text{Max } (o,\ x - cw) . \qquad (7.5)$$

Blue's counter-air operations are aimed at reducing the enemy's air force by bombing the appropriate targets. It is assumed that the number of aircraft destroyed varies with the number of attacking planes that penetrate the red defenses. It is also assumed that each blue plane that penetrates can destroy the planes of the enemy. Thus the extent of destruction of red planes can be specified as, at most,

$$b \text{ Max } (o,\ x - cw) . \qquad (7.6)$$

The number of red planes actually destroyed will depend on the number of red aircraft at risk at the time of the attack.[18]

The model also assumes that red's air force is reduced during the strike by features such as accidents and antiaircraft fire. If these losses are assumed to be proportional to the number of planes used by red, they can be described as aq, where a *is red's accident rate. Finally, it is assumed that, during the strike, red's air force may be increased by s planes.* Replacements are subject to blue's counter-air attack but are not available to be used by red during the strike. Given these considerations, the number of red planes at risk at the time of the strike is $q - aq + s$; hence, the number of red planes that blue's initial counter-air strike will destroy is

$$\text{Min} \left[q - aq + s, b \text{ Max} (o, x - cw) \right] . \qquad (7.7)$$

The air-battle aspects of the model are minimized. Planes used in air defense are assumed to survive, and aircraft that fail to penetrate air defenses are assumed to return to their bases.

Summing the losses and adding replacements, the size of red's forces after the strike is given by the expression

$$\begin{aligned} q_1 &= q + s - aq - \text{Min} \left[q - aq + s, b \text{ Max} (o, x - cw) \right] \\ &= \text{Max} \left[o, q + s - aq - b \text{ Max} (o, x - cw) \right] . \qquad (7.8) \end{aligned}$$

A similar calculation may be made for blue's inventory:

$$p_1 = \text{Max} \left[o, p + r - dp - e \text{ Max} (o, y - ku) \right] . \qquad (7.9)$$

Blue and red now have p_1 and q_1 planes to allocate for the second strike, which will give rise to new inventories p_2 and q_2 for the third, and so on until the end of the campaign.

It is now necessary to define a payoff to these operations. Suppose that blue's objective is to assist the ground forces in the battle area and that the results will vary with the number of planes allocated to ground-support operations. It is possible to construct a payoff function on m, the number of planes allocated to ground support. Obviously, the payoff will depend heavily on such characteristics of the target, as the concentration of troops, fortification of positions, and number of vehicles and other material. No attempt is made to give an explicit form to this function. It is assumed that the payoff $S(m)$ is a positive function that increases with increasing allocations. Blue's yield in ground support must be reduced in accordance with the number of planes n allocated by red to ground support. If $T(n)$ is the function that measures the distance gained by red's ground forces, in terms of his air support, then the net advance of blue's ground forces can be described by the expression

$$Y(m,n) = S(m) - T(n) . \qquad (7.10)$$

Thus the payoff for the entire campaign with N strikes is the sum of the net yields for each strike. This can be expressed mathematically as

$$M = \Sigma^N [S(m) - T(n)] . \qquad (7.11)$$

The problem faced by each side involves the trade-off between allocating large numbers of planes to ground support, thereby increasing the probability of advancing, and sending planes on counter-air operations to reduce the number of planes available to the enemy for ground-support missions in subsequent moves. In addition, each side has to provide air defense for its own air force as a counter to enemy attempts to destroy it. Thus M is a function of four variables and can be written as

$$M(x,u;y,w) = \Sigma^N [(p - x - u) - (q - y - w)] . \qquad (7.12)$$

Solving the model just described for optimal tactics is an extremely difficult mathematical task. Berkovitz and Dresher have accomplished this feat, however, as described in the following paragraph.

During the closing period of the campaign, both red and blue concentrate on ground-support missions. The same tactics are optimal for both regardless of their initial forces. At other times red and blue should behave quite differently. If blue is assumed to be the stronger side, then there exists a best way to allocate blue's air force among the three tasks; it is governed during the early period by a critical value of the ratio of blue force size to red force size. If the force ratio is less than this critical value, optimal allocation consists of splitting the stronger air force between counter-air and air defense and initially neglecting ground support. If blue's strength is high enough relative to red's, then it should divide its forces in a fixed way among the three tasks. The number of aircraft allocated to each mission depends on the number of strikes remaining. The weaker air force cannot use a single strategy but must bluff during all the strikes except those in the terminal phase. If it is not terribly disadvantaged, the entire force is concentrated either on counter-air or on air defense. If, however, it is very weak relative to the other side, then its entire air force is allocated to any one of the three air tasks, chosen randomly.

Berkovitz and Dresher correctly contrast this analysis with trying to run a simulation or an operational game for the same problem. They observe that in a game with m different allocations for each side at each of N moves, the number of possibilities is m^{2N}. A game with three allocations and five strikes would require approximately 59,000 plays. If there are t regions or segments of the battle area to which the m allocations are to be made, the number of alternatives very quickly becomes astronomical. For example, with $m = 3$, $t = 9$, and $N = 5$, there are 3^{45} possible choices, or approximately 2.9×10^{21}.

Berkovitz and Dresher argue that the odds are overwhelming that neither a simulation nor an operational game of this problem would enable an experimenter to spot counterintuitive tactics such as randomizing the allocation of forces. While this argument is undoubtedly true, another difficulty confounds the problem. Berkovitz and Dresher's illustrative work is notable for its high analytic quality and for its judicious emphasis on qualitative rather than quantitative results. There is some danger, however, that the qualitative aspect of the result may be only an artifact of the model. A slight change in the information conditions, which might easily take place in combat, could considerably alter the picture. A marked technological advantage on the part of one side's forces, a fact of life in rapidly changing conflict situations, could radically alter the analysis by upsetting the implicit assumption of symmetry underlying force capabilities. Even though a game-theory model may be elegant, the game description may not be sufficiently robust or sensitive to important contextual subtleties and changes.

The problems that can be investigated using this type of game theory are fascinating and interesting. In our view, continued funding of research in this area would contribute to improving the sadly deficient store of basic knowledge on which more "realistic" formulations, such as machine simulations, are based. Using the results to educate military personnel could be valuable if they were systematically challenged by the armed-forces students. On the other hand, applying these models directly to selected alternative force structures could be extremely dangerous if the all-important qualifications and limitations were forgotten.

Another type of model amenable to treatment through game theory is the search problem. For example, a surface ship must get from port A to port B. The opponent knows the approximate speed of the ship, the prevailing visibility conditions, the boundaries of the area in which the ship can be expected to operate, and the available methods of detection and jamming. If the opponent has k surface vessels available to intercept the enemy ship, what are the optimal search and avoidance procedures to be followed by both sides? A host of models can be built to represent this problem.[19]

It is impossible to know exactly how many people use game-theory models to solve problems of optimal military tactics or what is the general magnitude of work in this area. A crude approximation can be obtained by looking at the numbers of unclassified articles and their authors. About 100 to 200 articles are readily available in the open literature. Our best guess is that between 50 and 200 people in the United States are capable of making a serious contribution to this field.

Non-Zero-Sum Games and Other Mathematical Models

Only in combat situations characterized as short-term, tactical operations do models of pure opposition, like those described above, have much value. Lengthy campaigns and total wars cannot be represented accurately if the participants must be assumed to be in pure opposition, since both sides could easily lose simultaneously.

Defining the actual situation is frequently far more difficult than manipulating the mathematics purporting to solve it. The now classical prisoner's dilemma game serves as an example.[20] In this game, when each side pursues what appears to be a rational policy individually, the gains to each are worse than expected, and both sides lose ground. Thus communication and cooperation are stressed. Such considerations apply not only to long campaigns and wars but also, even more directly, to political, military, and diplomatic negotiations or "informal wars."

We believe that pure mathematical models have a role to play in the study of such situations, but only in three very special cases. They are valuable in basic research; they serve usefully as paradigms to illustrate counterintuitive properties in a situation or system; and they may be used as algorithms for larger models. Thus, for example, simple models may be used to illustrate the importance of coordination, to demonstrate why rational individual behavior can spell social disaster, to show the importance, or unimportance, of extra information in certain situations, or to clarify some of the difficulties involved in the operational definition of commonly used words such as *threat, bluff,* and *concession.* In all these cases, the expert and the decision maker continue to inhabit different cultures. The expert who knows the methods and weaknesses of formal mathematical modeling is generally not the person who is responsible for making decisions about policy. The lines of communication between the two are tentative, and discourse is impeded because they do not speak the same language.

Most work attempting to apply analogies from non-zero-sum games to various aspects of bargaining, competition, or warfare has been done in an academic setting, and much of the financial sponsorship for the work has emanated from research organizations such as the National Science Foundation (NSF) or the Defense Advanced Research Projects Agency (ARPA). The work has been performed by political scientists, international-relations experts, sociologists and anthropologists, and some operations researchers and mathematicians, most of whom have only an imperfect knowledge and appreciation of the detailed and formal aspects of game theory. A considerable body of experimental work has been done by social psychologists studying simple, non-constant-sum games (that is, games in which total gains and losses may vary, hence society as a whole may gain or lose as a function of the outcome). Some mathematicians and game theorists have also been working in this area. Nearly all of their investigations are best regarded as basic research. Most of it has been sponsored by NSF, ARPA, the universities, and private foundations. Roughly 1,000 to 2,000 articles have been published in this area.[21]

Other mathematical models do not fit neatly into any of the classifications just described. Some consider features such as the speed of learning and the capability of individuals or organizations to remember or process information. A certain amount of literature has been devoted to models of bargaining and negotiation.[22] Most of the models produced are intended for research or teaching purposes. They can be used to illustrate various principles, but they are generally somewhat removed from any direct operational application.

8 | Manual Games

There was nothing unusual about the idea of having war games—they are constantly being programmed in the game room of the Pentagon—these games were different, and all the players knew it; it was as if this was a dry run for the real thing.

David Halberstam, *The Best and the Brightest*

WAR GAMES have been manual games since their beginnings; however, as gamers realized that many of the problems confronting them in conflicts were not easily or productively analyzed by moving game tokens across maps or boards, demands for more satisfactory methods intensified. One method devised to examine problems that arise in the course of international conflicts is the manual game focused on political, diplomatic, and military issues.[1]

Such games are usually tailored to conform to a plausible conflict situation in the future and are played by teams under the direction of a control or referee group. A scenario describes key events preceding and contributing to the conflict and serves as a common pool of information during the play. The actions and reactions of numerous players are examined and woven together by a control team during the simulated conflict. Each team decides on specific moves after considering its options, objectives, and constraints. Moves are made in response to information presented in the scenario, to moves taken by the opposing teams, and to information and guidance provided by the control group. This group is the final arbiter of all moves and actions and also functions as Nature in the game setting; that is, it acts the part of fate.

These games never prove anything in the scientific sense; the proceedings have different motives and aims. It is generally agreed that games of this type help to portray the complexities of international conflict; that the role-playing aspects of the games provide insights into the special problems of command and control; and that such games are important educational experiences, during which the participants become aware of specific facts about possible conflicts. More precisely, discovery takes place. Positions, expectations, perceptions, facts, and procedures are typically challenged and improved as the game proceeds. Controllers and referees, who are often experts in particular areas, may question a decision or prevent individuals from making certain moves, but their actions are also open to challenge and debate. Thus imagination and innovation play a determining role in the drama of a manual game. The game may also be regarded as a type of brainstorming or intellectual interaction that allows players to uncover features of a problem not described in its scenario. The value of such exercises depends on many things, primarily the initial conditions created and the nature and quality of the controlling and playing groups. How good is the scenario? How professional are the players? How valid and inspired is the guidance of the control team, referees, and other contributing experts?

Although manual, free-form games originated partly because of the limitations of the traditional war game in dealing with political and other nonquantifiable factors in military situations, the focus of the more creative early efforts shifted quickly to include diplomatic, economic, psychological, and social factors as well. The shift increased the importance of the scenario and led to the relative devaluation of rote calculations of military outcomes.

Two apparently contradictory views have arisen about the data produced by manual, free-form games. One group believes that such games are nonscientific because they are not replicable and generate neither valid research data nor tangible research results. Analysis is not possible during play because the wishes of the control group and the momentum of the game override the researcher's desire to stop, speed up, or slow down activities for his own purposes. Measurement would, in effect, destroy or contaminate the thing being measured. The second group states that too much unsystematic information for postgame analysis is produced and that there are few effective means to manage and analyze it. Thus complaints arise on one side because there are not enough data; to the other side, there appears to be an overabundance. Resolution of the issue seems to depend on identifying reasonable, interesting, and manageable units of observation and analysis. Both groups at least feel that tangible research results might be obtained from manual games if effective procedures for the management, reduction, and analysis of data could be devised. This potential has not yet been tapped.[2]

There are five basic steps in free-form, manual gaming: preparing, starting the conflict, playing, exploring branches, and ending play.

The preparatory phase can be quite complicated and cover many months, or it may be simplified and abbreviated; the time required depends to a great extent on the information possessed by the experts selected to play. In addition to specifying the purpose of the game—a nontrivial matter—masses of data must be collected and arranged for use in the scenario and for ready reference once the game is under way. Developing the scenario is a demanding task that is too frequently left to the last moment, relegated to nonexpert personnel, or accomplished by dusting off and making marginal changes in some previous gaming exercise. Preparing for a game requires a preliminary check of the scenario to insure that it is convincing enough to sustain player interest and that it will not be rejected even before the game gets under way, as sometimes happens. Players are selected according to the various skills and perspectives they may contribute during the game. They are briefed about the game's purpose and provided with operating instructions. Background information, sometimes in the form of fact books or position papers, is provided at this point.[3]

The start of the conflict may be part of the scenario itself or may occur in response to preliminary moves by the opposing teams. In the first case, the scenario presents the teams with an ongoing conflict, and they are forced to make the hard choices needed to resolve the matter. In the second, more common case, opposing teams move according to conditions provided in the scenario, and the control team interprets and directs their moves to provoke the desired conflict, crisis, or confrontation. That variations exist, however, underscores the fact that this type of game is a tailor-made enterprise that depends heavily on the predetermined purposes of the controllers.

Game play is left to the control team's discretion, but players usually have opportunities to make requests and objections. Each team formulates its own moves; this process may take a full day or more, or it may be greatly compressed, as in a case when the players' likely reactions to the pressure of a simulated crisis were explored. Moves submitted to the control team may be highly detailed and formal and may resemble military estimates of the situation; they may be detailed and informal, stating various actions taken, requesting information, and stating intentions and expected outcomes (either honestly or deceptively); they may be brief directives ("launch two wings of B-52 bombers and hold at fail-safe for further orders"); or they may take a variety of other forms.

The control team reviews all moves submitted and determines the likely outcome of their interaction. It also responds to requests for information, generates information of its own, exercises its power as Nature, and handles other complaints and problems, both inside and outside the formal game structure. When its between-move activities are completed, time is advanced and the opposing teams prepare their next moves. During the control team's more active period, both teams of players have an opportunity to prepare contingency plans, to collect intelligence, and to consider their next moves. Edwin Paxson has outlined the main functions of the control team as (1) providing high-level political control and information; (2) adjudicating matters of credibility and relevance; (3) evaluating the operational and logistical feasibility of plans and moves; (4) evaluating the implications and impact of moves; (5) supplying intelligence to teams; (6) creating and sustaining pacing with respect to time, space, and the scaling of decisions; and (7) maintaining the integrity or realism of the game.[4]

The manual, free-form game has great potential—though it is rarely used—as a way of examining branch points, that is, the logical development of courses considered seriously by one of the teams but not actually submitted as a formal move during game play. Branches could be examined in real time (that is, during the play of the game) by outsiders conducting quick, informal analyses of the likely results of some contingent course of action; alternatively, they might be recorded and left for more detailed postgame analyses. In either case, the problems in gathering, managing, and analyzing information noted earlier in this chapter have inhibited the full exploitation of this feature of the manual game.

The game may be concluded in a variety of ways. It may have reached a natural end point recognized by most of the participants; control may end it; resources may have been depleted; or a prior determination may have been made to end the game after a fixed number of moves. Once the game is officially concluded, the control team prepares a summary of the game, or debriefing, and discusses the game with all participants. Together they recapitulate the game's key features and try to decide what has been learned and whether the initial purposes have been satisfied. This discussion need not be particularly formal, although the degree of formality will vary widely.

The design and execution of briefings and debriefings are demanding and time-consuming tasks. Both activities are obviously tied closely to the scenarios used in game play. Debriefing, for example, ought not be separated from a thorough analysis of the aims, conditions, proceedings, and results of the game. Nevertheless, many operational MSGs do suffer from such a dissociation. Debriefing sessions are often carried out mechanically in the shortest possible period of time, if at all, and the results of the game are then set aside, thrown away, or forgotten. Follow-up discussions and assessments of what various players learned from a game are relatively rare. Scientific studies based on the multiple leads generated during a game are also rarely pursued with a fraction of the concern and attention that go into game play. Improvement in these two areas might be accomplished if more time and attention were spent in documenting the game through histories or other records. Documentation should include the events of the game itself, the lessons learned by the participants, and a record of other analyses done as a result of the game. Current styles of documentation range all the way from no record keeping at all to masses of unstructured and unsystematic data—verbatim transcriptions of team and control discussions, videotaped debriefings, and so on.[5] No coherent standards exist to help the gamer with documentation; the matter is left very much up to the judgment of those conducting the game.

Deciding whether a game was worth the time, effort, and expense involved is a thorny and much-debated issue. At the very least, the answer depends on the game's stated aims and on whether the game's sponsors and users are satisfied that these goals have been achieved—a highly subjective matter. At its most basic, the evaluation boils down to deciding whether some idea or way of looking at the problem existed after the exercise that was not generally accepted before the game was played. The question is a difficult one, and also highly subjective.[6]

Structural Issues

Nearly all modeling and gaming activities involve scenarios; it is within the context of manual games, however, that this critical game component can most logically be discussed.[7] The scenario represents the model builder's basic conception of the process or system being analyzed; it is a positive statement of assumptions about its operating environment. Scenarios range in style and complexity from the elaborate, fully articulated version often used in free-form, manual MSGs to implicit scenarios embedded within all-machine MSGs. Ideally, they treat not only the important items selected for consideration in the MSG, but also those introduced for purposes of testing and evaluation:

> After all, it is from our anticipations of the environments in which our systems are to operate—the state-of-the-world, the conflict situations, and the tasks these systems are expected to accomplish—that many of our criteria for *evaluating* the *performance* of a given system emerge. Thus, having a casual attitude toward the scenario is often tantamount to having a casual attitude toward the selection criteria. If we accept the proposition that our

analyses can be no better than the criteria we employ, then we must accept the corollary proposition that our analyses can be no better than our scenarios.[8]

Generally speaking, a scenario is an account, usually written, of a context or situation created for use in a war game, a political and military exercise, or the analysis of a system of weapons, a strategy, or a military problem in a specific setting.[9] The term *scenario* was appropriated from the film industry and entered the official military lexicon in about 1965, when it appeared in the Joint Chiefs of Staff's *Dictionary of U.S. Military Terms.* A scenario describes the local and regional settings of a conflict situation and specifies the objectives of the concerned participants. It identifies the participants and the resources available to each of them, including the military forces likely to be called into action. It outlines the spatial boundaries of the conflict and establishes appropriate temporal sequences for events; it describes the initial levels of violence and the reasons why the conflict began; and it provides the overall framework within which a specific conflict can be studied.[10]

Little is known about the impact of a particular scenario on game play and outcomes. Even less is known about what constitutes a "good" or a "bad" scenario; the scientific investigation necessary to begin to sort these matters out has yet to be undertaken, in spite of the preponderance of bad scenarios.[11] Successful scenarios and scenario writers exhibit many of the characteristics of good historical accounts and good historians. Hence, a key to the development and use of better scenarios may lie in the historical approach, an insight provided by Goldhamer in his early work. If this view is correct, it has many important implications for training future generations of scenarists and integrating information gleaned from studying the writing of scenarios.

Emerging phenomena are unpredictable only in the strictly logical sense. They can, in fact, be anticipated using a consistent frame of reference or context.[12] With such a frame of reference, the scientific observer and analyst are able, in Harvey De Weerd's words, to exclude irrelevant materials and permit a concentration on the central problem under analysis. Unless one is dealing with present-day problems and can be assured that all members of a game or research team know precisely what the present situation is—and can agree on it—one needs a context to avoid wasting time in reaching a common approach to the subject. When dealing with future problems, it is even more desirable to have a context to provide a common understanding of what the particular future under consideration is like. Otherwise, each man will form his own ideas about the future and ideas can vary widely, making group research or game efforts difficult.[13]

De Weerd also reminds us that the specific details of any context are unique; thus making point predictions about actual events can be hazardous. Because key elements in any given context may never reappear in exactly the same form, it is uncertain that any given phenomenon will ever reappear. Predictions must therefore be based on a variety of approaches and methodologies, and conclusions must be drawn from several distinct, though related, levels of analytic detail.

If the details of a context are to be specified, the elements must be related to one another causally and with respect to their rates of change over time. A good historian or a good scenario writer will develop trend analyses that take this factor into account. In one version, the so-called reverse decision-tree analysis, the timing of events is determined by starting with the crisis to be modeled and working backwards to create plausible explanations for it.[14] Alternatively, the scenarist could begin with the present situation and work into the future, making sure that no changes occur in the existing situation that could not be reasonably accounted for. In either case, detailed knowledge of the context of past and present situations, a disciplined imagination, and judgment are required to make the account useful. These essential attributes are not easily taught, nor are they generally appreciated by quantitative analysts bent on producing MSGs that generate plausible numbers.[15]

Scenario construction and gaming have much in common

with the historian's art of constructing explanations for the single case. The scientific generalizations available to the historian merely provide "indications, and rough ones at that, of the sorts of factors which, under certain circumstances, we expect to find correlated with other factors; but . . . they leave open to historical investigation and analysis the task of eliciting the specific nature of those factors on a particular occasion, and the precise manner in which the factors are causally connected with one another."[16] In the game setting, the analyst usually does not have proven behavioral rules or laws to guide his investigation of past situations, let alone likely future ones; he is forced to rely on other means to project the present into the future. Games and models, properly used, can help to accomplish this task by exploring, identifying, and bounding the existing uncertainty.

Gaming, in effect, produces multiple factors, circumstances, and relationships in the form of highly conditional predictions about possible real and hypothetical events. The scenario serves as the statement of initial conditions, which generate an outcome based on moves, countermoves, and interactions among game participants (or representations of opponents, in the case of the all-machine MSG). Games and models generate synthetic histories in cases where available real data are insufficient to develop real histories. Because the outcome of the game or model is synthetic, it is important not to rely too heavily on the results; that is, they cannot be applied unquestioningly in a real situation. This is the area in which a historical approach to writing scenarios can make a strong contribution; it demands that the analyst be constantly aware that a multitude of factors impinge on the outcome of real world events and that no single scenario or single set of analytic results can be expected to reflect that reality adequately.

This observation relates directly to two current issues: the need for developing alternative future contexts and the logical importance of reexamining the scenarios now contained in the majority of operational MSGs applied to military problems.

Analysis and Research Topics

One of the most seriously underrated problems in defense research and analysis today is the tendency to ignore the less likely but more dangerous possible developments in future conflict situations. Under what conditions, for what reasons, and on the basis of what kinds of calculations would current and potential future opponents behave in unexpected or irrational ways? Such questions are not likely to be asked, much less answered, in the current situation where a few outmoded scenarios, unbalanced advocacy, and all-machine MSGs dominate and where only selected agencies of the Department of Defense conduct the analyses. In the words of John Diebold, "We should be both less dogmatic and . . . be more specific in our forecasts. We should have a variety of public and private forecasting institutes that set down lots of possible scenarios of the way things might develop, without committing ourselves with hysteria to saying that one scenario is more likely than another."[17]

Increased attention to the way games are developed and to the kind of information about possible real-world conflicts that responsible officials need would go a long way toward achieving these objectives. Toward these ends, the Department of Defense, along with other public and private institutions, should undertake critical appraisals of the assumptions on which past military planning and analyses have been based; it should also examine the policies and aims of present and possible opponents and consider the broadest possible range of opportunities and dangers.[18] Such inquiries could make profitable use of competently executed manual games. One fundamental problem with manual gaming exercises, however, is the difficulty of attaining credible results from them; the substantive problems treated in these exercises— that is, the social and political world of international affairs— are so tangled, complex, and uncertain that manual gaming simply cannot, unsurprisingly, provide instant, correct answers. This point is central; it leads directly to our recommendation that a variety of gaming experiences should be subjected to retrospective analyses and assessments. These efforts would increase understanding of appropriate ways to use games and to combine them with other, complementary, intellectual activities. Such evaluations might also identify erroneous assumptions made in both real and analytic settings, sort out good analyses from bad, and improve the future use of games and other analytic procedures.

This kind of analysis should be a routine procedure. If assumptions about an opponent's decision-making processes yield consistently incorrect results in a number of modeled situations, those assumptions obviously need to be reexamined. If past exercises produced incorrect results because of faulty assumptions, prospective analyses and exercises will probably do so, too.

In addition to the need for appropriate analyses, several important substantive topics appear to have been overlooked by the operational gaming community—topics whose intractability to other analytic approaches is rivaled only by their importance for international affairs and national security. In our opinion, most of these topics could be investigated, at least initially, by means of free-form, manual gaming techniques.[19]

For example, the issue of nuclear proliferation resulting from the wholesale, worldwide implementation of nuclear power stations is an obvious candidate for investigation by gaming. Terrorism, deception, and negotiation and bargaining strategies and tactics are equally appropriate topics.[20] The use of food, credit, and technology as weapons in the emerging world situation and the spread of sophisticated conventional arms are other subjects that require more thought and more attention to their wider ramifications than they now receive.[21] Similarly, the prevention and termination of regional and global conflict could be examined with a combination of manual games and related approaches.[22]

Political and Military Exercises

The manual political, diplomatic, and military game was developed largely through the efforts of Herbert Goldhamer. In this section, we shall concentrate on the events leading up to the decision to use this technique and on the methodological points and lessons learned throughout the whole process.[23] Goldhamer undertook the development of this type of game because he was unable to forecast the main lines of political evolution between the great powers in the 1955–1965 period by means of existing techniques; in other words, a substantive problem was the impetus for devising a new, more appropriate methodology. The magnitude of the problem far exceeded the intellectual powers of a single analyst, Goldhamer believed, and required the collective wisdom of many experts in political, diplomatic, geographical, economic, military, and other areas. The aim, then, was to create a cost-effective means that would enhance intellectual collaboration in the resolution of a complex problem of political analysis and forecasting.

Alternative modes of collaboration were carefully considered and set aside. Interviewing was rejected on the grounds that the issues were too involved for respondents to address the problem in sufficient depth. It was also feared that respondents might feel that they were being exploited and dissociated from their intellectual contributions, particularly in regard to complex matters requiring clarification and interpretation. Another possibility, soliciting papers on preassigned substantive topics, was considered and rejected on the grounds that it was not likely to produce focused information that could shed light on the primary task. Seminars were also considered and rejected; it was felt that it would be extremely hard to keep them focused on the main research problem and that they would in all likelihood generate more discussion and problems than answers.

Goldhamer eventually realized that his research problem was quite similar to that confronting historians. He was faced with the task of writing a "future history" to clarify his ideas about the motives and influences affecting the behavior of great powers, their leaders, and others in the real political world. His feeling that intellectual collaboration was essential stemmed in part from dissatisfaction with methods then commonly used to carry out political, diplomatic, and military analyses. When, as Goldhamer and Speier remarked, "it became clear that the simplification imposed in order to permit quantification made the game of doubtful value for assessment of political strategies and tactics in the real world," it seemed only natural to turn to the less simplified, freer form of the political and military exercise.[24]

The selection of competent professionals to participate in the political exercise proved to be critically important. This situation is analogous to that in chess or other games, when inferior players tend to consolidate their own bad habits rather than being stimulated to improved or inspired play. In any collective intellectual endeavor (the manual game is only one specialized variant), the results cannot be expected to be any better than those who produce them. This simple point seems to have been overlooked in the gaming literature, although Goldhamer and Speier were careful to indicate its importance: "We found that one of the most useful aspects of the political game was its provision of an orderly framework within which a great deal of written analysis and discussion took place. In describing our experience to others, we have continually emphasized that oral or written discussion of political problems that arise during the game is one of its most valuable features."[25]

The role of Nature—that is, of everything not explicitly treated in a game's scenario or assigned to the participating teams—has a far greater impact on this form of game than many would believe. While the decisions about Nature's role are based on knowledge or hunches about the events considered in the game, the best that can be expected is a crude sense of how various players will react. This point appears rather obvious, but there is a prevalent, and dangerous, tendency to ascribe validity to gamed results in which Nature has been subordinated or omitted.

Concern for the role and impact of Nature on game play and outcome focuses attention on the basic purpose served by conducting an effective manual game. The games in themselves are not especially good as forecasting or predictive devices, because these tasks require both tested theoretical propositions that are applicable to a variety of international phenomena and reliable theoretical or empirical knowledge to account for the role of Nature. The political game was intended basically as a means to organize intellectual collaboration, not to determine truth. Goldhamer has described the intent and the key limitations of manual games as follows:

> It is true, to be sure, that an effective mode of integrating the knowledge of various specialists can certainly lead to intellectual advances, but this is not always the specific feature of gaming to which enthusiasts seem to attribute their belief that political games can generate knowledge that previously did not exist. The game, then, may under favorable circumstances make more effective use of existing knowledge than other modes of intellectual collab-

oration, but it would be placing an intolerable burden on it to treat it as a machine that displaces theoretical thought and empirical research.[26]

Because of the interest aroused by the games they developed at Rand, Goldhamer and his colleagues were invited to describe their work at a variety of forums between 1956 and 1959. During this period, one of the group, W. Phillips Davison, visited the Massachusetts Institute of Technology and helped launch a series of gaming exercises.[27] In 1958, a key year, Professors Lucian Pye and Warner Schilling used a form of the Rand game to enliven and stimulate students in their foreign-policy course. In September 1958, Professor Lincoln Bloomfield and Paul Kecskemeti, a Rand employee, conducted the first POLEX (Political-Military Exercise) game—a crisis game involving a Polish nationalist uprising along the lines of the Hungarian revolt of 1956. This game led to others in the POLEX series and to a variety of other political exercises for various purposes and clients.[28]

Most of the players in these games were government professionals; student participation and input were limited. Nevertheless, greater stress was placed on the educational and training aspects of the experiences than in the Goldhamer exercise, the purpose of which was operational. As Bloomfield and Gearin stated in 1973, "evidence had accumulated that a well-designed and executed political exercise could have a substantial impact on a professionally-trained person in loosening up some of his policy assumptions by forcing him to 'live' realistically with an artificial situation not of his own choosing."[29]

SAFE: A Strategy and Force Evaluation Game

One of the most interesting manual games played at The Rand Corporation was SAFE, a Strategy and Force Evaluation game, one of several analytic efforts made in 1961 and 1962 to project changes in the size and composition, or posture, of the strategic forces for the upcoming decade. The SAFE games were exceptionally well documented, a fact that enhanced their usefulness at the time and that, more recently, enabled a thorough retrospective assessment and comparison of the game results with real-world developments—a rare occurrence.[30]

SAFE was played six times during 1962. One play lasted two weeks and used the talents of nine or ten professionals. All together, twenty-six different players were involved in the SAFE series; ten played at least twice, usually assuming the opposing role in the second round. The games involved two teams, red and blue, under the direction of a control team. All players were highly trained, experienced strategic analysts; all had already had considerable experience with games. At the starting point, both teams were provided with a budget, a "policy statement" to guide their decisions, a selection of strategic forces that could be developed or purchased over the decade considered in the game, and an account of the actual force postures of the United States and the Soviet Union in 1962, the initial period.

Moves were conducted over five periods, each standing for two years, during which the teams allocated their budgets to research and development, procurement, and operating expenses. Information about the opponent's actual and expected moves, that is, intelligence, was provided by control at the beginning of each move period. Negotiation between the teams was mediated throughout by the control team. Control also periodically assessed the relative capabilities being developed by the teams. While role playing and bureaucratic manipulations were eschewed, the blue team represented the level of the Joint Chiefs of Staff and the Office of the Secretary of Defense; the red team, a supposedly analogous group within the Soviet Union.

SAFE's basic purpose was clearly stated at the outset; the basic documents indicate it was adhered to throughout the game: "The purpose of the SAFE exercises, within the context of the ACWS [Alternative Central War Strategy] project, was to explore the extent to which alternative sets of strategic objectives would lead to distinguishable general war force postures. Each one of the six plays of SAFE was an instance of the implementation of a set of U.S. objectives in interaction with a particular set of SU [Soviet Union] objectives for given budget profiles."[31] The specific objective of the game was "to work out the rational consequences in terms of a strategic posture which could arise *given a policy and budget.*"[32] Having learned from prior gaming experiences, those responsible for SAFE set modest, attainable objectives for themselves. No one ever claimed or sought to pinpoint the single correct strategic posture for either side; rather, the game was played to generate shared experiences for researchers involved in the larger ACWS project. It was also intended to provide them with points of departure for focused seminars that would later be devoted to detailed examinations of policies and postures. In addition to the development of a common language, SAFE focused the players' attention on several relatively more important analytic and policy issues. "The result was a series of reports which led rather directly to the appointment of the project leader to a high post in [the Office of the Secretary of Defense] dealing with actual strategic forces."[33]

The retrospective assessments of differences between gamed and actual outcomes showed that for the ten-year period of the analysis (1962–1972), the policies actually adopted by both of the great powers were functions of changing personalities, bureaucratic structures, political events, and technologies. The historical impact of these dynamic factors and the suddenness of the changes strongly demonstrate the continuing need for analysts to reexamine the accuracy of empirical assumptions about the real-world context that have been embedded in games or models. While the need to update assumptions is readily seen and accommodated in a manual game such as SAFE, it is more problematic in the all-machine MSG where the embedded assumptions are hidden in a black box. Furthermore, the long and often costly phases of designing and constructing an all-machine MSG discourage such reexaminations. This important point is a major finding of the SAFE experience; it is especially important in a real environment, where "it was asserted that requirements could be calculated with reasonable precision, defining cost/effectiveness as the combat effectiveness of *each* system *per dollar of outlay.*"[34] Reliance on this level of accuracy is self-deception at best.

The SAFE results differed from the actual, historical events in four general areas. The blue team spent much more on civil defense than the United States government did; blue spent proportionally more on intercontinental ballistic missiles (ICBMs) than on submarine-launched ballistic missiles (SLBMs), which was not what actually happened; long-endurance aircraft were favored by both teams at various times, but none was ever actually produced; and both teams used mobile ICBMs, whereas none were ever really deployed.[35] In each case of contradictory results, changing institutional, political, personal, and technological factors were identified that accounted for the differences after the fact. The SAFE series and the retrospective assessment are remarkable examples of manual games that were carefully defined, played, and assessed. Complete documentation was the key to success, from both the methodological and the realistic points of view. Such success stories are extremely rare in practice.

Pentagon Games

In 1961, under the direction of William Jones, who was at that time a colonel in the Air Force, political gaming was begun in the Joint Chiefs of Staff's Joint War Gaming Agency. The games are typically free-form, controlled exercises involving two or more opposing sides and played according to an initial scenario. Specialists and high-level officials regularly participate in the games, of which five or six are conducted each year.[36]

A great variety of crisis situations have been gamed over the years, with settings including Berlin, Latin America, Thailand, Vietnam, and the Middle East. It was in response to one of a series of Vietnam games played in 1964 that David Halberstam commented that the games seemed to be "a dry run for the real thing."[37] During a game devoted to exploring the likely impact of the United States' bombing, it appeared quickly and decisively that North Vietnam would be especially resilient and resistant to bombing. The impact of the game and its findings on actual policy choices is moot.

The procedures for manual games at the Studies, Analysis and Gaming Agency (SAGA), which superseded the Joint War Gaming Agency, are highly routinized. Background material used in the preparation of an initiating scenario is collected and assembled into a scenario-problem paper, which is distributed to the players just before game time. Preparation may take two to three months, depending upon the specific crisis being considered. Two or more teams—the United States and the Soviet Union, blue and red, and as many others as are deemed necessary for the specific situation—are appointed. Each team is composed of from five to ten players; the teams meet several hours a day for three to four working days to plan actions and reactions based on strategies, objectives, capabilities, and plans either known or presumed to exist. Play extends for three to six cycles, or periods. A control team analyzes each move with respect to the world situation and other moves, determines the likely outcomes, updates the world situation in the scenario-problem paper, advances the game clock, and returns play to the active teams. Every game ends with a debriefing and critique, in which participants exchange opinions about actions taken or not taken in the course of the game. Extensive documents are then drawn up by SAGA personnel. This documentation includes not only a history of the game but also, in the case of the highest-level games, a half-hour film to be used at the convenience of the officials who participated or whose interests were represented in the game.

According to Jones and his immediate successor, William Thane Minor, these games have many obvious purposes and several that are not so obvious. The hypothetical crises are treated intensively, and the game environment serves the important additional purposes of stimulating communication among agencies and assessment of personnel in a real-world environment.[38] The following statement of purpose was cited in one of the rare public discussions of the SAGA manual games: "The basic purpose of the politico-military simulations is to provide a forum wherein key officials concerned with international security affairs can openly and candidly exchange ideas; examine controversial programs, objectives, and policies; and surface new approaches to the resolution of anticipated future problems. The intent of politico-military simulations is to alert, inform, and educate decisionmakers through the collective analysis of ideas, concepts, and selected aspects of national security policy."[39]

We are aware of the sensitive nature of these games and the related requirement to maintain strictest confidence in order to permit open and candid participation. Nonetheless, we believe that all documentation of SAGA games in the last fifteen years should be systematically reviewed by both in-house and external experts in order to determine whether the stated purposes are, in fact, being accomplished to the degree considered desirable and attainable; whether modifications are called for in the basic format and procedures embodied in these games over the years; whether others engaged in research activities are informed about unexpected results and interesting problems generated during game play; and whether they are charged with carrying out necessary follow-up investigations. Such assessments and the appropriate action resulting from them would do much to revitalize and strengthen these important activities.

Given some correspondence between a real international conflict and those aspects selected for inclusion in a gamed or simulated context, an individual player's own conceptions and limitations may be challenged, explored, and expanded. Problems of motivation, role-playing skill, and degree of sophistication notwithstanding, one purpose of manual gaming is to encourage creative, innovative thinking about problems that defy treatment with more conventional analytic approaches and methods. This basic goal has not been achieved to the extent that it could and should be. Creative exploration of analytic alternatives to manual gaming and their integration with the game experience are tasks that have not yet been tackled with even a fraction of the energy they deserve.

The suitability of manual gaming to a particular problem is determined by the difficulty and nature of the problem, the availability of alternative methods of attack, and the time and financial and human resources available. Can definite policy recommendations be made on the basis of manual games? Probably not, or only rarely and with stringent qualifications. Manual games have so many degrees of freedom and thus their results contain so much uncertainty that they are not reliable predictors.

Elaborate political, diplomatic, and military games are best perceived as key elements in a generalized problem-solving process. At present, the gaming community shows an unfortunate tendency to believe that a specific game will provide answers to a given problem—usually a crisis situation involving a limited number of nations. It seems more productive to view gaming as only one among many complementary problem-solving methods, no one of which necessarily dominates intellectually or practically, but all of which contribute to the fullest illumination of a given problem. If manual gaming were viewed as an exploratory or discovery activity, for instance, the onus of having to produce a firm set of recommendations or answers at the conclusion of play might be reduced; the game could then be appraised more clearly in light of alternative efforts and the nature of the problem being considered.

The primary objectives of this type of operational game should be to widen the range of possible problem-solving methods that can be considered individually and compared with other methods of analysis, to increase analytic flexibility, and to shake up existing procedural patterns and routines. Secondary aims should be to provide an arena in which the personal styles of current and potential decision makers could be observed at close range and without risk and to encourage players to come to terms with facts about potential conflict settings. These goals are valuable enough, in our view, to warrant continuing interest and support for games of this type.

9 | Man-Machine Games

The large print giveth; but the fine print taketh away.

American folk saying

MAN-MACHINE MSGS have generally been used by the armed forces either for operational or for teaching and training purposes. In this chapter, we shall describe several illustrative MSGs of this type. Man-machine MSGs may appear to be first-rate methods of solving particular problems when presented at high-level briefings; nonetheless, their success depends on the correct specification of key items like the accurate description of terrain, the correct assessment of human capabilities, and the careful measurement of a weapons system's firepower. This information can come only from a handful of extremely specialized technical experts, who are often neither willing nor able to spend a great deal of time making detailed assessments.

The degree of human participation and decision making in man-machine MSGs varies considerably. In computer-assisted manual gaming, the computer is used mainly as a bookkeeping device; the players are aware of the rules and details of the game and make all the decisions. At the other extreme, in man-assisted simulation, most of the game's structure is hidden in the computer program, which contains most of the rules for making decisions; the human player makes only decisions about overall policy. Games and simulations are nearly always tailored to a specific purpose or problem. Successful gaming and simulation depends almost entirely on the skill, integrity and judgment of the MSG's sponsors, builders, and users. There is no way to judge ahead of time whether an MSG will prove to be good or bad. In each case, its purpose, structure, components, and use must all be examined. The importance of these general warnings about man-machine MSGs is often poorly appreciated.

Of the 152 MSGs described in the most recent edition of the *Catalog of War Gaming and Military Simulation Models* of the Studies, Analysis and Gaming Agency (SAGA), nearly all were machine simulations.[1] Fewer than ten used human participants directly; most of these, strictly speaking, were manual political, diplomatic, and military games. Man-machine MSGs were not always so rare.[2] The Rand Corporation's Systems Research Laboratory, where many critical air-defense experiments were carried out with man-machine simulations, and its Logistics Systems Laboratory were important centers for man-machine gaming for experimental and operational purposes. Gaming at the United States Naval War College in Newport, Rhode Island, spans three generations of technology—manual and man-machine gaming and a man-machine–all-machine hybrid—applied to both training and operations. Finally, XRAY, an imaginative, man-machine, computer-interactive, political and military MSG was created and played at Rand in the early 1960s. The Navy Electronic Warfare Simulator (NEWS) at the Naval War College was phased out of operations during the mid-1970s and has been replaced by the Warfare Analysis and Research System (WARS); the Systems Research Laboratory is no longer in use, and the Logistics Simulation Laboratory exists in only the most rudimentary form; XRAY has ceased all operations.

The Systems Research Laboratory

The Systems Research Laboratory (SRL) was established at The Rand Corporation in the early 1950s. Its primary purpose was to study the behavior of integrated man-machine systems—in part as a reaction against a tendency then prevalent to conduct "component" investigations stemming from a mechanistic view of man-machine systems. SRL stressed an interdisciplinary approach; up to that time engineers, mathematicians, psychologists, and other behavioral scientists had approached the subject from widely different viewpoints and had seen the performance of man-machine systems partially, at best.[3] The goals of the laboratory were to develop ways of evaluating group performance, to identify the types of organization best suited to handling various tasks, and to find ways of identifying good policies and procedures and the methods best suited to teaching them. Players were assigned jobs that are found in any air-defense direction center—a vital communication and command facility for combat aircraft; radar operators, communications personnel, intelligence evaluators, aircraft controllers, and a center commander were all represented in the realistically equipped laboratory.[4]

From 1952 through 1954, four experiments were run by SRL. The first used college students; the other three, Air Force personnel. Each experiment simulated about six weeks of activity. The first, exploratory experiment demonstrated that college students did not have the background experience, level of professionalism, or motivation necessary to meet the defined goals of the experiment.[5]

Crews operating the simulated center had to defend an area of approximately 100,000 square miles. During each experiment, roughly 10,000 simulated flights were made over the area by friendly and hostile aircraft, variably combined. As the experiments ran, pressure on the crews was increased; in one instance the stress became overwhelming and a crew broke down. Other experiments, however, demonstrated that crews were able to learn and perform remarkably well under extremely difficult conditions.

The SRL experiments emphasized realism in the simulation of the center and in the organization of the crew. Surveillance personnel scanned radar screens and contributed their information to a central display area, where information about all the operational aircraft was portrayed for ready reference. Decisions about interception had to be made quickly and on the basis of many factors, including the ability to identify friend and foe; much of the communication was visual or face to face—just as it is in a real center. The preservation of a realistic military culture was, in fact, a central feature of the SRL experiments. For example, communications among the experimental staff and crew members were in precise Air Force form and style. In all experiments, the crew's behavior under a variety of plausible operational conditions served as the main object of study and analysis.

Many SRL experimenters were interested in whether a complex human organization could be simulated successfully and studied under laboratory conditions. Fortunately, a sponsor with a real problem that could be managed by means of a man-machine approach cooperated willingly in the exercises; the result was a mutually successful venture. Subsequent attempts to apply these methods to other, more complicated organizations were less successful.

System Development Corporation

The results of the exercises at SRL were encouraging enough to lead to the formation of the System Development Corporation (SDC), an institution comparable to Rand in size, the aims of which were the development and implementation of systems and training methods and the extension of research results into the operational sphere. Rand's primary focus has always been basic research.

SDC carried on the man-machine tradition and supported basic research and experimentation on organizations, as exemplified in the LEVIATHAN gaming and simulation system, a multiyear study the overall objective of which was the development of methods to investigate communications in a large social organization.[6] In 1963 and 1964, experiments were run on a hypothetical hierarchical organization with six levels of control. At the lowest level, 704 completely simulated robots worked in 64 squads, directed by live officers, staff, and staff assistants (sixteen group leaders, four branch heads, and a commanding officer). Graduate students were used as experimental subjects.

The idea of constructing an immense, highly automated laboratory for the general study of organizations and communications is attractive. Even when a relatively specific organizational context guides the simulated environment, however, the effort can easily absorb many millions of dollars and much time and require vast organizational skill and coordination. When the research is also expected to lead to results that can be implemented in the near term, communication and coordination among sponsors, researchers, and users—those responsible for the proposed implementation—must reach a new level. The lesson of SDC's experiences in general, and from LEVIATHAN in particular, is not that an ambitious attempt to study organizations turned out to be a waste of taxpayers' money or that money should not be spent in the future on large-scale systems research but rather that important problems of systems research and implementation are extremely difficult to deal with. The particular message of LEVIATHAN has to do with proportion and size. Either a more modest goal, with smaller-scale experiments and greater theoretical and analytic manipulation of organizational relationships, or, given the actual goal, a larger, more diverse group of talented professionals might have produced more viable results.

Looking back twenty-five years, many may feel that SRL and SDC did not fulfill the high hopes generated in the early stages of large-scale, man-machine experimentation. In the context of that time, however, we suspect that their efforts represented a gamble that was well worth taking. An in-depth, retrospective study of the successes and failures of these institutions could be of considerable value to the Department of Defense in guiding its future research into large-scale systems.

The Logistics Systems Laboratory

Rand's work in the application of man-machine MSGs to problems of both operational and experimental interest was carried out by the Logistics Systems Laboratory (LSL), primarily in the late 1950s. Various groups within the Department of Defense had already sponsored considerable research on problems of logistics and inventory management. There was, however, a large gap between the results of this research and their practical implementation. LSL was a man-machine approach to help bridge this gap. Basically LSL was intended to provide a sufficiently reliable representation of the real-world environment of Air Force logistics systems to permit testing and comparison of policies and procedures. It would also attempt to assist in transferring the results of research, modified by experience gained in the laboratory setting, to operations in the real world.[7]

Laboratory Problem I (LP-I) was LSL's first major task. It

was designed to test logistical policies and procedures for the Air Force and to indicate ways of implementing them. The potential policies were incorporated into a system (Logistics System 2) and compared with the actual configuration (Logistics System 1). The two models were evaluated under identical circumstances described in terms of numbers of aircraft to be maintained, flight programs, and other conditions; the comparative effectiveness of their policies and costs was also calculated.[8] Next, a rapidly changing aircraft program was simulated. The experiment provided for phasing aircraft in and out of inventory over a five-year period, during which use factors—frequency, duration and type of missions flown—for each aircraft were varied in ways assumed to be realistic. The properties of the simulated aircraft were derived from a study that selected 800 out of a possible 15,000 parts to reflect differences in price, demand, repairability, importance, and so forth. A special malfunction model was designed and used to give identical malfunction patterns for similar flights using either logistics system.

Each simulated day took about an hour of running time in the laboratory. The experiment ran for fourteen simulated quarters, during which two wars were simulated; it took four months to conduct. The staff of LSL included about thirty professionals, twenty clerks, and various supporting personnel to program and operate the computer. Fifteen players operated each of the two systems. Work began on LP-I in early 1957 and continued until the end of the year. In the fall of that same year, work commenced on Laboratory Problem II (LP-II) and continued until late 1958. Unlike its predecessor, LP-II stressed the development of systems; specifically, it was an attempt at a study of the Ballistic Missile System, which had not yet been fully developed. The basic aim of LP-II was to help develop a set of operating and support policies for the evolving system. In 1960, the Air Force created a team to evaluate LP-II and the techniques it had used, with the following major conclusions being reached:[9]

1. Laboratory simulations can be valuable tools for use in evaluating the design and application of military systems.
2. Benefits accrue from a reduction in the time and cost of system-development processes.

3. Combat effectiveness can be improved through better design of systems.

4. Laboratory simulation can be useful in generating and comparing certain classes of operational and logistical systems and policies.

5. Laboratory simulation does not eliminate the need for operational tests.

6. To be effective, facilities for laboratory simulation should be in close proximity to Air Force system-project offices. Constructing a single laboratory-simulation facility for the entire Air Force appears to be unsatisfactory, but there appear to be practical advantages to concentrating work in a few major installations.

7. Simulations of systems for Air Force decision-making purposes should be performed in house rather than by contractors.

A third problem, LP-III, was similar to LP-I. Its two major objectives were the specification and evaluation of policies and management procedures for the integration of an assortment of activities related to weapons support and the evaluation of different levels of responsiveness in the management system. A further experiment, LP-IV, was closer in spirit to LP-II and concentrated on projected logistical-information systems.[10]

Those responsible for LSL have taken two views of the place their efforts hold in the broader context of modeling, simulating, and gaming.[11] The first places LSL's activities along a continuum of abstraction ranging from the real world to pure mathematical modeling with the LP exercises falling in the middle range of this continuum (see fig. 9-1). The Laboratory Problem exercises are characterized in table 9-1 along with

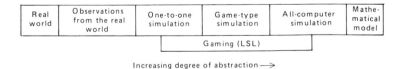

Increasing degree of abstraction ⟶

Figure 9-1. *The level of abstraction of activities at Logistics Systems Laboratory.*

Table 9-1. Characteristics of selected examples of simulation.

CHARACTERISTIC	HEURISTIC GAMES: MISSLOGS, BASELOGS	QUANTITATIVE SOLUTION ESTIMATES: MONTE CARLO	DEVELOPMENTAL PARTICIPATION TYPE: WAR GAMES	DEVELOPMENTAL OBSERVATION TYPE: LP-II, LP-IV	PROTOTYPE OR DEMONSTRATION: LP-I, LP-III	TRAINING: AIR-DEFENSE SIMULATIONS (SDC)
Computer preparation	Low	None	Low	Medium	Medium	High
Use and play	None	High	Low	None	Medium	None
Simulation of reality	Low	Low	Low	High	Medium	High
Degree of manual participation	High	None	High	High	Low to Medium	High
Specification of decision rules	Low	Complete	Low	Medium	High	Medium
Participation of arbitrator	Low	None	Medium	Low	Low	Low
Need for embedding organizations	Low	None	High	High	High	Medium to high
Time compression	High	Very high	Medium	Low	Medium	Low
Flexibility	Medium	Low	High	Medium	Low	Medium

Source: M. A. Geisler, W. W. Haythorn, and W. A. Steger, *Simulation and the Logistics Systems Laboratory* (Santa Monica, Calif.: The Rand Corporation, RM-3281-PR, September 1962), p. 9.

several other MSGs, some of which have already been described. The two heuristic games noted, BASELOGS (Base Logistics Management Game) and MISSLOGS (Missile Logistics Game), together with a board game called MONOPOLOGS (Monopoly-Logistics Game), were not man-machine MSGs but were designed and played by LSL personnel to improve their overall understanding of several general problems treated in specific detail in the contemporaneous LP exercises.[12] These relatively simple, exploratory MSGs did not require computer assistance and fulfilled two objectives very well: first, they helped define and explore several complex alternative models of logistics systems before any investment was made in large computer programs, and, second, they clarified many problems in the complex interactions between logistical support and operational units—problems that could very easily have been overlooked or assumed away had the modelers proceeded prematurely or hastily. A summary description of MISSLOGS illustrates this type of gaming activity.

> The game starts with a discussion of the rules. The player, acting as a squadron commander, discusses with the play director the squadron's objective: to maintain its missiles in a state of maximum readiness. They also discuss the resources available for pursuing this objective. The player is given a sum of money and a price list of all the items he may procure. He then allots his limited funds to that mixture of resources which he believes will accomplish the mission . . . He then must decide on an operational philosophy consistent with his policies on stockage and manning.
>
> Props, including representations of a squadron, missiles, silos, blockhouse personnel and spares, help the player visualize the course of events. A Squadron Status board is kept current and enables the player to experience the passage of time. Four days are simulated, during which missiles are checked, malfunctions appear and actions are taken.[13]

The Naval War College

War games have been played at the United States Naval War College since 1866, when manual games were introduced into the curriculum by William McCarty Little. Gaming was introduced into naval decision making at roughly the same time as parallel Army efforts; the concept was not readily accepted in either service, however.[14] Manual games were played at the war college from 1894 through 1957 and were known by a variety of names, including fleet tactical games, board maneuvers, and board games.[15] Eventually, the complexity of fleet operations outstripped the game's ability to represent real-world situations. Until that time, however, the manual games were extremely useful. In fact, Admiral Chester Nimitz is reported to have said, in a lecture at the war college, "The war with Japan had been re-enacted in the game room here by so many people and in so many different ways that nothing that happened during the war was a surprise—absolutely nothing except the Kamikaze tactics toward the end of the war; we had not visualized those."[16]

The Navy Electronic Warfare Simulator (NEWS) was built in response to the need for improved games and began operations around 1958. Because of increasing problems of reliability connected with its age and because of improvements in computer technology, NEWS began to be phased slowly out of operations in the late 1960s; replacing NEWS entirely has proved to be a difficult undertaking, however, and several of its constituent parts were still in operation as late as 1976.

NEWS was a computer-assisted analog war-gaming system designed to support the curriculum of the Naval War College and to conduct games sponsored by the fleet and operational commanders, usually during the summer vacation months. It therefore had both educational and operational purposes. Users of NEWS included students at the war college and other senior staff colleges as well as fleet, operational, and staff commanders; the facility was used for as many as fifty exercises each year.

NEWS was originally designed to play a two-sided map game in real time, at twice real time, or at four times real time. Its major subsystems were maneuver and display, weapon and damage computation, and communications. The facility occupied a large building containing player rooms, known as command centers, a command headquarters, and a separate room for the opposing side. An extensive control area was dominated by a large master screen covering the area of operations, on which moving images of all active forces were projected. As many as forty-eight active forces were available for maneuver, either single units, such as a ship or aircraft, or aggregations of task-oriented forces; in either case, each appeared as a single image on the master-plot display, which was photographed periodically for use in postgame debriefings. Weather conditions and other information needed to conduct naval operations were displayed, and a special-purpose analog computer was used to calculate the effects of employing various weapons.

The facility was used for two basic types of game: curriculum games, which are educational in purpose, and fleet games, which are operational and analytic. Francis J. McHugh's description of the original curriculum games played at NEWS illustrates their main elements:

> The first College curriculum games which were conducted on the NEWS involved, for the most part, task group plans. Players acted as task group commanders and staffs and as the commanding officers and staffs of ships, submarines, and aircraft (or flights of aircraft). From their flag plots (command centers), task group commanders issued orders and received reports over planned communication nets. Commanding officers of ships and aircraft, stationed in command centers, maneuvered their ships and submarines and aircraft, made detections on their scopes (azimuth range indicators), maintained plots, acquired enemy targets, fired weapons, sustained damage, and responded and reported to their game superiors. The subsystems of the NEWS, in accordance with programmed data, determined if and when detections were made, disseminated intelligence, evaluated interactions and assessed damage. The umpires monitored communications and interactions, initiated in-game programming, and compiled information for the critique.[17]

Subsequent curriculum games depended less heavily on the machine system alone for the development of the game; a larger role was given to the referees.

Fleet games are employed by operational commanders to

address problems such as the evaluation of contingency plans and the development of new procedures. In 1964, for instance, the Commander, Antisubmarine Forces, United States Atlantic Fleet, and the Canadian Commander Maritime Forces, Atlantic, jointly sponsored a fleet game to investigate problems of convoy escort and antisubmarine warfare; NEWS was used as an economical substitute for full-scale fleet exercises in this case. Fleet games enable a commander to try out many more operational possibilities less expensively and more quickly than he would otherwise be able to do—an increasingly significant consideration in an era of sharply escalating costs at sea. Lessons learned or procedures worked out in the game setting are routinely tried out and often put into action by the fleet.[18]

No matter how complex or expensive a gaming system is (and NEWS represents an investment of at least $10 million),[19] a sophisticated user will quickly find something that it cannot do. This failure may occur because the user becomes familiar enough with the system to begin testing its functional limits, or it may result from external events, such as a major technological shift not planned for in the system's original design. Frequently, the truly sophisticated user works out some modification to satisfy the immediate need. Others, including computer-systems salesmen and hardware buffs, are overly sanguine about what can be accomplished by bigger, better, and more expensive computer configurations. NEWS was a monument to engineering when it was built (and deserves its place in the Smithsonian Institution), but it quickly became a victim of technological changes, both in the computer business and in the business of naval warfare.

Serious discussions about a suitable replacement for NEWS were begun in 1966. The options considered included a major upgrading of NEWS; a reversion to manual gaming, with NEWS maintained to provide visual display; and the creation of an entirely new gaming system and facility using digital, general-purpose computer machinery. The final course was chosen, and the result is the Warfare Analysis and Research System (WARS). This third-generation gaming facility has been only partially implemented, and new operational capabilities and requirements have already reopened the search for an improved, fourth-generation system.[20] In electing to construct a new gaming facility based on large and powerful digital hardware, the developers of WARS very quickly entered the realm of all-machine MSGs and were faced with a set of problems not commonly confronted in the analog, man-machine system that WARS was intended to supplant.

The Master Simulation Program (MSP) is the heart of the WARS system; it was designed to contain all the basic information that might conceivably be required to model weapon platforms, that is, a naval vessel or aircraft: sensor configurations, weapons systems, motion constraints, logistics configurations, and environmental parameters. Task forces will be built up from these platforms, the basic unit or element of WARS. The gamer will be able to display platforms and units from 10,000 feet below to 200,000 feet above the surface of the earth anywhere on the globe. Game moves timed from real time up to forty times real time will be possible, as will every increment of time in between. WARS is intended to include flexible representations and interactions, from the simplest to the most complex, depending on the scenario. This is an all-encompassing task and one that has so far eluded the system designers. Figure 9-2 indicates the scale of tasks that WARS is expected to accomplish.

One somewhat optimistic assessment of the current status of WARS was offered by Lieutenant Commander Abe Greenberg in the official publication of the Naval War College: "[WARS] is far from complete. The system design and installation schedule were deliberately developed for phasing over a period of years to permit incremental evaluation before proceeding to the next step . . . the partially installed WARS and partially dismantled NEWS are now functioning as a frequently frustrating but remarkably improved hybrid, and a wide range of users are enthusiastic about the future potential of the ultimate full-digital system."[21] During interviews in July 1975, staff members of the war gaming department indicated that WARS is operational in conjunction with portions of NEWS but is less developed than originally planned. The result has been the retention of NEWS and the recognition of the weakest aspects of both systems. Only two of the five planned phases of development and implementation had been completed by July 1975, and work had slowed because of conceptual, software, and hardware problems. Twenty staff members

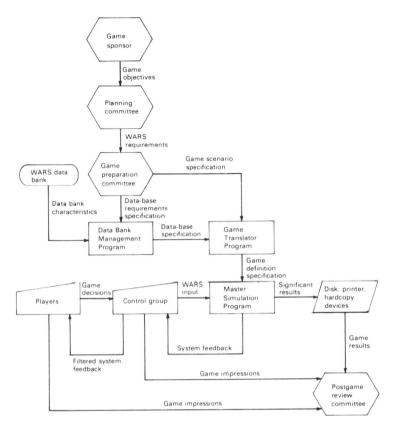

Figure 9-2. *The flow of data from the WARS game. (From Abe Greenberg, "War Gaming: Third Generation," Naval War College Review 27, no. 5 [March–April 1975], p. 75.)*

of LOGICON, a private systems-development firm, were on the site in late 1975, trying to work out problems that included bridging the gaps between pieces of hardware that were not intended to operate together; overcoming serious problems of reliability and maintenance; and developing software that would accomplish the large variety of tasks WARS was intended to accomplish. These are expensive operations. The United States General Accounting Office (GAO) estimated that the original plan for switching from NEWS to WARS would cost about $16 million; this figure may turn out to be conservative.[22]

Considerable differences in the technology of analytic,

man-machine, manual, and all-machine MSGs have meant that the integration of a variety of MSGs into WARS, one of the fundamental stated goals of the system, has not progressed smoothly. Writing the system software that would enable a relatively unsophisticated student gamer actually to use WARS is a formidable undertaking. Performing the necessary research to create algorithms describing the operational characteristics and interactions of weapon platforms is another. Generating the data needed by the Data Bank Management Program (see fig. 9-2) and designing and implementing the necessary amount and quality of display software and hardware are no less difficult. Accomplishing all of these tasks both simultaneously and well has so far proved to be impossible.

Staff members eventually concluded that there were too many conflicting goals for WARS and made a formal statement of the requirements of the system in 1974 (these were modified in late 1975).[23] Basing their judgment on these requirements, the staff estimated that the system would be developed in two five-year increments (1975–1980 and 1980–1985), each of which would cost about $10 million. That there is still no consensus about the basic purpose of the WARS or modified WARS system, however, was evident in the conflicting views of several staff members. One stated that "no analysis is done here; this is an educational facility"; another, who favored research, stated that the research games were "popular in the research-and-development community and well received in the hierarchy of the Navy."[24] Because of the considerable investments already made and those planned for the future, an understandable, but hazardous, trend has developed in naval gaming at Newport: trying to be all things to all people. Even an expanded and newly conceived WARS may not be able to provide operational gaming for the fleet, investigate gaming for the research-and-development community, and teach gaming for the war college.[25]

Although the Naval War College has endowed the William McCarty Little Chair of Gaming and Research Techniques, there appears to have been no major planning for a highly trained and experienced group to undertake research, development, and evaluation. The lack of importance attached to this function is suggested by the policies currently in effect for selecting and assigning personnel responsible for WARS. Many highly competent officers are currently charged with these responsibilities, but the system places the facility under the control of other, relatively transient individuals with quite diverse professional backgrounds and experience. Presently fewer than five full-time civilians are in residence; only one holds a doctorate in a technical area related to systems development. Even the first professor to hold the chair found his talents diverted to a variety of tasks not directly related to the design and implementation of the facility, as might have been predicted earlier. Changes in command at the war college have produced shifts in the types and purposes of games emphasized at the facility. Before 1974, operational fleet games were stressed; since then, tactical games have been favored. Such fundamental changes reflect personal tastes and preferences, but they also mirror current trends in the Washington naval-analytic community.

One of the real tragedies that resulted from not having a research, development, and evaluation group in place was the destruction of all game records held at the Naval War College in 1975. All documentation and histories of games before 1973 were thrown away; with them went all chances for evaluation of the games, for some much needed basic research, and even for an assessment of changes in the operational styles and capabilities of successive generations of naval leadership. Better procedures for documenting games are needed so that concern for storage will never again take precedence over concern about research and documentation.

XRAY

A new and imaginative type of man-machine MSG has evolved naturally with computer time-sharing and the development of computer-system networks. The potential inherent in these mushrooming technologies has not been well adapted to man-machine gaming, however. The operational possibilities of rapid, two-way interaction between a player and a computer, or among a number of interconnected computers, have been only slightly realized.

An early and striking exception to this state of limited development was the XRAY games conducted by Edwin Paxson in the early 1960s at The Rand Corporation (XRAY stands for the letter X, as used in the military's phonetic alphabet).[26] XRAY was a series of political and military exercises carried out at a highly aggregated level of strategic operations. In a typical exercise, separate teams represented major power blocs and were required to plan their strategic forces with limited budgets. Because of the extraordinary diversity of the information a team might need for this type of planning, a single run would have been either inordinately time-consuming or overly simplified. Ordinarily, the chances of running a man-machine MSG several times for comparative purposes decrease when the MSG is slow and expensive or when the players react adversely to an overly simplified setting. XRAY addressed this problem directly.

The concept underlying XRAY was to offer players computer-assisted planning information and a variety of computational routines, or submodels, on request. Large banks of data, submodels, and communication links were made accessible through an on-line, time-shared, multiconsole computer system.[27] Play was also operated in this mode. Among its components, XRAY contained a force-mix cost submodel that enabled the players to interrogate the system to find out the resource implications of various numbers and combinations of strategic offensive, defensive, sensor, and command-and-control forces for a projected ten-year period. Information generated by the computer was relayed and clarified by a control team. This mode of heavily machine-dependent gaming is a natural development; at the same time, the less players are aware of information and calculations, the more they must accept on faith. A serious flaw in a computerized model or data bank might not be discovered for some time. Placing a player directly in the analytic loop increases the odds that such flaws will be discovered early; it is difficult to be equally optimistic about the all-machine MSGs; in many instances, their results must simply be accepted or rejected and offer scant opportunity to question their constituent elements.

With sufficient skepticism, money, and diligence, the form of man-machine gaming exemplified by XRAY should pay off. Still, the interested but nonexpert sponsor should not necessarily sink resources into such work without considerable circumspection. It is far too easy to underestimate the expenditures necessary to construct a good data bank or analytic routine. Even such basic items as XRAY's force-mix cost submodel end up being oversimplified, costly, or difficult to build well.

The preceding discussion of man-machine MSGs is by no means exhaustive. Some man-machine gaming experts will probably find that we have omitted their favorite MSGs, and for this we offer our apologies. We are well aware, for instance, of the pioneering work of Harold Guetzkow and many of his students in the use of man-machine MSGs for educational and social-science research. Experimental man-machine MSGs have been built and operated in numerous university settings throughout the country. And man-machine systems have been used with spectacular success in training pilots, astronauts, and even would-be automobile drivers. The examples presented here are intended only to provide a fairly complete overview of the major activity in man-machine gaming.[28]

10 | Machine Simulations

Au coeur vaillant, rien n'est impossible.

MACHINE SIMULATIONS and computer modeling are where the largest proportions of money, staff, and supporting resources for MSGs are found. Much of the work is technical and unexciting; it is rare that any of it is publicized. As far as the nonspecialist is concerned, calculations of measures of effectiveness, the assessment of relative fire-support methodologies, and computations of CEP (circular error probable), FEBA (forward edge of the battle area), or AD (assured-destruction) ratios are of little interest. Such technical jargon is recognized, if at all, as an unfortunate necessity of modern life in a hostile world. Yet it is with such language that the contemporary military analyst evaluates weapons systems, checks out war-fighting doctrines, considers command and control problems, and ultimately tries to answer the question of what will be needed to ensure our security and defense.

Just as this language obscures the stark realities it is meant to describe, many basic questions about military computer models and analyses are obscured from public view: Who is responsible for them? How well are they doing? Do they know what they are doing? Does anyone really know enough about future wars to warrant trust in their calculations, or will they forever remain inaccessible to accurate comprehension? Even simpler questions about past wars continue to defy the most skilled analysis; it is doubtful whether anyone, for instance, will ever determine what combination of weapons and cir-

128

cumstances accounted for most casualties in Vietnam, Korea, or World War II, for that matter. That apparently simple question turns out to be as difficult to answer as it is important for our future security. This problem becomes trivial, however, when compared with the questions posed, difficulties encountered, and stakes involved in today's computer models of war. We can no longer afford the luxury, if we ever could, of presuming that someone else, somewhere, is taking care of these problems and answering the critical questions. Designers of weapons systems and military analysts, like undertakers, are groups the public generally avoids thinking about. Our national survival depends on the weapons business, however, and we dare not ignore it. Even if there were fewer unsolved problems concerning them, the sheer magnitude of our total investment and operational costs in weapons systems would require that the subject receive our fullest attention. This is one area in which a poor evaluation can result in the misallocation of billions of dollars; indeed, misallocated funds may be the least of costs.

Some of the machine MSGs discussed in this chapter were abandoned over a decade ago; others are still in the active inventory. Each has been chosen to indicate key points or lessons about the technology. For those who wish to examine these and other MSGs in greater detail, a surprising amount of information on machine MSGs is publicly available. While many studies contain classified information, most of the classified portions relate to numerical input data and to specific output and findings; separate, unclassified descriptions of the MSGs themselves can frequently be obtained.

Machine MSGs are used mainly for analysis, diagnosis, and operational applications. These three general purposes can be broken down into more specific categories, such as technical evalution, doctrinal evaluation, and force-structure analysis. Technical evaluation, for instance, often entails the evaluation of weapons—both current and projected components and systems; analyses of doctrines and force structures are directed toward the investigation of tactics and strategy, the coordination of weapons systems, command-and-control systems, communications, and the structure of forces. The Studies, Analysis and Gaming Agency (SAGA) of the Joint Chiefs of

Staff organizes its own work according to somewhat different categories, including MSGs concerned with strategic forces, general-purpose land forces, general-purpose air forces, general-purpose naval forces, general-purpose combined arms, logistics, personnel, communications and electronics, and politicomilitary matters.[1] Whatever the categorization, the field is immense, and studies may range from analysis of the minute characteristics of a single gun to attempts to divine the likely impact of our total strategic nuclear-warfare policy on national security.

The 1950s and early 1960s were, in a sense, a golden age for systems analysts and simulators. Nothing seemed impossible. Big enough models, run by big enough computers attached to evergrowing data banks would produce all there was to know, or so it seemed. Great improvements were made in planning and information processing, and the enabling technologies improved by orders of magnitude. One of the lessons from this era, however, was that even good large-scale models cannot easily be integrated into human organizations. A second lesson was that fundamental conceptual, modeling, and data problems that arose in every attempt to build large-scale models cast serious doubts on the possibility of using many of them except as experimental or teaching devices. The heyday of systems analysis has been celebrated in various accounts. Here we intend only to point out what appear to be persistent issues in the analytic environment that relate to the building and use of machine MSGs.

ABM: The Air Battle Model

The Air-Battle Model (ABM) originated in some small, exploratory mathematical models constructed in Rand's mathematics department in the late 1950s and quickly evolved into a large-scale simulation of a two-sided global war.[2] It consisted of a plan converter, the Air Battle Model itself, and a set of output programs. The first and last were simply packages for the preparation and analysis of input and output data. ABM itself contained seven routines: (1) missile launching, (2) bomber launching, (3) tanker operations, (4) bomber-cell handling, (5) attrition by enemy defenses, (6) target selection and reconnaissance, and (7) blast damage and radiation effects.

The model operated with up to 25,000 planes, of which 3,000 could be in flight, 1,000 offensive bases, 3,500 targets, 1,500 local defense installations, 1,500 radars, 31 separate bomb types, and 32 different kinds of aircraft. The task of merely preparing the input for a run was considerable. The enormous amount of data required by ABM presented serious problems in gathering and validating data, as well as basic conceptual problems.[3] As with other very large MSGs, the problems with ABM highlight the need for sensitivity analysis, outside professional review, and even simple data checking. It requires a leap of faith for anyone beside the model builders, who know what is in the computer programs they have constructed, to apply and use the output from such simulations.

TEMPER: Technological, Economic, Military and Political Evaluation Routine

The Technological, Economic, Military and Political Evaluation Routine (TEMPER) originated at Raytheon Company, was funded mainly by the Joint War Gaming Agency (JWGA), the predecessor of SAGA, and cost betweeen $1 million and $1.5 million. An all-machine MSG, it was intended to simulate international conflicts, including cold and limited wars. Data for 117 nations were needed, and the operational context was the world, divided into three blocks that were segmented into twenty conflict regions. Seven categories—military, economic, political, scientific, psychological, cultural, and ideological— were used to describe each nation. The model required thousands of (mostly unverified) input values. TEMPER was an effort literally to model the world.[4]

Several questions about TEMPER are particularly interesting and important, even today: What justifications might there be for embarking on such a project in the first place? On what level of theoretical knowledge would such a model be based? What type of data were needed to structure and operate the model? Did such data exist? These and other, more technical, questions were raised by two outside consulting groups who evaluated TEMPER for the Defense Department before the model was abandoned. Their findings are discussed below; considering the variations among them, however, it is surprising that they were looking at the same model. That the TEM-

PER project was terminated implies that the model had failed to accomplish the ambitious operational tasks for which it was intended. It is possible that the exercise might have done a better job if these tasks had been different, but the postmortem analysis was not especially encouraging on this point.

Before we consider alternative goals that might have been chosen for TEMPER, we should explain why we may seem to be belaboring this example. In many of its key concepts, TEMPER differs only slightly from most existing, large-scale MSGs designed to treat strategic conflict interactions. While TEMPER displayed our collective ignorance about central aspects of war openly, successor MSGs are less readily understood and treat many critical matters by assumption, exclusion, or concentration on trivial but measurable features of the world. Fred Iklé, former director of the United States Arms Control and Disarmament Agency, has captured the essence of this point:

> In particular, it is usually assumed that the essential features of deterrence can be calculated in advance, e.g., the familiar calculation of so-called "missile exchanges" that are often noted in scholarly literature and discussed in congressional debates.
>
> The prominence of the calculations continues because we know how to make them. Much as in a freshman's algebra test, we have tailored the problem to our capability to calculate. The seemingly rigorous models of nuclear deterence are built on the rule: "What cannot be calculated, leave out." For example, "missile duel" calculations usually ignore fallout; they seldom confront critical details regarding reliability; nor can they fully encompass other nuclear forces, such as bombers and sea-based missiles, and their many possible interactions.
>
> . . . Curiously, we are far more skeptical in accepting the calculations of traditional conventional military campaigns than the calculations of nuclear warfare. In fact, the more battle experience and information military analysts have, the more modest they become in predicting the course of conventional war. Such modesty is missing for nuclear war, where pretentious analyses and

simplistic abstractions dominate and blot out the discrepancies existing between abstractions and possible reality—a reality that for so many reasons is hard even to imagine.[5]

Large-scale model building and simulation can easily be a valuable research and learning device for people developing basic theoretical ideas; in the case of TEMPER, this group would have included social scientists working in the areas of economics, political science, and international relations, among many others. Preparing a logically consistent and complete model for computer simulation is a demanding task that forces researchers to try to clarify their concepts as precisely as possible. Such exact specification is often extremely difficult, and the first efforts to construct such a research model usually only point out what has been omitted or misunderstood. At this stage, the usefulness of the model does not depend on the accuracy of the data base; the key task is simply to establish the logical consistency of the formulations. If a researcher needs numbers during this phase, he can invent them.

Most scholars would agree that the study of international relations is in a prescientific state. Simulation offers the international-relations expert an interesting methodological device with which to undertake his research projects. This use of simulation is important; it is one on which it might be worthwhile to spend several million dollars.[6] Furthermore, a legitimate case can be made for spending even larger sums to solve some of the conceptual problems that inhibit the gathering of meaningful statistics and the building of useful data banks. We often talk loosely about concepts like the level of morale, the degree of hostility between nations, the extent of patriotism, the climate of revolution, and the mood of the mob. Do we need to measure these concepts, and, if so, how should we measure them? Supporting basic research does not guarantee that operational advances will directly result. The idea of TEMPER is imaginative and interesting, but only in the context of a group established to conduct pure research in the social sciences, adequately supported by money and machinery, and allowed the freedom to work without severe pressures to produce something useful. Sponsoring such work in any other context, as was attempted in the case of TEMPER, calls for a convert's faith in the scientific possibilities of simulation and systems analysis.

Two external evaluations of TEMPER were carried out for the JWGA, one by the Simulmatics Corporation and another by Mathematica. Their assigned tasks were somewhat different. Simulmatics was asked to evaluate the international-relations aspects of the project; Mathematica, to concentrate of its models of conflict.[7] The Simulmatics report was positive and ended with this encomium: "TEMPER is an accomplishment, for, despite all the errors, the model produces output that is a plausible, if not a probable representation of what might happen. One may be sanguine about TEMPER. For as the obvious errors are changed, a few equations simplified, and some others expanded, TEMPER should become a useful analytic device"[8] The Mathematica report, on the other hand, was strongly negative. After carefully documenting errors in logic, problems in modeling, insufficient attention to technical and analytic flaws, serious problems with data, and other difficulties, it recommended that TEMPER be abandoned. How could two evaluations, each conducted by reputable professionals, arrive at such different conclusions? The Simulmatics report compares TEMPER with the Wright brothers' flight at Kitty Hawk—not at all the message transmitted in the Mathematica report. The difficulty stemmed not from carelessness or dishonesty but rather, we believe, from fundamental differences in the beliefs and interests of the two groups.

Simulmatics was committed to large-scale simulations, as are many modeling firms and agencies, and its reviewers were confident about the virtues of simulation as a methodology. In addition to the commercial and ideological reasons underlying their hopeful assessment of TEMPER, they felt an understandable desire to carry on with this type of work. Many social scientists dream of receiving funds from an operational agency to do the kinds of research work they are interested in. It is not all that difficult to rationalize this dream: operational agencies should be willing to pay for basic research without expecting the results to have immediate operational value. The system of funding research in the United States even encourages this view; it is sometimes easier to obtain funding for basic research with euphemistic operational goals than for outright operational research. This system is dangerous. Not only is the importance of basic research denigrated, but the work that results is often not satisfactory either as basic research or as an operational product.

Mathematica's reviewers were not primarily in the business of simulation; if anything, the group was biased toward applied mathematical models. Their report applied strictly scientific standards in judging the value of TEMPER and did not consider the more general question of whether the JWGA should have been sponsoring this kind of work.

CARMONETTE: A Computer Simulation of Small-Unit Combat

CARMONETTE, a computer simulation of small-unit combat, is one of the longest lasting families of MSGs in the Defense Department's active inventory. The patriarch of the family was TIN SOLDIER, which was developed in the early 1950s. Since then, the new generations have been named CARMONETTE I through VI, of which the last is the currently active version.[9] TIN SOLDIER, which became operational in 1954, was a hand-played game modified to include computer-assisted treatment of random elements. All subsequent versions have also depended on the computer. CARMONETTE I (1958–1963—dates are approximate and indicate its period of main use) simulated ground combat at the level of battalions or smaller units and considered tank and antitank operations; CARMONETTE II (1963–1966) added infantry operations; CARMONETTE III (1966–1969) added armed helicopter operations; CARMONETTE IV (1969–1972) introduced new capabilities in communication and night vision; and CARMONETTE V (1972–1974) emphasized cost considerations for alternative configurations of weapons.

This description of CARMONETTE VI, reproduced from the *Catalog of War Gaming and Military Simulation Models*, indicates the minimal amount of technical and professional information needed to characterize an operational MSG:[10]

TITLE: CARMONETTE VI—Computer Simulation of Small-Unit Combat

PROPONENT: U.S. Army Concepts Analysis Agency (CAA)

DEVELOPER: Research Analysis Corporation

PURPOSE: CARMONETTE VI is a computerized, analytical model designed to simulate small unit battles (up to two battalions per side) with emphasis on unit movement, target detection, weapon firing and assessment of results. The model's chief focus of concern is the assessment of different weapon mixes with different kinds of weapon effects. In addition, it is also concerned with the assessment of the effects of tactics and of sensors and detection devices on battle outcomes.

GENERAL DESCRIPTION: CARMONETTE VI is a two-sided model involving land forces and armed helicopters. It is primarily designed to consider units ranging from the individual soldier or vehicle up to units of platoon size. The lower limit of this range may be manipulated to make the smallest group considered as large as a platoon, and the upper limit may be altered to consider up to two battalions. One minute of CPU [central processing unit] time is required to game four to six minutes of battle. Simulated time is treated on an event store basis. The model is stochastic, using as its primary solution technique random number determination of success and of time duration for certain events.

INPUT: Troop lists; weapon lists; weapon accuracy; weapon performance data; weapon lethality; sensor performance data; vehicle mobility characteristics; vehicle vulnerability; tactical scenario; terrain characteristics. A total of 35 inputs must be completed.

OUTPUT: Output is in the form of computer printout listing all events assessed, with a summary of all casualty events, and summation of kills by target type and weapon types. Also available are summaries of weapon engagements (firings) shown by target type, rounds fired, personnel and vehicles killed for each of the selected range brackets.

MODEL LIMITATIONS:
Maximum of 36 weapon types (both sides)
Maximum of 48 weapons units (each side) with up to 63 killable elements (personnel) per unit

Maximum is 63 × 62 grids of selectable size (5m to 250m)

Does not treat logistics

Player cannot change tactics during a single game; must write a new scenario and a new game

Results are highly dependent on detailed input

HARDWARE:

Computer: CDC 6400, or CDC 6000 Series, UNIVAC 1108

Operating System: SCOPE 3.3, EXEC VIII

Minimum Storage Required: 65K words in memory

Peripheral Equipment: 3 tape drives, 1 disk

SOFTWARE:

Programming Languages: FORTRAN and COMPASS

Documentation: CARMONETTE III—RAC R28, in 3 volumes (volume 1, AD8222400L; volume 2, AD827900; volume 3, AD825000). CARMONETTE IV—The Use of CARMONETTE IV in Assessing the Combat Effectiveness of Small Units Equipped with Night Vision Devices (in draft: AD514519L). CARMONETTE V—Equal Cost Firepower (in draft). CARMONETTE VI—Both user's documentation and technical documentation are complete, although not available in one document.

TIME REQUIREMENTS:

1 month to acquire base data

2–3 man-months to structure data in mode input format

300 seconds playing time for 50-minute battle

150–600 seconds CPU time per model cycle

2–3 months to analyze and evaluate results

SECURITY CLASSIFICATION: Unclassified

FREQUENCY OF USE: 200 times per year

USERS: Principal: ASCFOR, CDC CONFOR GP

POINT OF CONTACT:

U.S. Army CAA

Bethesda, MD 20014

Telephone: (202) 295-1645

MISCELLANEOUS: CARMONETTE VI supplies assessment data to RAC's Division Battle Model (DBM). CARMON-

ETTE game results are processed by linear regression techniques to generate assessment equations for DBM.

Keyword listing: Analytical Model; Damage Assessment/Weapons Effectiveness; Land Forces; Air Forces; Computerized; Two-Sided; Stochastic Event Store

The conceptual and empirical problems of studying ground combat in detail are so enormous that even a fanatical proponent of simulation must, at some point, ask himself a tough but obvious question: When does the magnitude of probable errors caused by poor data, inappropriately chosen aggregation, omitted factors, and weak conceptualization of basic modeled elements make the simulation useless in answering operational questions? In other words, when does science become science fiction? Criticizing the work of others is easy, and a natural response to such criticism is to ask for better alternatives. We believe one such alternative is to continue work in simulation but to invest much more time and money on the investigation of basic conceptual problems, the definition of key indices, research into gathering and validating data, and reviewing, analyzing, and criticizing the MSGs actually in use.

FAST-VAL: Forward Air Strike Evaluation Model

Another example of detailed small-unit simulation is Rand's FAST-VAL, or Forward Air Strike Evaluation model. Its chief developer has described FAST-VAL as "designed to bring together military situations developed through war gaming, and weapon assessment possibilities permitted through the use of computing machinery. FAST-VAL thus permits the extension of gaming from situations in which weapon effects must be developed."[11] The model has been used for more than ten years, both for research and as an operational device. It deals with what are called close-support or battlefield-interdiction situations and was intended to help assess the effects of air power using conventional weapons against a ground unit.

The basic spatial unit in the model is 10,000 square feet, which is small enough to show the effects of ordnance as small as a 750-pound bomb. These areas are coded from detailed maps by applying a 100' × 100' grid. Regiments are characterized by 600 to 800 data points. A "snapshot" shows a regiment's deployment at any given time. A variety of targets may be assigned to any specific geographical location—combat troops, gun crews, tanks and other vehicles, artillery of various types, and supplies, for example. Army firepower score numbers are assigned to the various weapons and may depend on their positions. Each modeled element can be regarded as a target and hence has some form of damage-criterion index attached to it. The model's methodology has been checked against information collected from actual instances of infantry combat in Korea and Vietnam. FAST-VAL can be used in a computer-assisted mode; thus a staff planner can consider a specific deployment of troops, call for several different configurations of air support, and obtain an assessment of damage in each case. These can be displayed by transparencies overlaid on the operational map.

FAST-VAL is a robust MSG that treats a few key aspects of land combat, specifically the interaction of air and ground elements. Like any other model, it has limitations. It is not meant to assess real-life trade-offs among firepower, communications, reconnaissance, and different organizational configurations. While it is used to help understand new ordnance, it cannot evaluate combinations of air and ground weapons systems. Changes in Army weapons capabilities must be treated outside of FAST-VAL's domain, since developers believed that incorporating substitutions of weapons would have overcomplicated an already large model.

SUBDUEL: Submarine Tactical-Simulation Model

SUBDUEL, a submarine tactical-simulation model, was sponsored and built by the Center for Naval Analyses (CNA).[12] Its primary purpose is the detailed study of encounters between submarines, with attention to the stages of detection, approach, attack, and kill. Secondarily, SUBDUEL is used to study engagements between a submarine and a surface ship. The model is a two-sided Monte Carlo simulation (one treating random elements) that relies on fairly detailed information about the acoustic configurations of opposing submarines and their operational capabilities. The model generates summary, detailed, and diagnostic output. Summary output lists only the overall probability of outcomes from the engagement; detailed output provides both this information and specific details of the vessel's course, speed, location, weapons status, ranges, and bearings and the times required to pass through the stages of the encounter. Diagnostic output contains all these factors as well as whatever data have been ordered for study. The model does not consider air-sea interactions.

BALFRAM: Balanced Force Requirements Analysis Model

Our final example is BALFRAM, or Balanced Force Requirements Analysis Model, constructed by the Stanford Research Institute (SRI). BALFRAM, which became operational in 1972, is a major modification of the earlier Force Requirements Analysis Model. It was sponsored by the office of the Commander-in-Chief, Pacific (CINCPAC—the overall military command in the Pacific Ocean area) to assist staff planners in determining force requirements and evaluating the assignment of forces. BALFRAM is a deterministic simulation (that is, it does not treat random elements directly) that generates estimates of the outcome of large-scale engagements. Attrition in these engagements is calculated from expected values, and the user may choose either of two distinct fire laws, depending on assumptions made about information possessed by the opponents. The first, or linear, law implies that a unit cannot determine the casualties it has inflicted on its opponent and hence cannot concentrate fire on the survivors; the second, or square, law assumes that this knowledge is available. The empirical justification of either fire law, or of different versions of them, is presumed. The output from a BALFRAM run provides a battle history and a summary of the end of the campaign.

The MSGs described above are only a few of the hundreds of operational machine simulations. Our intention has been to give the nontechnical reader a general picture of their nature and a sampling of the many diverse questions they try to answer. Persistent scientific difficulties bedevil the construction of MSGs, and this issue lies at the core of many of the more obvious human and management problems related to their use. Simply improving organizations and communications will not solve all of these problems. Many hard-core simulators (and many engineers and physicists) automatically equate objectivity and the scientific method with tightly defined computer models and tables of numerical input and output. This scientific approach contrasts sharply with that of free-form gamers (and many social scientists), who often do not even define all of the rules prior to play but rely instead on teams of referees and experts to determine the reasonableness of certain moves and to comment on game play. Free-form gamers tend to regard simulators' compulsion to define what they consider undefinable and to quantify what is not clearly measurable as manifestations of rigidity and a lack of understanding of the true problem. The truth, in fact, lies in between. Nevertheless, the current predominance of all-machine MSGs indicates a clear preference among users for the hard-core approach and perspective. In our view, it is time to step back and assess some of the more pervasive and potentially costly results of this dominance.

All-machine MSGs may be counterproductive in the important but subtle sense that they focus attention on the quantifiable aspects of a problem to the exclusion of significant nonquantifiable aspects. Iklé has commented, "We have tailored the problem to our capability to calculate."[13] The time, resources, talent, and hard work needed to construct an MSG as complicated as those discussed in this chapter are sufficient to obscure this common shortcoming. SUBDUEL, for instance, does not address the important context of air-sea battles in its analysis of antisubmarine warfare.[14] By concentrating on details of submarine maneuvering and on the physical characteristics of its environment, the model prevents attention from focusing on the conditions under which one would want to destroy an opponent's submarine; these conditions are probably not the same as they were in World War I and World War II. The question of whether we really need a killer submarine and the complementary problem of defending against a killer-submarine attack are not raised, with the result that many other potentially critical issues are passed by. Rather than thinking about the likely future employment of the weapons system, we are distracted by detailed considerations of noise, speed, submarine configurations, and other measurable elements, as if those were the real problems. They may very well not be.

Building models of any type involves abstraction, which calls for aggregation and simplification. Aggregation and simplification, in turn, lead to problems of defining variables in observable and measureable terms—and then collecting and processing the data so defined. A gap forms almost immediately between groups concerned with what the numbers are and those concerned with what they mean. Objectivity is not the exclusive property of either the quantitative or the qualitative approach. If the scientific problems posed in measuring the relative effectiveness of weapons systems were straightforward, the related organizational problems would be more readily solved. As it is, deep differences remain among opinions and perceptions about the worth of most MSGs. If the current professional standards and criteria of the disciplines using MSGs were routinely applied to their construction and use, the worst work would be discovered and set aside. Without such standards, however, bitter debate will continue about nearly every aspect of the analysis of weapons systems—including the worth of the MSGs described here.

Complicated problems may never be able to be simplified. There may never be a magic simulation that will solve everything. The nature of the subjects examined may allow genuine scientific and organizational advances to be made, but this is by no means certain. Qualified experts representing different approaches and perspectives will always be found, in all likelihood, to help bolster the individual and collective objectives of military commanders, their staffs, and their supporters. In spite of our reservations, however, we are essentially optimistic about the future of MSGs. Procedures for making decisions and the use of scientific methods of analysis in the Department of Defense appear remarkably rational when compared with activities in other organizations like the Departments of Energy or Health, Education, and Welfare. Even so, improvements can be made; the key to such advances is a better understanding of the decision-making process.

PART FOUR

A Survey of Operational Models, Simulations, and Games

11 | The Contextual Map

Lieutenant A: Did any event out of the ordinary occur dur-
                   ing your passage to this port?
Le Commandant: Le surlendemain de notre départ, nous avons
                   été pris par un ouragan avec une grosse plise
                   et une mauvaise mer.

United States Naval Academy, *Naval Phraseology*

WHILE THE HYPOTHETICAL Lieutenant A probably did not understand that his companion had experienced foul weather and rough sailing, the commandant was able, despite the language differences, to get the information he needed, thanks to a map (or "chart," in true naval parlance). Its contents provided him with a picture of the whole route and detailed information about specific hazards along the way. Comparable communication problems also arise among those who speak the same language. Unfortunately, for the technical experts and military decision makers who concern us in this book, no comparable map exists, although they face many rocks and shoals and an occasional shipwreck.

Experts and Decision Makers: Two Cultures

Decision makers must be encouraged to appreciate the costs of their not having a clear view of the world. Their usual inability to answer questions like these indicates, at least roughly, the extent of these costs: What kinds of models, simulations, and games have been funded, built, and used? How have resources, in the aggregate, been expended over the years for various classes of MSGs—free-form, man-machine, all-machine; tactical, strategic, political and diplomatic; fine-grained, coarse-grained; or land, air, sea, and joint operations? With what payoffs? To whom? Where in the process of constructing and using MSGs are there weaknesses that require

145

top-level managerial decisions for correction? Who is responsible for making these changes? What kinds of activities have
been oversubscribed? Undersubscribed? According to whose
standards and criteria? Where are there pockets of excellence? Of ineptness? What rewards and penalties encourage
the former and discourage the latter? What general management concepts and institutions are required to sustain needed
professional and operational improvements? What might
these be? Who is, and who should be, responsible for them?
None of these questions can be answered without a relatively
clear view of the whole field. Immersion in one or even a few
of its aspects makes it impossible to assemble the information
needed to answer these questions and then to come to grips
with the issues underlying them.

At the moment, no single individual or group makes these
determinations, and hence, no one takes overall responsibility
for the operation of the system of military study and analysis.
Everyone involved is to some extent to blame for the various
problems implied in this list of unanswered questions, but no
one is responsible for doing anything about them. Even partial
maps of the context are seldom communicated. Not only is
there little or no communication among groups and individuals; there is also virtually no institutional memory to transmit
specific lessons from one generation to the next within the
same organization. Clearly, much can be done to develop better information about specific activities and better devices for
transmitting it so that MSG experts can be used more effectively in the future. The hard-won and often costly lessons
learned in specific settings must be documented so it will not
be necessary for those in other areas of responsibility or those
in succeeding generations to relearn them.[1]

Technical experts also need to become more aware of costs
incurred by operating with an incomplete map of the context.
As with the decision makers' culture, various questions illustrate the nature and extent of these costs: If the person who
developed the MSG did not produce a set of input data himself
by field testing or other direct empirical means, who did? Why
were the numbers initially generated? How often and by
whom have they been used? What are their inherent weaknesses, biases, errors? If an MSG is dependent upon theoreti-

cal estimates for specification of input values or for its structure, whose theory is it? Why should the assumptions underlying the estimates be believed or rejected? What standards guide the construction of an MSG? For example, are data-formatting, software, or computer-language norms in general use? If so, where does one find out about them? If not, why haven't they been established? How should an MSG be documented? Who is responsible for documentation? Where does one go to get documentation? Where can one find a summary of basic knowledge in a specific substantive area (firepower indices, human factors, or negotiation styles and strategies of likely opponents, for instance) in order to make a preliminary judgment about the appropriateness and feasibility of modeling versus other analytic or investigative methods? How are common research needs recognized and translated into research undertakings?

Certain practical questions also apply to the areas of responsibility shared by experts and decision makers. Among them are these: Who is funding, building, and operating various classes of MSGs? With what payoffs? To whom? To what extent do salesmen and managers dominate the interface between those who actually build an MSG and those who actually use it? With what effects, both in specific instances and in terms of the general status and development of the profession? To what purposes are MSGs applied by various decision makers and their organizations? Can systematic patterns of misuse be ascribed to any of these? Who inside and outside the uniformed segment of the analytic community really knows what he is doing? Who does not? Where are working conditions, professional standards, development opportunities, or pecuniary benefits relatively better or worse than the average for the industry? Who decides about the norms, and who keeps track of individual conditions and standards in order to help others make these comparisons? Once again, none of these questions can be answered in ignorance of key components of the context. Furthermore, no individual or group is currently able to make these determinations; responsibility for the overall operation of the system has thus neither evolved nor been assigned.

Because modeling is an underdeveloped field in many ways,

problems in its growth and development should be expected. Creating and using a map of the whole context may lessen the effects of these inevitable problems, however. For instance, technical specialists within the military explored time-shared, man-machine gaming in the early 1960s; however, the technical breakthroughs that made possible a network of players in separate locations interacting in real time through a computer were not shared with other technical specialists. A decade later, nonmilitary specialists in educational and research modeling and gaming were painfully reinventing many of the old programs and hardware configurations.[2] Scarce research talent and resources were thus wasted—not as a result of any individual's actions but because the profession as a whole is unnecessarily fragmented. A better view of the whole context would, we believe, bring about improvements in many specific technical matters, not the least of which is the allocation of scarce talent and resources to areas of relatively higher priority and more likely benefit. These areas obviously cannot be chosen on the basis of a fragmentary view of modeling as a whole.

The Complexity of the System

The study and analysis bureaucracy is a complex social system—that is, "roughly, one made up of a large number of parts that interact in a nonsimple way. In such systems, the whole is more than the sum of the parts, not in an ultimate, metaphysical sense, but in the important pragmatic sense that, given the properties of the parts and the laws of interaction, it is a nontrivial matter to infer the properties of the whole. In the face of complexity, an in-principle reductionist may be at the same time a pragmatic holist."[3] While it is difficult to understand the entirety of any social system in terms of its parts, the operation of no one part can be understood without comprehending the way the whole system operates. The situation is all the more difficult because human beings have only a limited capacity to deal with complex systems as wholes. George Miller, a noted social psychologist, has phrased it this way: "It seems to me that the very fact of our limited capacity for processing information has made it necessary for us to discover clever ways to abstract the essential features of our universe and to express these features in simple laws that we are capable of comprehending in a single act or thought. We are constantly taking information given in one form and translating it into alternative forms, searching for ways to map a strange, new phenomenon into simpler and more familiar ways."[4] In short, the complexity of the subject matter, on the one hand, and our limited capacity, on the other, require us to simplify; yet the implications of doing so are seldom considered, in either an analytic or an operational sense.

There will always be a need for specialization and for simplifying assumptions and procedures, but these simplifications are costly. The study of complex systems has a quality of wholeness, just as the systems themselves do. A meaningful analysis of the field cannot be limited to any single purpose, since each study necessarily makes assumptions about the results of studies with other, specialized purposes. For instance, a rational analysis of strategic interactions, which might be conducted to determine assured-destruction values, depends either implicitly or explicitly on the results generated in other studies on such topics as human factors related to weapon delivery, weather conditions, command and control parameters—the whole, in fact, of an incredibly long list of limited but critical factors. Similarly, the parts of systems selected for analysis must not be limited by any single empirical approach or methodology, since none deals with all the phenomena that are important in explaining the behavior of systems. Thus, although simplifications are necessary, so are communication and coordination among areas of specialization and assumptions and procedures that enable us to deal more adequately with complex problems.[5]

THE ANALYST'S VIEW

The analyst's general view of his subject matter is crucial in determining how the subject will be perceived, simplified, analyzed, and interpreted. The analyst who has a predilection for seeing linear, orderly, static, and rather simple patterns in the world—as a statistician or actuary might—will choose different methods and will have different abstracted views of the world from those held by the analyst who looks at the world as composed of a small number of important elements, related in nonlinear, deterministic ways—as an engineer might see it. Selection has its logical consequences. The choice of topics, the organization of the problem, the application of a method, and the formulation of results all eventually hinge on the judgment, knowledge, and skill of the analyst in carrying out each of these tasks.[6] This fact has generally been neglected, and the importance of the analyst has been overshadowed by a misplaced emphasis on techniques. The construction and interpretation of formal models, for instance, are basically judgmental processes.[7]

An expert is a person who has acquired highly detailed, often esoteric skills in a particular area; a specialist is one who has concentrated on a very limited field of knowledge. Striving to know more details about fewer basic topics—that is, specialization—creates a dilemma for those interested in making use of the detailed knowledge that results. Grave mismatches are common among the narrowly defined, highly detailed information dealt with by an expert or specialist, the somewhat more general and comprehensive information required by a military decision maker, the broad and general information required by an elected official, for whom military affairs are one of a long list of substantial issues, and the average citizen, whose very survival is at stake in the issues under consideration.

Different scientific disciplines rely on somewhat related but different methodologies.[8] Specialized disciplines may generate specific, narrow insights about selected aspects of broad, complex, and poorly understood phenomena. This narrow view is seldom sufficiently robust to comprehend the phenomena or to locate them within a broader context as a basis for making decisions. Thus a physicist or an engineer well grounded in physics can extend his technical expertise to other areas, such as the terminal-ballistics aspects of weapons design, and can often offer valuable insights to assist the military decision maker. The same physicist, however, pondering the less technical, less familiar aspects of a broader subject—perhaps that of command and control over the warheads or missiles he had previously designed—might try to extend his models and concepts to the new area without generating any truly productive insights at all. Nevertheless, many users place a disturbing and inappropriate reliance on technical experts who are working beyond their substantive competence, especially when they are doing so with methods and techniques that are rigorous and hard to understand. In the same way, the economist is often moved to extend his theoretical expertise into areas where the theory is, at best, only partially applicable; the results are often questionable or even counterproductive.[9]

It is not the case, naturally, that diverse theories and methods cannot occasionally provide insights when extended to areas different from those in which the basic work attained legitimacy. The incontrovertible complexity of war remains, however, along with many other factors that create obscurity and uncertainty. Rather than being thoughtful or even circumspect about the dangers of inappropriate methodology, the military modeling community tends to rely increasingly on MSGs the underlying assumptions of which are often at odds with the actual nature of the subject matter. Their proliferation doubtless arises from a combination of factors, some of which have been discussed in earlier chapters. Fundamentally, it suggests considerable immaturity about the need to understand the subject matter; the situation warrants increased concern with and consciousness about methodology and its relationship to knowledge.

THE DECISION MAKER'S VIEW

The decision maker's view is also important, but it is insufficient in itself to provide the required levels of understanding and knowledge. As the analyst's view of the world is shaped by a variety of factors, including training, personality, and past experience, so is that of the decision maker. The world view of an Army lieutenant colonel recently transferred from commanding a line battalion to a three-year studies and analysis post in the Pentagon will be strongly shaped by field-oriented environmental cues, incentives, and pressures. His language will be entirely different from that used by the technical expert; difficult problems of respect, communication, and coordination between expert and decision maker regularly result from such differences.

The ever present constraints of budgets, time, organizational demands, and personal and career motivations enter into any consideration of the complex social system we have labeled the contextual map. Our representative colonel needs an occasional glimpse of his and his organization's location in the bigger picture, but no existing institutional mechanism provides it. He needs to understand that the specialists on whom he relies are not communicating among themselves very well and, furthermore, are speaking different languages from his own; there is no way, however, short of hard-won, on-the-job training, for him to learn about these problems. He needs to understand the theories and methods he is buying and using far better than he typically does; he must at least grasp their comparative weaknesses, strengths, and costs. The current system, however, gives him little help in these matters.

Simplification and Modeling

The need to simplify is evident even in MSGs used to represent war in all its complexity. Figure 11-1 summarizes, in simplified form, a process commonly encountered in building and using MSGs.[10] As one moves down the left-hand column, highly selected aspects of a substantive problem are retained and much information is deleted as efforts are made to represent the problem formally or mathematically. Moving across the bottom row and back up the right-hand column, presuming that something has resulted from the previous exercise, we see that information is being added back onto the analysis. At points A and A' key interactions between decision makers and experts occur, with all the attendant language problems that

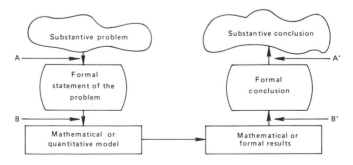

Figure 11-1. *A simplified paradigm of modeling.*

we have noted earlier. Subsequent translation steps (noted at points B and B') are dominated, even under the best of circumstances, by the expert. The step at point B is routinely taken for purely technical, rather than substantive, reasons; that the step at point B' is critical for any analysis is poorly appreciated.

Bias enters at every stage and leads to distortions of the analysis and the interpretation of the analytic results. In order to define the substantive problem, for instance, choices must be made about what is relatively more important often by decision makers on the basis of their own special views of the world, by analysts on the basis of their own perceptions of the problem and the world (modified somewhat by the degree to which the decision maker's concerns have been taken into account), and then by the technical imperatives of the method employed to specify the MSG. The MSG itself further biases the results. Although strong statistical assumptions may underlie the measurement and structure of parameters and variables, we are seldom informed either about them or about their consequences for the analysis.

As the process moves back up the right-hand column in figure 11-1, additional information permits the results already generated to be interpreted. At the topmost level, the communication issues raised by the existence of two cultures once again color the outcome.

At best, any MSG provides a single perspective on a problem, one that is highly colored and qualified by the steps taken to create it. These logical distortions are seldom sufficiently heeded. Once the logic of the problem has been laid out, alternative perspectives should be generated and examined for their technical and informational content. Thus thorough documentation is necessary so that technical details can be independently assessed; entirely different groups of individuals should be working through all of these steps to illuminate the problem according to their own distinct biases, purposes, perspectives, and expectations. Currently even the basic technical information, including documentation, to carry out the necessary appraisals is lacking. Thus the discourse required as a preliminary to the longer-term goal of remodeling the same or closely related problem situations cannot be undertaken. If realized, this accomplishment could lead to a fuller understanding of the problem, to alternative possibilities for solution, and to a more open discussion and exploration of concepts and policies.

Unverified findings from an MSG built and used by one organization are often accepted as facts by a different organization and used as input for the latter's own MSGs. These data may combine subtle concepts, subjective evaluations, and limited but hard evidence based on actual physical testing. Even the testing, however, may have been undertaken for purposes very different from those of the next study group.[11] Although such uninformed recycling is common, the difficulty it presents is generally not sufficiently appreciated by the decision maker or other users. If asked often enough, questions like the following might be used to expose faulty practices and improve the current situation: Does a given number or set of numbers result from an MSG or from physical measurement? If it is part of the output of an MSG, to what extent is it an untested and therefore contestable hypothesis? That is, has the MSG been validated by some independent source and test? If the MSG has not been independently validated, then what is the structure underlying it—that is, what is its implicit theoretical base? If the MSG has been tested, or if the set of numbers derives from some physical test or other empirical source, what was the experimental design and what are the possible errors resulting from the instrumentation of the previous effort? What reporting methods were employed? How were the data filtered and aggregated as they moved through the bureaucratic hierarchy? If the subjective assessments of individuals comprise some of the data, who were these individuals and what is their experience and what institutional affiliation?

Raising these and related questions would easily bring into focus the limited empirical and theoretical bases upon which most MSGs are currently constructed. In the absence of a complete view of the context and without even minimal documentation, however, these questions are simply not being asked. If they were, the need for better and more empirical work, including operational testing whenever possible, would plainly be great enough to require major reallocations of talent from model building to fundamental work. The resources have not yet been reallocated, primarily because no one has yet obtained a complete enough view of the process; no one's contextual map has been drawn on a sufficiently large scale.

The real payoff from raising and answering these and related questions is an institutional one. Better empirical work could lead to the creation of institutional mechanisms meant to check the assertions that flow from MSGs, including those used to justify technical-performance specifications for new weapons systems. If past experience, which often seems to have been forgotten, is a valid indicator, better empirical efforts will suggest reasons and ways to structure new and better MSGs.[12]

The Nonmilitary Implications of the Map

The foregoing discussion has implications far beyond the military area.[13] Many lessons can be learned from the experience of the military with MSGs; if they are learned well and soon enough, perhaps they need not be relearned later. Among them are the need for vastly improved professional communication and coordination through institutional mechanisms that do not yet exist; for constant assessment of all MSG activities so that top-level decision makers and technical experts will have a timely sense of who is doing what in all substantive areas of endeavor; for an enlarged base of knowledge on which MSGs can be constructed; and for a serious effort to promulgate technical and professional standards to ensure that the best possible work is produced and then appropriately used.

Because most problems, military or nonmilitary, likely to be addressed with these analytic tools are extremely complex, they are not likely to yield to the intellectual powers of one or a few groups of experts. The need to create alternative perspectives on these problems is as urgent as it is obvious. Counteranalyses are needed—analyses developed from different perspectives than those associated with the few agencies now active in the area of MSGs. An adversary point of view that would emphasize legislative, public-interest, and perhaps even international values and expectations should be developed. Within the federal legislative branch, the Office of Technology Assessment (OTA) and the Congressional Budget

Office (CBO) might serve appropriately as institutional bases and funding sources for some of this work. Universities have a clear but often unfulfilled role in this regard; the same is true of UNESCO and other international bodies. Nearly all of them have failed to recognize the threat presented by one-sided analyses of complex social phenomena; virtually none is actively and diligently attempting to counter that threat.

Adversary analyses might take several forms. Full-scale construction and use of MSGs would be one direct means of entering the lists; however, this plan would necessitate capital outlays for talent and machines far beyond the capabilities of many concerned groups (this is not an acceptable rationalization for continued noninvolvement on the part of Congress). A second, less costly method would be the evaluation and reinvestigation of one group's work by another with different institutional and professional imperatives and orientations. As we discovered, classification of even military analyses is not a real barrier to this kind of examination; so far the full potential of the various freedom-of-information laws has not been realized with respect to nonmilitary problems.

There is no reason to believe that a unitary view of the world is going to be the correct one. On the contrary, it is likely to be quite inaccurate, as a result of the innate complexity of most of the problems that are commonly analyzed with the techniques and methods discussed here. The more professionally competent and well-articulated views there are, the better. All the issues discussed above are important when considered in the light of the magnitude of the issues being analyzed and the importance of decisions based on these analyses. They are, quite literally, matters of life or death for millions of people.

The Survey

To begin answering many of the questions posed earlier in this chapter, we spent nearly five man-months from 1970 through early 1971 designing and testing a survey questionnaire.[14] Our initial concern was to be sure that our questionnaire was comprehensive, comprehensible, and appropriate for the diverse population of military models, simulations, and games being used by the Department of Defense. Although we did not know it at that time, the General Accounting Office had been asked by the House Appropriations Committee to assess the kind, extent, and application of war games being used by the military; their initial probings of these matters had not progressed far when we discovered the complementarity of our interests and decided to collaborate. Our first formal contact with auditors from the General Accounting Office occurred during a conference of military modelers and gamers that we hosted at The Rand Corporation in early 1971, the general purpose of which was to bring some of the key participants together for three days of taking stock of and summarizing the status of the art and profession at that time. During the latter part of 1971 and early 1972, we worked closely with the auditors, providing them with a refined and expanded version of our questionnaire, helping them to identify operational MSGs in the active inventory, and training members of their staff, who subsequently went into the field to administer the questionnaire. As soon as all questionnaire replies had been completed and returned to the auditors, a separate listing of responses was prepared for our use, and the two investigations proceeded on separate courses.

Together with the auditors, we identified approximately 450 active military MSGs.[15] Finding them was a difficult job, only partially facilitated by several Department of Defense and armed-service catalogs and inventories—none of which was comprehensive and most of which were outdated and incomplete. From this pool of 450 MSGs, we chose a sample of 150 (later reduced to 135); members of the General Accounting Office audit team made inquiries to identify the most knowledgeable individual or the directly responsible agency in each case; finally, the auditors administered each questionnaire. We received 133 replies, one of which gave too little information to be usable. Thus, unless otherwise noted, the survey findings reported in the following three chapters and noted occasionally in the remainder of this book are based on this respondent population of 132 active, operational MSGs. The sample was chosen to include several of the larger or more heavily used simulations and games. It was biased somewhat toward the Army (the respondents included 59 Army, 26 Air Force, 35 Navy, and 11 other Defense Department staff members). As a result, extrapolations from this sample to the total population should be made carefully.

Our survey and supplementary investigations into the past, present, and likely future of military modeling and gaming (including an extensive regimen of interviews, searches and reviews of the literature, and participation in several gaming exercises) suggest that there are eight distinct and interrelated phases in the general life cycle of MSGs used operationally in the Department of Defense: initiation, promotion, prescription, production, operation, use, evaluation, and termination. That process, or sequence, of decision making is considered at length in chapter 16. For the moment, however, our main focus is on details discovered in our survey that relate to the purposes for which MSGs are being constructed, the means used to construct them, the ways they are employed, and the benefits and costs involved.[16] The next three chapters consider these details as revealed in our survey results. Here, however, we shall attempt to present a broad view of the map of modeling, simulation, and gaming before exploring its details in depth.

Total reported development costs in our survey were approximately $32 million, but approximately 30 responses did not provide appropriate or clear information about costs. These 30 included several of what we believe to be the larger simulations. Estimating about $8 million for these, total development costs approximate $40 million.[17] Since the sample represents roughly 30 percent of the total inventory by very conservative estimates, a crude approximation of the total investment would be $130 to $140 million for all MSGs in active use by the Department of Defense at the time of the survey. Before our questionnaire was circulated, the General Accounting Office made a preliminary estimate of $170.5 million, which seems plausible, on the basis of other costing criteria.[18] The inventory represents, on the average, a three- to four-year supply of MSGs (an average MSG lasts three to four years); hence we estimate that $30 to $40 million a year was expended for construction costs during the mid-1970s. These estimates are not only necessarily rough; they are presently somewhat out of date. Since, however, no one has made an effort to replicate or improve on this survey, to the best of our knowledge, they represent the only figures available.

Expenditures and number of activities do not provide all the clues to the importance of the work done using MSGs. Many other criteria are needed to judge these activities, but valid standards have not yet been formulated for the profession. With these caveats in mind, we turn to a detailed description of our findings.

12 | Purposes and Production

> ... When we mean to build,
> We first survey the plot, then draw the model;
> And when we see the figure of the house,
> Then we must rate the cost of the erection;
> Which if we find outweighs ability,
> What do we then but draw anew the model
> In fewer offices, or at last desist
> To build at all?
>
> Shakespeare, *King Henry IV, Part II*

DETERMINING THE PURPOSE of a model, simulation, or game is a necessary first step toward understanding it. Because there is so little agreement about fundamental definitions, we felt it was especially important to find out what terms and concepts the professional community currently uses to describe the rationale or aim of various MSGs. The purpose for which an MSG is built bears directly on its subsequent production, use, validation, and appraisal. Those who provided answers to our many questions (summarized in appendix B) must be identified before we present their answers.

When the final version of our survey questionnaire was set, the staff of the General Accounting Office (GAO) audit team met with personnel in the Department of Defense, described the purpose of the survey, and asked that the person most knowledgeable about any given MSG be assigned to answer the questionnaire. If one person could not respond, groups or committees were acceptable substitutes, as long as the answers were as up to date and accurate as possible.[1] As it turned out, most questionnaires were filled out by one person, and most respondents filled out only one questionnaire. In a few instances, one person was responsible for two or perhaps three separate responses. One did yeoman service by answering questionnaires on six or seven different MSGs.

Respondents were most often users (42, or 31.8 percent) or designers and builders (41, or 31.1 percent). The next largest classes of respondents were funders and sponsors (19, or 14.4 percent) and caretakers—individuals responsible for an MSG but not fitting any of the other respondent categories (13, or 13.6 percent). The average length of time required to fill out the questionnaire was 10.5 hours. The modal time was 4 hours, and 84 respondents were able to answer in 8 hours or less; however, a few respondents stated that they took as much as 70 hours.

We feel that this group of respondents was as well as or better qualified than any other available group to provide reasoned and valuable replies to the questionnaire. The replies relating to purpose and production are discussed below. Those concerning operations, benefits, uses, and costs of MSGs are discussed in chapters 13 and 14, which also present our opinions about certain hypothetical innovations in the gaming profession.

Reported Purposes

We began by asking each respondent to identify his MSG as a model, a simulation, a man-machine or manual game, a mathematical analysis or study, or, if none of those categories fit, some "other" type. As figure 12-1 indicates, most were identified as models. The usage of that term and concept is vague, however; one respondent noted that to him a model

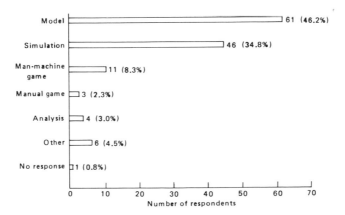

Figure 12-1. *Respondents' primary classifications of MSGs.*

was any regression equation, and the universe of models was therefore so large as to be virtually unbounded. In short, the word *model* has little referential utility. This terminological problem is underscored by the GAO's initial lack of success when it asked the military services to provide data on war games. The GAO found that practically no war games are played; rather, models and simulations are built.

Another striking finding is the small number of man-machine and manual exercises in the Defense Department's active inventory—only 14, or 10.6 percent. While our sample represents only 132 of the some 450 active MSGs, we are reasonably confident that this figure accurately reflects the current low level of man-machine and manual, or free-form, activity. Multiple choices were allowed; that is, a respondent could call his MSG both a model and a man-machine exercise, for instance. Only 26 indicated a second choice, however; of that group, 19 chose simulations; 3, "other"; 2, models; and 2, mathematical analysis. No one selected man-machine or manual game as a secondary choice.

Because the concept of purpose is inherently complex, our questions were detailed and intentionally redundant. Respondents were asked to describe in their own words the major stated purpose of their MSG and to cite two specific questions or operational problems that the MSG had been used to answer. Next, they were asked to check off appropriate characterizations of purpose from a list of eight categories. We also asked them to indicate the degree of certainty of response—from low to absolutely certain. Several questions later, purpose was mentioned again, this time with reference to who initiated the work, what he wanted, and how well he specified his wishes. Finally, still later, we asked whether the MSG was initially designed for experimental or educational purposes. The results of this repeated probing are revealing, especially when tabulated against other descriptive categories, such as who paid for, built, or used the MSG and at what cost.

The primary purposes of the MSGs surveyed, as described by the respondents, are shown in figure 12-2.[2] None of the respondents indicated that his MSG was intended primarily for military, political, and economic purposes or for training and education. In fact, only one MSG was listed under

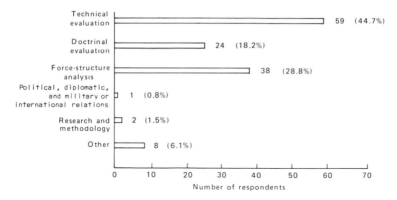

Figure 12-2. *The primary stated purposes of MSGs.*

political, diplomatic, and military or international-relations purposes. Given current concern about the limitation of strategic arms, perpetual tensions in the Middle East, and the expansion of Sino-American relations, that is a startling finding. Even when secondary and tertiary purposes are taken into account, the findings are not much different. Sixty-one of the MSGs, or 46.2 percent, had only one purpose; of the remainder, one was described as having secondary political, diplomatic, military, or international-relations purposes and one, training and education. Of the MSGs with three purposes (36, or 27.3 percent), two were intended for military, political, and economic uses, one for political, diplomatic, military, or international-relations uses, and one for training and education. Research and methodology received similarly scant attention; it was the primary purpose of two MSGs, the secondary purpose of five, and the tertiary purpose of ten.

By far the greatest emphasis in current activity within the Department of Defense is on all-computer technical evaluations (59, or 44.7 percent), force-structure analysis (38, or 28.8 percent), and doctrinal evaluation (24, or 18.2 percent). When it comes to secondary purpose, the ratio changes. Of the 71 MSGs with more than one stated purpose, 32 were intended to study doctrine; 28, for force structure; and only one, for technical evaluation. Thirty-six tertiary purposes were reported—17 for force-structure analysis, 10 for research and methodological development, and the remainder divided among other purposes.

Technical evaluation turns out to mean the evaluation of weapons systems, at least as described in the written descriptions of each MSG's major stated purpose and the examples of its use. Such activities require checks to see, first, whether the data are valid and available for scrutiny by responsible persons and, second, whether scientific criteria and procedures, such as replication, external review, and documentation, are being followed. If such rigor is not assumed, much effort is probably going to build unevaluated MSGs that support specialized points of view. The scarcity of attention to research, training, and more or less political matters might lead to the conclusion that the Department of Defense is modeling problems that are easily quantified and sufficiently understood that no new theoretical research is needed to explain them. If so, then either the problems confronting the Defense Department are in fact being managed in a rigorous, scientific fashion or, as appears to be the case, intangible, intractable, or "soft" issues are largely being overlooked. The majority of the respondents (105, or 79.5 percent), were highly confident or absolutely certain about their MSG's purpose, but 27 (20.5 percent) either specified low to moderate confidence in their answers or did not respond at all. Considering the composition of the respondent population and the inquiry's intent and sponsorship, that figure seems inordinately high.

As figure 12-3 shows, the initiators of MSG development strongly favored analysis and diagnosis as a primary purpose (108, or 81.8 percent). Far fewer favored operations (14),

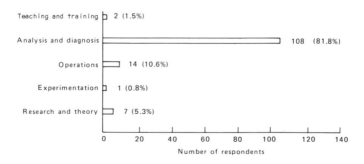

Figure 12-3. The MSG initiator's primary purpose.

research and theory development (7), experimentation (1), or teaching and training (2). That finding is consistent with the heavy emphasis on technical evaluation and force-structure analysis already observed. When asked how tightly (that is, how clearly) funding sources specified their intentions or purposes, 77 respondents replied with either high or absolute certainty that 33 of the sample MSGs, or 25.0 percent, were tightly specified; that is, the funding source defined exactly what it wanted for its money. In 26 of the cases, or 19.7 percent, however, the respondent either did not know or did not respond to the question (see fig. 12-4).

A full 114 of the MSGs, or 86.4 percent, were not intended for experimental purposes; 121, or 91.7 percent, were not intended for educational purposes. The sample MSGs may thus be tentatively characterized as operational machine models and simulations used for technical evaluations and force-structure analysis. Research, experimentation, and training and education are all of considerably less importance.

We were able to make crude comparisons between MSGs sampled based on differences in their year of initiation, thus glimpsing several shifts in emphasis between the newer and older MSGs in the inventory. The fundamental purposes of MSGs have shifted somewhat since 1966. Technical evaluations have declined from 50.0 percent of all MSGs initiated in 1966–67 to 38.9 percent of those initiated in 1971–1972; force-structure analyses have increased from 13.6 percent to 38.9 percent; and doctrine evaluations have remained rather

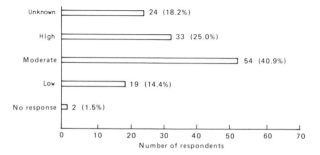

Figure 12-4. *The degree of specificity of the initiator's purpose.*

steady at about 22.0 percent of the total. Since 1966, not a single MSG of those reported in our survey was initiated for teaching and training purposes. MSGs intended for analysis and diagnosis have held steady at about 85 percent of the total.

That respondents knew in general what their MSGs were supposed to do is clear when primary purpose was cross-tabulated against the respondent's confidence in his reply. Some 89.5 percent were either highly or absolutely certain about the MSG's purpose; however, 10 of the 38 force-structure MSG respondents indicated low or moderate confidence or did not answer at all (χ^2 $p < .024$; chi-square is a statistic indicating the significance of a given measurement; in this case, there is only a 2.4 percent chance that what is described occurred because of random factors). The reason is not clear, but it may be that force-structure MSGs are not well documented or are one-shot affairs the initial purpose of which is no longer remembered by the organizations responsible for them. We shall reexamine that hypothesis later.

Of the MSG funding sources, it appears that the Navy concentrates most heavily on technical evaluation (26 out of 33 MSGs funded, or 78.8 percent); the Air Force divides between force-structure analysis (12 out of 23, or 52.2 percent), and technical evaluation (10 out of 23, or 43.5 percent); the Army is evenly divided between technical evaluation (18 out of 56, or 32.1 percent), doctrine evaluation (16 out of 56, or 28.6 percent), and force-structure analysis (16 out of 56, or 28.6 percent); and the Joint Chiefs of Staff funded 5 MSGs on force structure and 1 on political, diplomatic, and military or international relations (χ^2 $p < .001$). No direct Department of State or National Security Council funding was noted, a fact that reinforces our earlier observation about the sample's apparent lack of explicitly political or diplomatic substance.

Cross-tabulation of the initiator of the MSG with its purpose requires some explanation. Model builders or researchers acting as individuals may propose the construction of an MSG to an appropriate funding source. In-house work, on the contrary, is limited either by the needs of the eventual users or by a nonuser management source acting for the users. An outside agency may ask an organization either to build an MSG for its use or to build and use an MSG for the initiator's own purposes. Individual researchers initiated 24, or 18.2 percent, of all 132 MSGs in the survey; this group was fairly evenly divided among those intended to be used for technical, doctrinal, or force-structure evaluation and analysis. Of the 40 MSGs initiated by in-house users, 18, or 45.0 percent, were intended for technical evaluation. This group and the MSGs initiated by users outside of the building agency together account for 34 of the 59 technical-evaluation MSGs, or 57.6 percent. Thus it appears that users tend to initiate their own technical-evaluation MSGs ($\chi^2 p < .011$).

Tabulation of the initiator's purpose—teaching, analysis, operations, experimentation, or research—against the MSG's purpose or category of intended use shows that the penchant to do analysis and diagnosis runs evenly through all MSG activity. Of the 59 technical-evaluation MSGs, 50, or 84.9 percent, were intended for analysis and diagnosis; 21 of 24, or 87.5 percent, for doctrine evaluation; and 30 of 38, or 78.9 percent, for force-structure analysis ($\chi^2 p < .001$). The one surprising finding is that in those cases where the initiator's purpose was research and the development of theories (7 of 132, or 5.3 percent), the primary purposes of the resulting MSGs were technical evaluation (4 of 7), force-structure analysis (2 of 7), or doctrine evaluation (1 of 7), rather than the development of research or methodology ($\chi^2 p < .001$). Even when the development of an MSG is motivated by a serious research problem, it is apparently not reported as geared primarily to research. In the cases of the 2 MSGs the prime purpose of which was listed as research and methodology, the initiators intended analysis, diagnosis, and experimentation, not research as such ($\chi^2 p < .001$).

The tabulation of purpose against the extent of documentation was highly significant ($\chi^2 p < .001$) and suggestive. By the respondents' own assessment, 15 of the 59 technical-evaluation MSGs had weak, poor, uneven, unavailable, or unknown documentation; 9 of the 38 force-structure MSGs fell into those categories. That information is not conclusive, however, because roughly equal numbers in each category responded that their MSG had excellent, very good, or average documentation. While the distributions are flat, the fact that 25.4 percent of the technical-evaluation and 23.6 percent of the force-structure MSGs were acknowledged to have weak documentation, or worse, seems important.

Cost data were coded and tabulated against purpose. We were immediately struck by the fact that 25 of the respondents, or 18.9 percent, were unable to supply any information whatsoever on costs. Of the remainder, 50 MSGs were reported to have cost $100,000 or less; 22, $100,000 to $249,000; and 17, $250,000 to $500,000. Eighteen MSGs cost more than $500,000, of which 6 were technical evaluations, 5 were doctrine evaluations, 5 were force-structure studies, and 1 was used for political, diplomatic, and military purposes (χ^2 $p <$ .012). Cost considerations are taken up in more detail in chapter 14.

Unstated and Retrospective Purposes

Several pitfalls are routinely encountered when one tries to describe and evaluate models, simulations, and games. First, and most important, it is essential to be aware of the many unstated but important purposes that underlie MSG activities; it is even more revealing to discover that there may not even be a clearly perceived or stated purpose. While we are not claiming that unstated purposes overwhelmed the activities for the MSGs we surveyed, we do believe that an outside evaluator should at least consider three possible uses: (1) to rationalize and provide scientific window dressing for a decision already made; (2) to keep a professional staff occupied or to use up funds that would otherwise have to be returned at the end of the fiscal year; and (3) to provide a way to delay making a decision.

Purposes can be assigned after the fact in at least two major ways. First, a sponsor may be sold a bill of goods by a model builder who has time and a technique in search of a problem. The problem of matching a research or operational question and the immediate analytic purpose with the appropriate research technique is seldom clearly articulated. Analysts become accustomed to certain techniques and are hired by firms to join others who are proficient in them. Because the invested intellectual capital, for the individuals, and the professional commitment of the firms for which they labor are so extensive, no one bothers to figure out whether these techniques are the best suited to the purpose at hand. Many users feel uncomfortable with sophisticated research methods and even with the researchers themselves; it is nearly impossible for them to determine whether or not the skills and techniques involved are in fact the right ones for the operational problems in question.

Rationalizations of purpose after the fact also result from the discontinuities in personnel inherent in most long-term, complex activities in the bureaucracy. A new group may be left holding the bag, in effect—finding themselves with an analysis or study that they did not order but for which they now have responsibility. Without a clear understanding or appreciation of the initial purpose for the work, they may find it expedient to devise a purpose that fits their own current interests and needs.

Production Factors

How long does it take to build an MSG and how much does it cost? Depending on who is asking the question and the purpose for asking it, there are several different answers. When a contract to develop an MSG is drawn up, the accountant and the lawyer fix a date on which the MSG or its results are to be turned over to the customer. This process is well defined and generates a set of numbers and some evaluation of the overall effort. How meaningful they are if used for control purposes depends on many factors other than those treated by the lawyer or accountant.

In the model-making business, there is a considerable difference between a legally fulfilled contract and an operationally useful product. The two major resources expended in the construction of a model, for both planning and evaluation tasks, are time and money. The relevant costs and time needed to carry out a project in a bureaucracy cover the period from the decision to act until the receipt of a usable finished product. Thus the difference between a legally acceptable product and a useful one is measured in terms of cost overruns, new contracts to find out what the original work was intended to do, briefings, and other modifications.

An interest in the costs of previous work is not merely historical if future work is expected to have similar properties. The costs of research-and-development work are notoriously hard to calculate. Although we believe that we have some relevant and worthwhile comments to make concerning production and costs, we cannot overstress the need for outside evaluators who understand the details of the business. The General Accounting Office—one of the very few sources of external evaluation—is able to generate tables of statistics that may result in extra audits or an occasional comment from the Congress. Because they lack thorough technical and conceptual understanding of the work, however, the GAO auditors merely reinforce the prevalent view that the Congress and the Pentagon must always be engaged in an adversary process. What actually results is an uneven struggle between lawyers and accountants, on the one hand, and flag-ranked officers and their large technical staffs, on the other.

All would stand to gain if the GAO had technical and scientific assistance, so that people who know what the numbers actually mean would be available for ongoing external reviews of MSG production.[3] Challenges concerning new weapons systems and other military expenditures could then be moved from an adversary process, in which one side is basically ignorant of the technical facts of life, toward a more evenly balanced technical assessment. For a slight additional effort, significant social gains could be realized.

Some production questions, such as what MSGs preceded or followed the investigated MSG, are straightforward and easily answered; others are not. When discussing development time, for example, it is difficult to be both precise and accurate. Our definition of development time as the elapsed time between the decision to build a given MSG and its first production run grossly underestimates the total when an MSG continues to be developed even while it is being used. Another conceptual difficulty arises in estimating expenditures of human resources. One must distinguish between total man-years, professional man-years, and programmer man-years to understand what kinds of talent have been involved in the construction of an MSG.

In an attempt to understand our survey sample better, we asked respondents to describe scenarios, mathematical difficulty, timing, levels of resolution, use of random events, and supporting data. Taken together, their answers provide valuable insights into current production practices.

RESULTS

About three-fourths of the sample had at least one directly antecedent MSG, a fact that indicates the cumulative nature of much of the work in this area. While the sample was biased to include many active MSGs, in 45 cases a spin-off was reported to have been developed. These activities are clearly not discrete events but represent an ongoing process of initiation, production, and use.

An assessment of alternative procedures was elicited by asking the respondents to imagine achieving the objectives of the MSG by different means. As figure 12-5 shows, analysis was the most common alternative; this finding reinforces our earlier observation of the widespread use and acceptance of the term *analysis*. The fact that 22.0 percent of the respondents believe that no alternative existed supports the view that much of this activity is of the nature of a methodological last resort; that is, many of the problems are not tractable by other means.

A large number of the MSGs in our sample—59, or 44.7 percent—were constructed by the armed forces themselves.

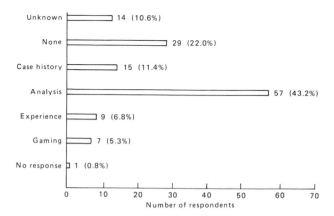

Figure 12-5. *The best alternative method to that used.*

Profit-making organizations built 37, or 28.7 percent; nonprofit organizations contributed 29, or 22.0 percent; and universities accounted for 7, or 5.3 percent. Development time (time elapsed between initiation and first production run) varies widely, from less than 3 months to more than 42 months (see fig. 12-6). Since 63.6 percent were developed in 18 months or less, it appears that decision-making lead times are most likely to run under 2 years. It took 2 to 5 man-years to develop 31.8 percent of the MSGs in the sample. Human-resource expenditures are depicted in figure 12-7. Professional man-years and total man-years are nearly equivalent, suggesting that most development activity was carried out by professionals themselves. Indeed, written profiles of professional teams support this point nicely. About 1 computer programmer man-year for each MSG was the norm.

Our next set of questions dealt with characterizing the MSGs and their data bases. A summary of the findings revealed that 54 percent used numerical scenarios only. Judg-

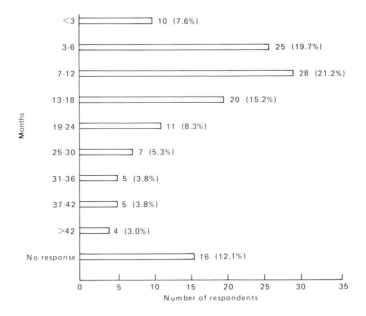

Figure 12-6. *MSG development time.*

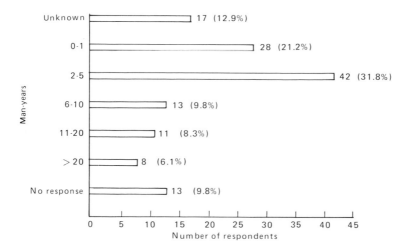

Figure 12-7. *Human-resource expenditures in MSG development.*

ing from the analysis and written replies to the questionnaire, little attention appears to be paid to intangible assumptions or to qualitative factors in the studies. Further findings are presented below.

In spite of a popular belief that advanced mathematical methods are taking over, the level of mathematical sophistication required to work with the MSGs was described as high in only 8 percent of the cases.

The time setting for 52 percent of the MSGs was either an unspecified time or the future.

Approximately 45 percent of the MSGs were directed toward the study of combat at the engagement level, 10 percent at the battle level, 11 percent at the campaign level, and 14 percent at the level of war.

The level of the temporal resolution was rather fine; 79 of the MSGs, or 66.8 percent, were detailed down to either minutes or seconds. Spatial resolution was also fine-grained; about 35 percent were based on meters, and some 27 percent were detailed at the kilometer level.

The sample was split about fifty-fifty on the use of random elements.

We were surprised, given the quantitative and qualitative advances in computer languages, that so many MSGs, more than 80 percent, were still written in Fortran. The remainder were spread among SIMSCRIPT, ALGOL, ASSEMBLY, COBOL, and several other languages.

On the average, the MSGs are either very large (36, or 27.3 percent, had over 10,000 instructions contained in the model itself—less any data input) or moderately small (24, or 18.2 percent, had 2,000 or fewer); 45, or 44.0 percent, contained fewer than 4,000 instructions, or about two boxes of standard-sized computer cards.

The difficulty we experienced in gathering information about these MSGs was not caused by classification problems; 72 percent were unclassified as long as data input values were not attached. (With input data, 88 percent were classified, predominantly at the "Secret" level.) Thus, classification problems present little or no reason for withholding most of the sampled MSGs from scientific scrutiny.

Indications are that problems of data sources and validity are acute. Careful gathering of field-test data or experimental information tends to be expensive and time-consuming, especially the preparation of planning factors; few of the sampled MSGs benefited from such measures. The most common procedure is to have other military agencies supply data, without any follow-up or cross-checking by the user agency. In fewer than 30 percent of the replies was there any indication that additional effort had been made to check the validity of the data.

Development time for the MSGs developed since 1966 has fluctuated to the extent that no clear trends are apparent. A slight trend toward fewer technical evaluations and more force-structure analysis is evident; doctrine evaluations have been relatively stable. The technical characteristics of MSGs are all quite stable. That is to say, no discernible changes have occurred in the proportion of numerical versus verbal scenarios being used, in the level of mathematical sophistication built into the MSGs, in the level of temporal resolution, or in the proportions using and not using random elements.

Of the 59 MSGs constructed in house, 31 were for the purpose of technical evaluation, 17 were for force-structure analysis, and 8, for doctrine evaluation. Of those built by profit-making organizations, 11 were technical evaluations, 11 were force-structure analyses, and 8 were doctrine evaluations. Nonprofit organizations built 11 of 29, or 37.9 percent, for technical evaluation; 10 of 29, or 34.5 percent, for force-structure analysis; and 8 of 29, or 27.6 percent, for doctrinal evaluation. Universities concentrated 6 of their 7 MSGs on technical evaluation. Of the 2 research MSGs, 1 was developed by a university and 1 by the armed forces (χ^2 $p < .007$).

Multiple authorship or participation in the construction phase was noted in 17 instances. Nonprofit organizations produced 11 of these group efforts, mostly on a piecemeal or consultative basis, and 8 of them were intended for technical evaluation. The remaining 6 multiple-author MSGs resulted when several agencies of the same armed force contributed significantly to one final product (χ^2 $p < .016$). It appears that the nonprofit firms are occasionally utilized to back up in-house construction activities in the armed forces. Given the scope, magnitude, and cost of many of these MSGs, the extent of multiple authorship is less than we had expected. In fact, it may arise from what appears to be a harmful compartmentalization and overspecialization in activity.

When the military service responsible for an MSG is tabulated against a range of construction-related descriptive variables, certain patterns are evident.

Construction and purpose. The Army is rather evenly split among the three purposes of technical evaluation, doctrine evaluation, and force-structure analysis; the Air Force is doing more force-structure analysis (50.0 percent) and technical evaluation (42.3 percent) than doctrinal evaluation (7.7 percent); the Navy is largely constructing MSGs for technical evaluation (77.8 percent), to the exclusion of other types (χ^2 $p < .0001$).

Initiation. Navy MSGs are initiated either by external users or by the builders themselves to a far greater extent than is the case in the other services. The Army accounts for 11 of the 17 of the external, nonuser initiations, or 64.7 percent. No particular pattern is discernible for the Air Force; that is, initiation comes from a variety of sources (χ^2 $p < .03$). There is also no observable pattern in Air Force specification of the purposes of its MSGs. The Army, on the other hand, accounts for two-thirds of those that are tightly specified. The bulk of Navy work was noted as being specified in "moderate" detail (χ^2 $p < .002$).

Construction site. While these two variables are not significantly related (χ^2 $p < .15$), on a percentage basis the Air Force does more of its own work in-house than do the other services; the Army uses profit-making organizations more than expected and more than the others; and the Navy's involvement with Johns Hopkins University makes it the dominant university user.

Development time. As noted earlier, about two-thirds of the sampled MSGs were developed in 18 months or less. The Army accounted for 21 of the 36 MSGs built in 6 months or less. Navy construction appears normally to take from 6 months to a year, while no distinct pattern is evident for Air Force construction. At the other end of the scale, no one service stands out as taking particularly long to develop its MSGs (χ^2 $p < .05$).

Source and validity of data. Navy data, as indicated by the respondents, are most likely to have been cross-checked, field-tested, or experimentally derived (27 of 36, or 75.5 percent, of the Navy MSGs underwent some form of validation). For the other services, it was a toss-up whether data were checked or not. The MSGs built by or for the Joint Chiefs of Staff were about three times as likely not to have their data checked as all others in the sample; in fact, in 10 of the 11 MSGs identified as "other Department of Defense," the data were not cross-checked or were unknown or no response was given. Validation procedures were not significantly related to the specific services, although no fewer than 38 respondents, or 28.8 percent of the entire sample, reported that validation was not undertaken or was unknown or gave no response.

Data type. Examples of each of the three basic types of data—hard, moderate, or soft—were provided. Only eight MSGs used mainly soft data or soft data in combination with numbers of greater certainty, a point already noted. Generally, Air Force MSGs used hard data to a greater extent than did those of the Navy or Army ($\chi^2 p < .01$).

Construction and security classification. If an MSG without data input was classified at all, and about one-fourth were, it was most likely labeled "Confidential" (17 of 37, or 46.0 percent) of "For Official Use Only" (9 of 37, or 24.3 percent). More Army MSGs are unclassified (81.4 percent) than Air Force (69.2 percent) or Navy (64.0 percent) ($\chi^2 p < .01$). When data input is added, a full 85.6 percent of the entire sample becomes classified, mostly at the "Secret" level (78, or 59.1 percent). On a percentage basis, the Air Force has more classified MSGs (92.3 percent) than expected for the entire sample, and more than either the Navy or the Army ($\chi^2 p < .002$).

Size. The bimodal distribution noted for the whole sample held for the individual services with only minor variations; the Navy, with 33 percent, had a higher proportion of MSGs in the largest size category (those with more than 10,000 instructions) than did either the Army (28.8 percent) or the Air Force (19.2 percent). Most Air Force entries were in the range of 1,000 to 2,000 instructions (9 of 26, or 34.6 percent). If Army MSGs were not large, and 17 of 59 were not, they were in the range of either 2,000 to 4,000 or 4,000 to 6,000 instructions; each category had 8 of 59, or 13.6 percent ($\chi^2 p < .001$).

Level of resolution. The Navy is building more of its MSGs at a finer level of temporal detail than are the other services; all are cast either in seconds (22 of 36, or 61.1 percent) or minutes (8 of 36, or 22.2 percent) with the remaining six not responding ($\chi^2 p < .001$). The spatial detail of most Army MSGs is at the level of kilometers, the Navy's at that of meters, and the Air Force shows no clear preference. In keeping with the fine grain of much of the sample, most MSGs were cast at the engagement level. Battles, campaigns, and wars, increasingly large levels of resolution for military activity, are mainly the province of the Army, which accounts for 85.7 percent, 40.0 percent, and 61.1 percent of the activity, respectively (χ^2 $p <$ .001).

When MSG category was tabulated against the ratio of model time to real time, 30.3 percent of the respondents either did not know or failed to answer. Of the remaining MSGs, those that compressed time extremely were generally simulations; real-time representations were fairly evenly divided among the categories; and expanded MSGs were man-machine exercises or models (χ^2 $p <$ .03).

About 73 percent of the smallest MSGs, those having fewer than 1,000 computer instructions, were models. More than half of the man-machine exercises (54.5 percent) were in the largest size category, while only 33 percent of the simulations and 21 percent of the models were as large (χ^2 $p <$ .02). We looked at the incidence of intangible assumptions and MSG size and found that for the largest category, intangible assumptions were made nearly 20.0 percent more often than would be expected for the whole sample (χ^2 $p <$ .001).

New Production versus Inventory

The production of MSGs is very much a hand-tailoring process. The better the MSG, the less likely it is to be a general-purpose device. Useful MSGs tend to be built to answer well-defined and relatively specific questions. Thus, even if there appears to be a large inventory of MSGs available, there is no guarantee that a new project can be completed simply by modifying an old, existing work. Developing MSGs is usually harder and more time-consuming than anyone initially estimates—particularly when the basic research question is not well defined or understood. It is even more true when the project is a large one. Acknowledging this fact, what can be done about reducing the time required for program development? The answer frequently given by cost-conscious outsiders is to use someone else's computer program. Modifications are almost invariably needed, however; depending upon the size of the original program and the extent of the modifications, it may well be easier, cheaper, and more efficacious to start over again. The choice between starting over and making do with minor modifications to an old program is not likely to be resolved with any general rule of thumb. The importance of carefully defining and thoroughly understanding the research question cannot be overlooked or overstated. An example may help to clarify this point.

Depending on the question, a trade-off between speed of MSG response and accuracy may favor speed—an eventuality that is not well appreciated. Edwin Paxson emphasized speed in his XRAY series of games, for example, so that players could have more or less instantaneous interaction with the underlying MSGs.[4] The trade-off is not well understood, and speed is usually sacrificed to apparent accuracy by the realities of model design and construction. In the broader sense of the discussion, speed could be obtained through the judicious use of MSGs in the existing inventory. More specifically, the desire for speed will generally result in the production and use of many small MSGs, each of which is well understood, designed around very specific objectives, and quite flexible in its operation and in the ease with which input values and specified relationships can be changed. Time-shared MSGs become appropriate in this situation.

In addition, it might be useful to invest time at the beginning of a project in a review of similar work in the field in order to determine what others have thought were the important issues and problems and to be sure that unnecessary duplication does not take place. If this initial review process is to be routinely carried out, information about extant MSGs must be adequate and easily accessible. In our opinion, sources of such information do not presently exist in sufficient quantity or with adequate professional and technical scope and magnitude to make this process as automatic as it should be. A trade-off also exists between search time and thoroughness. The MSG builder cannot waste too much time in hunting for information before beginning work; no one, however, can afford to miss turning up a gem that would be of significant, direct use. This problem highlights the need for reliable retrieval and documentation of existing MSGs to allow more of them to be scanned in a fixed period of time, thereby increasing the probability of turning up an essential fact.

On the whole, the analyst must decide whether there is an existing MSG that would suit his specific research need. A problem with so-called general-purpose models is that there is a strong tendency to bend the research question to fit the model. If a large MSG is readily available, it is usually easier to distort the problem than it is to do the one-time analysis that would best answer that question—especially where extensive resources have already been invested in MSG production. No one, however, appears to compute the costs involved in such activities.

13 | Operations

Those who are not mathematically learned can read
the Propositions also, and can consult mathematicians
concerning the truth of the Demonstrations.

Newton, *Principia*

OPERATIONS ARE THE PROVINCE of the
mathematically learned technical specialist.
The truth of any MSG is difficult enough to divine, yet this determination is further complicated by some
current operational practices.

MSG operation requires attention to many technical details
the cumulative importance of which cannot be overemphasized. For instance, the structural and behavioral properties of
the MSG should be thoroughly explored and systematically
determined before any applications of results is attempted. Is
the MSG correctly and concisely specified? Are the inevitable
simplifications required to specify an MSG known and documented? Have their likely effects on the operations of the
MSG been documented? If not, can anyone other than the developer of the MSG locate and identify these mechanisms?
Are the MSG's output values reasonable for only a very select
and narrowly constrained set of input values? That is, if certain input values are altered slightly, does the MSG begin to
generate wildly improbable output numbers? Does its behavior become unstable?[1] Are the numbers used, both to specify
the MSG and to set its initial input values, accurate and appropriate for the task at hand? Is documentation of the steps
taken to construct the MSG, including data sources, procedures used to specify the structure, and tests used to estimate
input or initial values, available? Are technical modifications
that have been made throughout the life of the MSG noted in

an understandable and accessible format? All of these questions relate to the documentation needed during the production and operation phases. They are an essential part of any effort to replicate, transfer, and check out the operation of an MSG.

Replication is essential for the building and operation of any model; without it, no such activity can be considered a scientific enterprise. While unreplicated MSGs may be capable of generating numbers, both the numbers and the MSGs must be treated cautiously. Our concept of replication differs somewhat from that used for a scientific experiment. We are speaking not of reproduction according to a given sequence of precise operations but rather of the reproduction or rerunning of an MSG in a different site by different individuals from those who built it; there must also be some assessment of its ability to regenerate equivalent output values. Before this assessment can be made, the MSG needs to be transferred from one site to another, a process that in itself implies adequate documentation and suitably configured hardware. Without documentation, there can be no transfer and therefore no external, scientific, professional review and evaluation.

In our survey of military MSGs, questions related to operations dealt basically with two broad matters: scientific standards and technical and procedural issues. Our major concern was with the testing and professional controls employed to ensure the fidelity of MSGs. Our questions addressed such issues as whether sensitivity testing was carried out, whether the operations of a given MSG could be transferred to a comparable location elsewhere, and whether an independent professional review had been carried out. Questions about the MSG's need for special facilities, languages, or documentation pertained more to techniques and hardware.

Results

Sensitivity analysis is an important operational control, particularly when the number of variables in an MSG is large and the model is complex. It is necessary to know the effects of alterations in input parameters on MSG behavior. This is especially true when the precision of the data is questionable, where data variance is large, or where random perturbations are treated explicitly. Nevertheless, 45 percent of the MSGs we surveyed had not been tested for sensitivity. Such testing is generally expensive and time-consuming, but it is essential to a determination of the MSG's usefulness and validity.

About 14 percent of the survey respondents used generally acceptable, adequate means of checking on the accuracy and quality of their input data. About 28 percent of them used less thorough measures, with questions remaining about the precision of some numbers actually being used. For another 30 percent, the written commentary and categorical assessments indicated that at least some effort was made to check out data. Data validation was not attempted in 16 percent of the cases, and 13 percent either did not reply or did not know whether data validation had been attempted. The survey of nonmilitary MSGs reported somewhat more widespread efforts to validate input data. Of the 189 project monitors or directors who answered this question (310 were asked), 65.6 percent attempted some kind of external checking of data; however, the extent and quality of these checks were not reported.[2]

Documentation is a major control function that has received inadequate attention. Figure 13-1 presents the respondents' assessments of their MSGs' documentation; many of the favor-

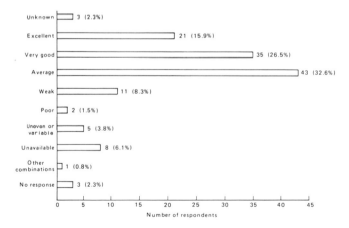

Figure 13-1. *Respondents' assessments of the quality of MSG documentation.*

able evaluations would be shown to be unrealistically optimistic if the documentation were put to an operational test. In fact, as figure 13-2 shows, only 18.2 percent of the MSGs were generally transferable. The administrative issue is the obvious one of avoiding redundancy; 52 percent of the respondents indicated that they were not aware of any closely related MSG, and approximately 4 percent did not respond to the question. Their lack of awareness is of little consequence, however, because nearly half of the respondents did not know what it would cost to transfer operations (see fig. 13-3).

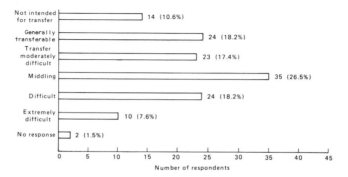

Figure 13-2. *Respondents' assessments of the transferability of MSGs.*

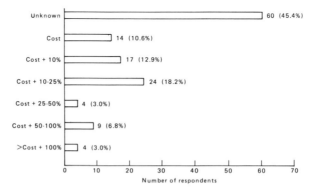

Figure 13-3. *Estimated transfer costs (production cost plus increment) for MSGs.*

Gary Fromm's nonmilitary survey appears at first glance to show that nonmilitary MSGs have better documentation and transferability than military MSGs; 39.9 percent of the nonmilitary MSG respondents reported excellent documentation, and 37.7 percent reported it to be average.[3] A question was raised in this survey about the difficulty of transferring MSG operations—the "transfer constraint." No such constraint was thought to exist by 27.5 percent of the respondents; 39.2 percent thought that there would be minor problems; 25.4 percent foresaw moderate difficulties; and only 7.9 percent thought it would present severe problems.[4] Digging more deeply into this survey, however, we find serious contradictions to these optimistic self-assessments, especially in terms of the kinds of existing documentation. Of the nonmilitary MSGs, 82.0 percent were not documented in a publishable book; 78.7 percent did not have a user manual; 86.1 percent had no available program decks; and 34.4 percent were not documented in even a publishable report.[5] This problem is evidently a general and pervasive one that requires considerable professional attention.

Responses from our military survey indicate that nearly half of the MSGs received no external review. The actual figure is undoubtedly higher, since this sample is biased toward Army models, which probably benefited from the efforts of the ad hoc Army Models Review Committee to increase the outside professional review of MSGs. At best, there is less than a fifty-fifty chance that any active model in the inventory has been reviewed (the question was not asked in the nonmilitary survey). The elapsed time since the most recent review for those that received them is shown in figure 13-4.

Special facilities were required to operate about one-third of the MSGs surveyed. About 16.6 percent needed dedicated computational systems; 13.0 percent used specialized languages or libraries; and 2.3 percent required special buildings or laboratory facilities. We feel strongly that MSGs should be made more transferable than they are, since there are few valid technical obstacles to replication.

Since 1966 there has been a significant decline in the incidence of external professional review, in spite of the Army initiatives. The trend in MSG review activity is summarized in table 13-1. The percentages of MSGs not intended for transfer and MSGs that are generally transferable have also decreased

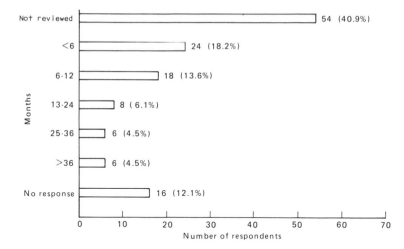

Figure 13-4. *Time elapsed since most recent external professional review.*

somewhat. The extremes appear to be moving toward a middle category of difficulty of transfer. The proportion of MSGs for which there is no information on transfer costs has remained steady at about 40 percent in the same period. In other words, a consistently high percentage of respondents had no idea what it would cost to replicate their MSG elsewhere.

The attributes of data sources, data-validation procedures, extent of documentation, and incidence of sensitivity testing described by the respondents remained stable over the period of the analysis. Very little has ever been published in journals or books about the military or nonmilitary MSGs that have been developed. Since 1966, however, the percentage using the Defense Documentation Center, a general-purpose archive, has increased. The primary form of documentation, reports, has been relatively stable over time at 25 to 30 percent, and user manuals have consistently accounted for slightly less than 10 percent of the MSG documentation, but documentation in user manuals combined with program decks has increased from 13 to 28 percent during this period.

No significant relationships were observed between the service responsible for the MSG and ease of transfer, cost of transfer, incidence of sensitivity testing, or the need for specialized facilities.

Differences in the frequency of external professional review

Table 13-1. *Trends in the external professional review of MSGs.*

	PERCENT OF MSGs SURVEYED		
RESPONSE	1966–1967	1971–1972	PERCENTAGE CHANGE
No review	22.7	50.0	+27.3
Review	29.1	38.9	−20.2
No response	18.2	11.1	− 7.1

Table 13-2. *MSGs receiving external professional reviews, by service.*[a]

SERVICE	MSGs NOT REVIEWED	MSGs REVIEWED	No RESPONSE	TOTAL
USA	15	36	8	59
USAF	18	5	3	26
USN	13	21	2	36
Other Defense Department	7	3	1	11
Total	53	65	14	132

a. $\chi^2\ p < .003$.

initiated by each service were significant. Based on the average for the entire sample, Air Force MSGs are the least likely to have been externally reviewed (see table 13-2); in the case of over 80 percent of the sampled Air Force MSGs, no external review was undertaken or no response was given. The frequency for Army MSGs shown in table 13-2 indicates the influence of the Army Models Review Committee's activities; the table also shows a low rate of review for other Defense Department MSGs. The Army MSGs also had a significantly higher incidence of recent professional review; 25.4 percent of the Army's entries were reviewed within the six months prior to the cutoff date of the original MSG survey, while of the 5 Air Force entries that were given external professional review, 3 were last looked at between one and two years prior to the survey's cutoff date, 1 more than three years prior, and 1 less than six months prior. The proportion of Navy MSGs reviewed was consistent over time ($\chi^2\ p < .05$).

The relationship between external professional review and other characteristics of the sample is also revealing. While MSGs used for analysis and diagnosis, teaching and training, or operations stood about a fifty-fifty chance of being reviewed, those with research applications did not fare so well. Only 1 of the 7 research or experimental MSGs surveyed received a professional review. Curiously, the few explicitly scientific examples that were reported in the survey were not subjected to this rudimentary scientific control precedure.

Professional reviewing was not significantly related to transferability, transfer cost, size of the MSG, total cost to build, extent of documentation, type of data used, or incidence of sensitivity testing. There is, however, a significant relationship between an MSG's data sources and the incidence of external review. If an MSG underwent a data check, derived from field exercises, or used data from a variety of experimental and operational sources, its chances of receiving a professional review doubled ($\chi^2 p < .005$). Similarly, if the data-validation procedures described in the respondents' written commentary were highly or moderately rigorous (55, or 41.6 percent, were so classified), the chances of subsequent professional review were also nearly double those of MSGs with less rigorously validated data ($\chi^2 p < .02$). This finding suggests that concern for rigorous design and production carries over into operational control procedures as well.

That concern does not appear to carry over to sensitivity testing, which was not clearly related to professional review in our survey responses, although it was strongly related to MSG size. The relatively small MSG entries, that is, those with fewer than 4,000 instructions, were about twice as likely not to have had sensitivity testing as the larger MSGs (with 4,000 to 10,000 instructions). The largest MSGs—those with more than 10,000 instructions—were evenly split on the question ($\chi^2 p < .001$). We could find no apparent reason for the lack of sensitivity analysis for the smaller MSGs, which are probably more readily and inexpensively tested.

Documentation and the incidence of professional reviews were related in several interesting ways. Documentation for MSGs that had been reviewed was twice as likely to be available at the Defense Documentation Center as that for others. Comparing assessments of data-validation procedures with the location of documentation for the 65 MSGs that did receive an external, professional review produced a highly significant finding: of the 34 MSGs reported to have high- and moderate-quality data validation, 19 did not have generally accessible documentation; documentation was controlled directly by a nonprofit organization in the case of 3; for another 3, it was controlled by a proprietary organization and could be obtained only by contacting its author; in 10 cases, documentation was limited by official classification and available only with special permission from the author; in 2 instances, no one knew anything about it; and it had gone out of print in the last case (χ^2 $p < .001$). These figures indicate, once again, the isolation of much of this activity. Of the 35 MSGs with documentation publicly available in the Defense Documentation Center, only 15 were reported to have high- or moderate-quality data validation, significantly fewer than those with inaccessible or limited-access documentation (see table 13-3 for the full tabulation).

Major Issues

Several aspects of MSG operations require more attention from those responsible for the construction and use of operational models. First of all, on the basis of the evidence found in our survey and other sources, documentation appears to be poorly appreciated and inadequately developed. Requiring that the documentation of MSGs meet certain specific criteria would cost little in comparison with the significant improvements it would bring about in management control and professional practice. The need is particularly great in the case of very large simulations. When generations of programmers perpetuate inconsistencies and errors in poorly updated documentation, the simulation can very quickly become useless.

Validation of MSG results is also deficient. Not only are empirical tests dubious or nonexistent, but, in addition, few efforts are being made to provide or correct missing or questionable input data or to execute sensitivity analyses according to an appropriate experimental design. The lack of sensitivity analysis is related to deficiencies in estimating the validity of input parameters. Even in those cases where a sensitivity test is performed, frequently no record of the outcome

Table 13-3. Cross-tabulation of location of documentation and quality of data validation for 65 externally reviewed MSGs.[a]

LOCATION OF DOCUMENTATION	QUALITY OF DATA VALIDATION						TOTAL	PERCENT OF TOTAL
	UNKNOWN	HIGH	MODERATE	WEAK	NOT DONE	NO RESPONSE		
Unknown	1	1	1	2	1	0	6	(9.2)
Out of print	0	1	0	2	0	0	3	(4.6)
Proprietary or nonprofit organization	0	0	3	0	0	0	3	(4.6)
Proprietary or under author's control	2	1	2	0	1	0	6	(9.2)
Proprietary (classified) or under author's control	0	4	6	1	0	0	11	(16.9)
Public or in Defense Documentation Center	2	3	12	8	9	1	35	(53.8)
No response	0	0	0	0	0	1	1	(1.5)
Total	5	10	24	13	11	2	65	—
Percent of total	(7.7)	(15.4)	(36.9)	(20.0)	(16.9)	(3.1)	—	(100.0)

a. $\chi^2 = 61.83$, with 30 degrees of freedom; $p < 0.0005$.

is kept. The majority of the MSGs we surveyed have not been subjected to any external review, with the result that many are based on implicit, intangible data the existence of and rationale for which have not been documented in any way. The institutional memory in the general system is not extensive; even for fairly recent MSGs it is difficult to obtain reliable answers to technical questions and questions about cost. A comprehensive exploration of these issues and strong corrective measures should be instituted. At present, advocacy seems clearly to predominate over scientific evidence when choices are made about the construction and use of MSGs.

DOCUMENTATION

Everyone agrees that documentation is a good thing, but there is little professional literature on the subject. Moreover, key issues have not been carefully enough defined to enable them to be studied more intensively. Along with unresolved conceptual problems, many practical problems of documentation reduce the operational efficiency of MSGs. Resources are wasted when MSG activities are not well documented. Even though documentation is tedious and difficult, it is still critical, particularly in an environment heavily oriented toward the needs of users.

The General Accounting Office has noted many of the problems caused by poor or inadequate documentation, among them the excessive time required to change or modify existing programs and the general impossibility of sharing or reusing programs in other settings.[6] Other difficulties mentioned in its survey arose from the unnecessary redesign of systems or rewriting of programs, a pervasive inability to perform internal evaluations, impediments to management review, and excessive delays in completing assignments. The GAO's report describes the problem as follows: "The aggregate cost incurred, which could have been avoided with proper documentation of the systems involved, is difficult to estimate but, in view of the number of cases, we believe it would be high."[7]

While the GAO's inquiry concentrated on computer systems, it attempted to assess the impact of poor documentation on about 100 MSGs bought and used by the federal government in New England. For about one-third of the MSGs where some joint usage was required or expected, documentation did not exist at all. Of the remainder, documentation "was poor and impeded converting the programs for use on another computer configuration and using the models for other than the original specific purpose."[8] As we have noted earlier, if an MSG cannot be reproduced and checked out by people not directly responsible for its construction and use, it is highly unlikely that it can ever be evaluated effectively, a point stressed in the findings of the Army Models Review Committee:

> It became evident to the Committee members that in many cases the available documentation, together with discussions with the model groups, were inadequate to thoroughly evaluate the models. This was particularly true with regard to models that were developed some time ago and where the original development team could no longer be identified. In some cases, models have been used occasionally, then retired and then are used again by different individuals. More continuity of personnel associated with a useful model is required.
>
> In many cases models were not subjected to detailed technical review and are not validated in any other way. Some of the complex simulations contain many implicit inputs such as detection factors, decision factors, transition probabilities. The rationale for such inputs in most cases is not documented and they have never been reviewed, improved or updated. There is rarely enough funding for sensitivity analyses and, if performed, they are not documented.[9]

VALIDATION

Professional standards of validation have not been sufficiently developed to encourage their routine and widespread application to MSGs. The fact that many of the data used to build and operate military models are questionable, however, clearly demonstrates the need for more stringent data validation in the field.

Critical uncertainties, unjustified assumptions, and errors

frequently occur in calculating the quantifiable features of an analytic setting or defining them on the basis on historical information. Such matters as the rate at which an infantry battalion marches against various degrees of opposition and in different kinds of terrain may have been faithfully recorded in a wide variety of actual circumstances and may be used to generate reasonably useful planning factors or rules of thumb. Nonetheless, these conditions and assumptions must occasionally be reexamined to ensure that a sufficiently good correspondence between a past and a likely future empirical setting justifies the reuse of old data. Certain questions must be asked: Where did a set of data originate? Under what conditions were the data gathered? What were the initial purposes, conditions, and uses of the data? Who was responsible for taking the measurements? How have the data been used subsequently?

Our working premise is simple: if the data on which an MSG is based can be shown to be suspect, inappropriate, or error-ridden, there is no point in being concerned about the operation of the MSG itself. With poor data, the most elegant operational MSG in the world quickly becomes useless. This principle has too frequently been overlooked in the rush to build and use bigger and better MSGs. As J. A. Stockfisch has written,

> The analysis of conventional military affairs presently suffers from an inadequate empirical endeavor, an apparent misuse of what empirical data there are and a large-scale production of "pseudodata." Further, there appears to be a widespread practice of using "data" generated from models, or by a priori methods, as numerical inputs for other models, which in turn, may be either unverified or inadequately tested. In some instances, the outputs of the prior model, although adequate for the questions initially addressed, may be inappropriate for subsequent refinements, formulations, or uses of the data made at a later time and, often, by a user other than the one that conceived the model or did the related empirical work. In other instances, empirical data based on historical experience may be inadequately assessed, analyzed,

and modified so as to serve properly the analytical purpose at hand.[10]

While the problem of data validation unquestionably im-
pedes the operational modeling of conventional warfare, the
issue is even more striking for MSGs concerned with strategic
situations. The basic difference lies in the fact that strategic
models rely on theoretical estimates of the performance of
weapons whose effectiveness is also estimated theoretically.
In conventional settings where theoretical estimates have
been measured against empirical information, the dominant
finding has been that the estimates exaggerated attainable
performance, frequently by a great deal. The lesson, with respect to present-day strategic models, is that similarly faulty
estimates are likely to lessen the operational utility of a model.
This problem appears not to be openly discussed in the professional literature or in the currently available documentation of operational military MSGs. Some attention has been
given to the scientific problems of verifying and validating
data for use in MSGs.[11] In most instances, however, the necessary expansion of research has not been matched by actual
modeling operations.

The validation of computer programs is another aspect of
the more general issue. It implies demonstrating that there are
no errors in the program, that is, that it performs as intended.
In some sophisticated settings, program validation has been
shown to consume as much as 40 to 50 percent of all the resources devoted to software development.[12] The computer industry has worked on program validation, and the software
community is aware of the importance of accurate specification, testing, and debugging.[13] Our experience indicates, however, that these efforts are not integrated into operational
modeling as well as they might be; certainly, current documentation practices give little indication of whether or not
program validation has been undertaken, with what results, or
at what cost.

Sensitivity analysis is a form of validation that allows the
behavioral characteristics of a formulation to be observed
under a variety of known and controlled input situations. It
might show, for example, that an MSG is valid only for a nar-

row range of input values, beyond which unlikely or clearly erroneous results are generated. Thus the user can be made aware that the input data must be precisely measured if the MSG's structure is to be adequate for the research and operational purposes at hand. Sensitivity analyses may involve large-scale, time-consuming, and costly experimental designs or Monte Carlo runs to test model performance under a variety of uncertainty conditions; they may also be handled analytically or in a more qualitative format.[14] However sensitivity analyses are conducted, they should be routine in virtually all cases; if they were, improvements would probably follow in MSG design, operation, and use. Some record of these analyses would occur naturally in thorough MSG documentation and provide users with valuable information on the behavioral properties and operating characteristics of particular MSGs. Validation may also take the form of checking an MSG against alternative models and other forms of analysis. This process helps a user to determine whether a given MSG is a better and more useful device than other options; the answer, of course, depends largely on the user's aims.[15]

EXTERNAL REVIEW AND TRANSFERABILITY

The current lack of MSG transferability and external professional review strongly suggests the need for better practices. Some proposals have already been made. The Army Models Review Committee's recommendations, for instance, if followed conscientiously, would do much to improve the situation. Transferability is important for two primary reasons, one scientific and the other practical. First, scientific standards demand faithful replication of procedures in diverse locales. Initial lack of replication casts doubt on the findings, and repeated failures to replicate tend to confirm this suspicion. If a modeler wants to justify his work and his product as scientific, he must be prepared to subject that work to scientific standards and procedures. Models that do not or are designed not to transfer cannot meet this key requirement, a fact that cannot be ignored even on the basis of a security classification.

The second, practical reason for transferability is to minimize unnecessary duplication of effort. Rather than pressing for general transferability, it might be more realistic to require that an MSG be able to operate at one of three or four facilities, such as the Federal Simulation Center, the National Bureau of Standards. Independent validation could thus be undertaken; other interested users could gain access to the model; and the type, amount, and quality of documentation could be standardized.

14 | Benefits, Uses, and Costs

> None calleth for justice, nor any pleadeth for truth: they
> trust in vanity, and speak lies; they conceive mischief, and
> bring forth inequity.
>
> Isaiah 59:4

T HE SUCCESS OF AN MSG depends on a complicated set of organizational, communication, and technical issues; unfortunately, it is seldom if ever possible to separate them clearly in determining how well an MSG has been used in a large organization. Relying on simple statistical or technical tests to determine success fails to account for many difficult questions. What, for instance, does the user want? When does he want an answer? How accurate must it be? Only when general questions like these have been raised and resolved is it appropriate to be concerned about specific technical assessments of an MSG.

Equally thorny are matters of cost. To a great extent, MSGs cost whatever the bookkeepers want to make them cost. The development of an MSG involves many invisible costs, overhead costs, shared facilities, and jointly used products; thus formulating a meaningful procedure for calculating costs poses deep scientific and practical problems that are far from being resolved. Many of the respondents to our survey found it difficult to give even a description of the cost of their MSGs. Accounting figures may be available, but it is not a simple matter to make sense out of what these figures actually mean.[1]

While we make no claim to settling either of these broad issues, we shall at least open them up to scrutiny and begin the hard job of trying to resolve them.

Uses of Models

Four distinct levels of use may be identified. The first, for strategic, high-level decision making, is exemplified by the political and military exercise. Even though its value is an open question, it is intended specifically for the use of those at the top strategic level.[2] Studies and simulations of the procurement of weapons systems are designed implicitly for use at this level; to some extent they appear to be used to bolster the arguments of those on one side of the budgetary decision-making process. After an evaluation of a weapons system has been performed by means of a large-scale simulation, the results tend to be used primarily, if not exclusively, by generals or admirals rather than by civilian participants. This process is not necessarily either good or bad; it is merely usual.

The second level of use is operational, bureaucratic, and scientific. Most studies and simulations, along with much work investigating human factors, fall into this category. Here contractors and subcontractors work closely with their opposite numbers in the bureaucracy of the Department of Defense. The problems that are addressed are meant to be operational and relatively specific. A third level is at the interface of scientific and advisory functions with operations. A fair amount of the work at this level is sponsored by the Defense Advanced Research Projects Agency (ARPA). Investigations, such as some human-factors studies, are typically not concerned with immediate applications but, rather, focus on building a supply of basic knowledge. The fourth level is that of purely scientific and experimental work that utilizes top professionals in a scientific advisory capacity. When an adviser is called in, he is expected to be, if not actively engaged in basic research, at least actively aware of scientific developments. This level includes basic work in experimental psychology, programming, game theory, hardware and laboratory developments, and human-factors studies.

In addition to asking whether the application of an MSG corresponds to the major purpose for which it was constructed, we have devised a market measure of use: Will the MSG sell? Is its funding regularly renewed? Although it is not ideal, this is a crude, pragmatic measure of the client's satisfaction and his willingness to buy and use more of the same type of MSG.

Two operational questions approach the matter slightly differently. The question "How many briefings were given on the basis of the results produced by the MSG?" may suggest how much stock a user places in a particular MSG. If no briefings resulted, that fact reveals something about how key participants assess a given enterprise. The corollary question "How many times is the MSG referred to in making specific operational decisions?" further refines and clarifies this measure. To make this approach an ideal criterion, it would be necessary to ask all major participants precisely how an MSG related to a specific decision, who advocated it, who voiced reservations, and what official rationalizations derived from it. Questions about who initiated the MSG and why dramatize the actual use of the MSG. Others, such as whether the MSG is active or not and how often it is operated, provide further important information. Operations and use overlap when one considers what kinds of documentation are located where, how easy it is to transfer the model from one site to another, the rate at which an MSG becomes obsolete, and the reasons why it does.

RESULTS

The primary categories of actual use reported in our survey are shown in figure 14-1. The emphasis placed by initiators on

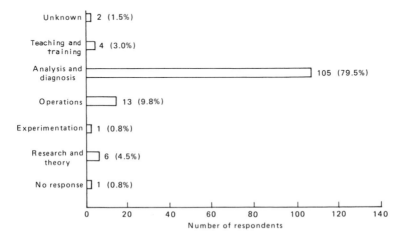

Figure 14-1. *Respondents' primary classifications of MSG use.*

the use of MSGs for analysis and diagnosis, reported earlier, is reflected almost exactly in the actual uses indicated by respondents. Other categories together account for less than 22.0 percent of the sample. Respondents indicated that 42 of the MSGs, or 31.8 percent, have secondary uses and that 13, or 9.8 percent, have tertiary uses. Of the secondary uses, 30 were listed as operations; 5, analysis and diagnosis; 4, research and theory development; and 3, experimentation. About 80 percent of the respondents were highly or absolutely certain about how their MSGs were being used. Questions about the MSGs' genealogy revealed that nearly three-fourths had a direct antecedent and about one-third had already produced offspring. The market measure of use tells us, roughly, that business is good and clients are sufficiently content to keep funds flowing.

Several questions focused on briefings. The total numbers of briefings based on particular MSGs are shown in figure 14.2; 11.4 percent of the respondents said none were given, and 42.4 percent did not know. For some models the number of briefings may not be a good measure, but for games and simulations it usually is. Frequently, a briefing may be no more than

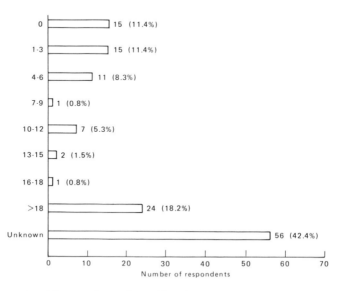

Figure 14-2. *The total number of briefings based on MSGs.*

a superficial performance, but it indicates, at the very least, that someone thought enough of the work to publicize it.

Respondents were asked to comment on the organization and personnel level and the purpose of the briefings. Briefings related to the 61 MSGs for which answers were given were commonly for the project staff and an immediate superior in the organizational hierarchy; occasionally flag-level officers and their civilian counterparts at the top command levels of the services were briefed. The purposes were not reported consistently enough to allow simple categorization, but some of the common replies were that the MSG was used for input to other studies, for strategic-posture choices, for information on F-15 performance, for selection of weapons for DLGN-25, a nuclear, guided-missile frigate, and that no decisions were based on the model. Generally, briefings appear to have been organized for one or a few colonels or generals, or their naval and civilian counterparts, whose roles include studies and analysis. What further use these audiences made of the briefing information could not be determined from the answers to the questionnaire. Nearly half of the MSGs surveyed, however, did not produce a single briefing.

The issue of who initiates the development of an MSG was discussed in chapter 12; as figure 12-3 showed, analysis and diagnosis predominate among initiators' purposes. Comparison of those data with the responses displayed in figure 14-1 suggests that, to a marked degree, initiators are getting what they requested.

The frequency of MSG operation is another measure of use. A distinctly bimodal distribution of average annual frequency is evident in figure 14-3. Limited documentation and transferability do little to promote widespread use. The respondents to our survey indicated that public availability was concentrated in the Defense Documentation Center, that no MSG was documentated in the Library of Congress, and that only one had been written up in a journal or book. Multiple sources of documentation were listed, but only three respondents checked two sources and only two checked three.

The cost of keeping an MSG up to date and, to a lesser extent, the average cost of running it affect how much it is used. To obtain annual update costs, we asked for information on

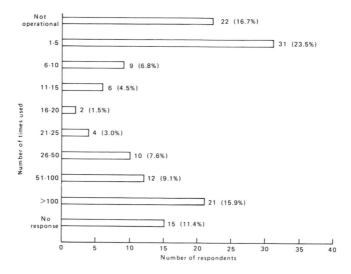

Figure 14-3. *The frequency of annual MSG operation.*

total dollars, professional man-years, and programmer man-years expended over and above normal operating costs. Cost data for the 71 MSGs for which replies were given are summarized in figure 14-4 and make it clear that updating is not a trivial matter; similarly, the sampled MSGs are generally expensive to run. Figures on the cost of a single MSG run, assuming minor variations at most in input values, are shown in figure 14-5.

The availability and location of MSG documentation have changed somewhat since 1966. A higher percentage of documentation on MSGs that have become operational in the last decade is now being located in the Defense Documentation Center, but more is also owned and controlled by individuals or institutions, classified, and available only from the author. However, fewer MSGs have documentation that is proprietary, both available from nonprofit firm and proprietary, or both unclassified and available only from the author.

Average annual update costs are changing in significant ways. A smaller proportion of MSGs (16.7 percent) are updated for less than $10,000 now than in 1966 (36.4 percent), but no MSG updates currently fall in the $50,000 to $100,000 range.

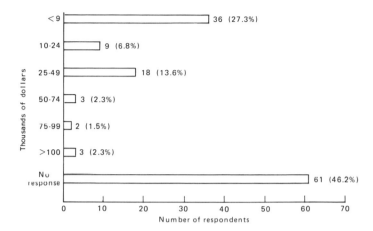

Figure 14-4. *Total annual MSG update costs.*

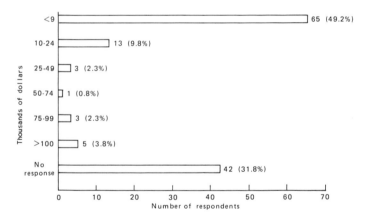

Figure 14-5. *The cost of single runs of MSGs.*

Thus MSGs in the two intermediate cost ranges have increased (see table 14-1). Other trends in use are not so easily discernible.

As already noted, respondents were highly or absolutely certain about the actual use of an MSG in nearly 80 percent of the cases. No significant association was noted between category of use and level of confidence. The correspondence

Table 14-1. *Trends in the cost of annual update.*

	PERCENT OF MSGs SURVEYED		
COST (THOUSANDS OF DOLLARS)	1966–1967	1971–1972	PERCENTAGE CHANGE
<10	36.4	16.7	−19.7
10–24	9.1	11.1	+ 2.0
25–49	9.1	22.2	+13.1

between the initiator's intended purpose and the actual use to which the MSG was put was strikingly consistent. If someone wanted an MSG for analysis and diagnosis, he got it in 97 out of 108 cases, or 89.8 percent of the time; 3 of the other 11 were used primarily for teaching and training, 3 for operations, 1 for experimentation, 1 for research and theory development, and in the case of 3 the respondent did not know or did not reply ($\chi^2 p < .001$).

When the respondent's role was tabulated against his assessment of the quality of his MSG's documentation, we found that funders and sponsors tended to claim excellent documentation (7 of 19, or 36.8 percent); users most frequently indicated that documentation was very good (16 of 42, or 38.1 percent); and designers and builders considered documentation average (14 of 41, or 34.1 percent) or very good (12 of 41, or 29.3 percent) in nearly equal measure. Caretakers, on the other hand, indicated that documentation was either average (8 of 18, or 44.4 percent) or poor (4 of 18, or 22.2 percent) ($\chi^2 p < .001$). While several interpretations are plausible, those farthest removed from actual MSG use—that is, funders and sponsors—seem to give the most glowing assessments of documentation quality.

On the average, about one-third of the respondents did not know whether their MSGs had been described in briefings or not. Table 14-2 compares MSGs in this category with those for which briefings were given for each military service. The relationships are not statistically significant, but the data suggest either that the MSGs in this sample are not being used or, more likely, that people responsible for their use are not keeping track of how often they are used.

Table 14-2. *Briefings based on MSGs, by service.*

SERVICE	MSGs NOT BRIEFED OR UNKNOWN	MSGs BRIEFED	TOTAL
USA	34	25	59
USAF	12	14	26
USN	14	22	36
Other Defense Department	11	0	11
Total	71	61	132

Annual frequency of operation and update costs vary according to the individual services in significant and interesting ways. The bimodal nature of annual use holds for all services. About 25 percent of the time, a given MSG will be operated one to five times a year, if at all; at the other extreme, an MSG has about a 15 percent chance of being operated more than 100 times a year (χ^2 $p < .05$). Annual updating costs are approximately the same for all services: 30.5 percent of the Army's MSGs cost less than $10,000 to update, compared with 34.6 percent of the Air Force's and 22.2 percent of the Navy's. The next most frequent cost range is $25,000 to $49,000, which accounts for about 12 percent of each service's MSG updates (χ^2 $p < .005$).

This discussion of MSG uses has naturally included an initial treatment of costs, as the topics are highly interrelated. Costs are so underrated and misunderstood, however, that they require more detailed, separate consideration.

Cost Considerations

In spite of many profound difficulties, we can give approximate costs for each type of MSG. Analytic models tend to be relatively inexpensive—realistically so, for the overhead support they require may consist of as little as a pencil and pad of paper, or chalk and a board, for a single professional. Frequently what is needed are "quick and dirty" analytic models that do not look elegant but do contain useful concepts. The

medium is not the message; models are the message. To encourage thought and flexibility, quick creation and frequent
destruction of models are recommended. In any event, analytic model building becomes expensive only when a poorly
thought-out, tentative formulation is prematurely hardened
into a computer simulation. The value of all-machine simulation, at least as presently carried out, is probably inversely related to the cube or the fourth power of the output. In addition,
cost is probably directly related to the cube or fourth power of
the number of parameters and variables used in the MSG.

A consistent difficulty in calculating costs is that of data
gathering. Generally, the total cost of an MSG depends to a
large extent on whether it can be built using information from
ongoing activities or whether special data-gathering efforts are
required. The costs of gathering data can be assigned in essentially any way. The standard model builder's plea that analyzing data can save untold millions of dollars for the relatively
trifling costs of acquisition and manipulation ignores an important bureaucratic cost. People do not like to have their organizations and procedures disarranged merely to enable
outsiders to collect data.

Man-machine simulation has more or less the same spotty
record in the area of cost-effectiveness as all the other types of
MSG. While both all-machine and man-machine simulations
are expensive, cases can be cited in which the expense was
distinctly worth the effort; all seemed to depend on one or two
reasonably well defined questions, asked early in the process,
that generated important answers. Furthermore, the principals
in these cases were able to recognize an important answer
when confronted with it. In a large-scale simulation, important answers may appear but go unnoticed. After deciding
what the question is, it pays to ask what a reasonable answer
might look like. Costs for free-form MSGs are relatively low,
although the publicity they receive is disproportionately large.
Because levels of expenditure are low in both absolute and relative terms, a few additional dollars spent on this type of activity may be justified.

How big are the sums involved? Our guess—based on wide
reading in the area, on responses to our questionnaire, and on
comparable responses for nonmilitary MSGs, but not on much

inside information—is that free-form gaming accounts for less than $1 million per year. All other MSGs account for between $150 and $300 million per year, depending on the ways the terms are defined and the accounts totaled. These figures were confirmed, to a large extent, by a survey of nonmilitary MSGs, sponsored by the National Science Foundation, that used the questionnaire described in this volume. "Although the majority of models required less than $50,000 for development, the price tag ranged over $3 million," the survey report states. "The average cost was around $140,000 . . . extrapolating to the total universe from which the sample was selected, the overall cost would approach $100 million."[3] Discussions of "unattributable costs" and the cost of data were similarly varied and imprecise.

The different costs of MSGs are summarized in the checklist that follows (the term *MSG* is used, although most of the items apply to simulations and games, rather than, strictly speaking, to models).[4] It provides a gross breakdown of items that must be considered in creating a comprehensive account of costs. They are discussed in some detail below.

Research-and-development costs
MSG design and preconstruction testing
MSG construction and programming
Debugging, test running, and evaluation
Major MSG modifications
Laboratory design and modifications

Investment costs
Equipment
  Computer
  Peripheral equipment
  Other special instruments (audio, visual, etc.)
  Office equipment
Laboratory facilities, buildings
Stocks
  Library
  Supplies
  Spare parts
Personnel training

Miscellaneous
  Travel and transportation
  Other
Operating costs
Maintenance and replacement
  Computers and peripherals
  Laboratory and buildings
  MSG-specific equipment
  Other specialized equipment
Salaries and payments
  Direct salaries and wages
  Payments to players
  Indirect salaries and wages
Services and miscellaneous
  Transportation and travel
  Other variable costs
  Other overhead

Research-and-development costs are the expenditures (not including equipment) required to bring an MSG to a stage where it can actually be used for its stated purpose. Estimates of these costs are often the most difficult to make, especially when completely new systems are being built. The difficulty is compounded by the practice of producing a lengthy study comprised of many integral models or component MSGs. Not only is it difficult to identify and assign costs to any particular component, but the components may be separated from the inclusive study and subsequently resold to other users—or to the same user after some period of time has elapsed and after a certain amount of turnover has occurred in the staff of caretakers and users. This situation highlights the need for management control, including thorough cost accounting.

A related anomaly is the high incidence of military MSGs that cost between $100,000 and $500,000 to develop. This range may provide comfortable revenue levels to a contractor while keeping his activities at a low level of visibility. Other interpretations are possible, but this one seems entirely plausible and uncontrollable given the current poor to nonexistent accounting and management-control practices. The same phenomenon appeared in the survey of nonmilitary MSGs, but costs were an order of magnitude lower (34 percent of the nonmilitary sample cost less than $25,000 and 56 percent, less than $50,000).[5] These data and the practices that they appear to reflect require further scrutiny.

Investment costs are one-time outlays that must be made to implement and use an MSG. While they do not present any extraordinary difficulties in comparison with other classes of cost, they may be significant. Investment costs might, for example, include the purchase of a dedicated (or single-purpose) computer to maintain control of classified materials used in an MSG.

Operating costs include all salaries and charges involved in running and analyzing an MSG. If it is used intermittently, storage and reprogramming costs may be incurred as equipment is modified and old programs are updated or revised for use on new equipment. An example of one of several unresolved issues in this area is the case of a frequently used program originally constructed for a second-generation machine but now running on an advanced third- or fourth-generation machine. Should this program's costs be calculated in terms of its inefficient implementation on the newer and faster machine? Should the client or user pay to have the program rewritten and run the risk of errors in reprogramming and downtime for the MSGs using the program? How are reprogramming costs allocated? The list of unresolved questions relating to costs is large.

Another difficulty in calculating operational costs concerns what economists call opportunity costs. If an empty office or auditorium can either be used for a gaming exercise or left empty, what charge should be made to the game for its use? If the space could be rented for some amount, perhaps $500 per night, is this charge attributed to the MSG? If the space could be rented during the day but never at night, when the exercise is run, should a charge be assessed? The concept can be examined from the point of view of wages as well. Suppose a major who participates in developing an MSG has a Ph.D in operations research, a technical aspect of gaming and simulation. His opportunity cost may easily range from zero to many times his salary; the problem here is in making a reasonable and consistent assessment.

Difficulties in Calculating Costs

Four major difficulties confront the cost analyst: (1) unallocated costs; (2) opportunity costs of special resources, including personnel; (3) overhead and joint cost allocation; and (4) the confusion of costs and benefits. Unallocated or unattributed costs make up a significant percentage of the total expenditure of resources for an MSG. We did not include any specific questions on this topic in our survey of military MSGs; however, the nonmilitary survey found that as much as 43 percent of the costs of projects totaling between $25,000 and $50,000 and 17 percent of those in $100,000 to $250,000 range could not be attributed.[6] Research-and-development time, player time for free-form and man-machine MSGs, and computer time are among the more likely items for which no costs are assigned.

Opportunity costs, mentioned above, are particularly important when special resources cannot be moved. For some reason, the importance of opportunity costs is not often appreciated or understood, even by highly trained technical personnel. Assigning a physical input a zero opportunity cost must be distinguished from ignoring its cost. In the first case, the explicit enumeration means that a replication elsewhere will at least recognize the need for the resource, which may not be free in another location. Thus ignoring a zero opportunity cost may lead to a serious underestimation of MSG costs. The cost of personnel used as players in an MSG is no simpler to calculate. Usually either no cost is attached to player personnel or the hours of participation are directly charged according to the individual's salary rate. Neither of these methods is completely satisfactory. Empty offices, borrowed facilities, second- or third-shift computer time, and the time of personnel are all items that, under certain circumstances, should be figured into opportunity cost. Presently there are no well-established guidelines for accomplishing this goal; indeed, the basic concept appears not to have been appreciated in the sample of MSGs included in our survey.

Large bureaucracies invariably have large overhead costs, which are assigned in widely varying ways. MSGs that require data generated in other parts of an organization are particularly inconsistent in this regard. Depending on the whims of the administrators, such input may be supplied at no charge or at an extraordinarily high cost.[7] The problem of opportunity cannot be totally disassociated from that of joint costs and arises in situations when the costs of a jointly used facility must be allocated. In addition, joint costs must be shared by the different MSGs operated in the joint facility.

Finally, costs and benefits are different. Certain experimental MSGs intended and operated for educational or entertainment purposes, for instance, can actually be run at a positive net income. This statement does not mean that costs will be negative; instead, it means that revenues will exceed costs. Arguments against calculating the cost of the participation time for top-level personnel because they gain more than the time is worth may be correct, but they only increase confusion between cost accounting and the evaluation of a product. An accounting system is valid only with respect to a set of questions it is meant to answer. Calculating costs in order to attack a project as a waste of money on the basis of its inefficiency is a different process from using cost figures to whitewash a project that may have wasted resources. Calculating whether or not it is feasible to perform a piece of work within a specified project is different from justifying a work program by means of its costs.

Overall, at least three forms of cost calculations should be considered. The first merely lists the value of the physical resources used. The second assigns monetary costs to reflect the costs of investment, research and development, and operation at a specific location over a specific period of time. The third evaluates the costs of transferring and running an MSG elsewhere.

RESULTS

Our questionnaire contained a large number of questions relating to cost. Besides attempting to characterize the nature of costs using several plausible dimensions and categories, we wanted to determine the amount of attention currently paid to costs and the general level of knowledge about costs in the profession. Answers to questions on all three issues were disappointing. More than a third of the respondents did not answer the cost questions; among those who did, the replies varied widely and the level of confidence was low. If qualified professionals being asked questions by the GAO on behalf of the House Appropriations Committee could not come up with some sort of figures, it is unlikely that anyone else can, unless cost records are required to be kept with the work.

Although nearly three-fourths of our MSG sample had at least one direct antecedent, 62.1 percent of the respondents either did not know about the costs for these MSG families or failed to respond to the question. Moreover, uncertainty about the answers was high among those who answered; over half had a low level of confidence in their responses. This evidence suggests that cost considerations are discontinuous, that is, that costs are not accumulated, even though changes in the MSG may be marginal from one version to the next. Costs easily become separated from substance. Direct funds—that is, money formally assigned for construction purposes—were used in 61, or 46.2 percent, of the sample. The distribution of these funds is shown in figure 14-6. Confidence levels were low in nearly half the cases.

Total costs—direct, imputed, and unimputed—are shown in figure 14-7. The confidence level for this roughest approximation of costs was slightly better than for the other, more detailed cost categories but considerably worse than for other variables. On the subject of MSG purpose, for instance, 80 percent of the respondents were either highly or absolutely

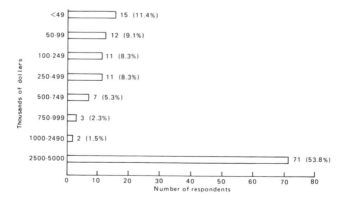

Figure 14-6. *Direct funds for MSG construction.*

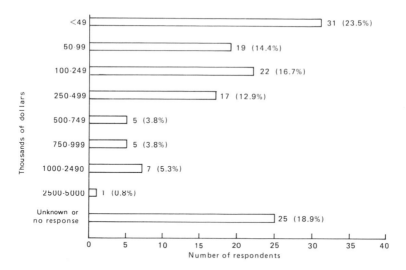

Figure 14-7. *Total MSG costs (direct, indirect, imputed, unimputed).*

certain; on the question of total costs, only 20.4 percent were as confident.

Because so little information was given, fewer cross-tabulations were made for cost than for other descriptive variables. No significant associations were found between total costs and the incidence of professional review, data sources, or general MSG type. The results of tabulating the military service against direct costs are shown in table 14-3. When the process was repeated for total costs, the pattern shifted somewhat (see table 14.4). The relationships shown in table 14-4 are not statistically significant (χ^2 $p < .09$) but are nevertheless interesting.

All the evidence on costs only confirms our impression that (1) generally accepted, simple accounting definitions do not exist; (2) insufficient attention is paid to costs to manage MSGs effectively; and (3) few people know how much money was invested in their MSG, how much is being spent to operate and maintain it, and what monetary benefits are accruing. Elementary questions like what was bought for how much are apparently seldom asked.

Table 14-3. Cross-tabulation of military service and direct costs.[a]

	DIRECT COSTS (THOUSANDS OF DOLLARS)									
SERVICE	49	50–99	100–249	250–499	500–749	750–999	1,000–2,490	UNKNOWN	TOTAL	PERCENT OF TOTAL
USA	12	12	4	7	5	0	1	18	59	(44.7)
USAF	5	0	2	0	0	0	1	18	26	(19.7)
USN	8	10	9	1	2	2	1	3	36	(27.3)
Other Defense Department	1	1	3	1	1	1	0	3	11	(8.3)
Total	26	23	18	9	8	3	3	42	132	—
Percent of total	(19.7)	(17.4)	(13.6)	(6.8)	(6.1)	(2.3)	(2.3)	(31.8)	—	(100.0)

a. $\chi^2 = 47.42$, with 21 degrees of freedom; $p < 0.0008$.

Table 14-4. Cross-tabulation of military service and total costs. [a]

SERVICE	TOTAL COSTS (THOUSANDS OF DOLLARS)									TOTAL	PERCENT OF TOTAL
	49	50–99	100–249	250–499	500–749	750–999	1,000–2,490	2,500–5,000	UNKNOWN		
USA	15	6	7	7	4	1	4	1	14	59	(44.7)
USAF	10	6	2	7	0	0	1	0	6	26	(19.7)
USN	4	6	10	8	1	2	2	0	3	36	(27.3)
Other Defense Department	2	1	3	1	0	2	0	0	2	11	(8.3)
Total	31	19	22	17	5	5	7	1	25	132	—
Percent of total	(23.5)	(14.4)	(16.7)	(12.9)	(3.8)	(3.8)	(5.3)	(0.8)	(18.9)	—	(100.0)

a. $\chi^2 = 33.36$, with 24 degrees of freedom; $p < 0.0965$.

PART FIVE

The Military
Analysis System

15 | Individual and Institutional Participants

> If the body was tense and driven, the mind was
> mathematical, analytical, bringing order and reason out of
> chaos. Always reason. And reason supported by facts, by
> statistics—he could prove his rationality with facts.
>
> David Halberstam, *The Best and the Brightest*

MODELING ACTIVITIES are conducted by individuals, but the individuals act on behalf of institutions. These, in turn, exhibit many well-known bureaucratic characteristics and several that are not so familiar.

Humans have relied on technical analyses for the solution of hard problems throughout their history. With the apparently increasing number, diversity, and complexity of problems thought to be amenable to expert technical scrutiny, however, the issue has taken on added importance. If we agree that the number and diversity of topics that need expert treatment are increasing, then the reasons for the proliferation, fragmentation, and further specialization of expert roles are relatively clear. A working proposition on this issue may be stated simply: many more difficult problems are confronting responsible officials, who are coming to rely on many more highly specialized skill groups to advise on and help resolve those problems. There have always been costs associated with the delegation of responsibility for problem solving; as the problems themselves have become more numerous and difficult, it is not surprising that these costs have also increased.

Decision makers rely on whatever help they can get. Basically, they will use anything that simplifies information and packages it in intelligible, easily digestible chunks.[1] A rumor, a national opinion poll, advice from a friend, suggestions from a benefactor, a consultant's recommendation, and a scientific

219

study are all examples of the preprocessed data that decision makers receive. Because access to the raw facts from which this information has been derived is so limited, the decision maker may be accepting most of it on blind faith; this trust is misplaced, as it turns out, for many of those who build and operate MSGs. Indeed, an underappreciated skill in modern decision making is the ability to pick one's experts so that the chance of getting a useful morsel of information is increased. Data that are assimilable and that help a decision maker to make the correct choices are rare, yet consistently finding them and using them effectively are essential to legitimate, responsible, and positive decision making.

Experts

The fact that the problems confronting defense policymakers are numerous and complex helps to explain the proliferation of experts involved in decision making.[2] Unfortunately, efforts to confront complexity routinely add to the overall confusion about what a problem is and what reasonable answers to it might be. Analytic experts, for instance, resort to simplifications—emphasizing some things and overlooking others—according to their temperaments, perceptions, and professional training. Far from reducing complexity and clarifying policy choices, such experts often end up creating bigger and more complicated theoretical and analytic structures.[3] As we have noted already, analytic experts seldom view the world in the same way as decision makers; even competing experts may disagree among themselves. These differences reflect the disparate ways in which experts and decision makers perceive, order, and interpret common settings.

As problems demanding attention and resolution become more complex, decision makers find themselves less able to manage or even understand them. Naturally enough, approaches to such problems proliferate. Resorting to tried and true response routines, making incremental adjustments, and doing nothing at all are three common ways decision makers simplify and attempt to cope with problems that they and their expert advisers do not understand or disagree about. A wide chasm exists between what should be and what actually is known about most of these problems. If the gap between scientific work and the information required by decision makers were not so wide, these unsatisfactory responses would be less common.[4] To the extent that perspectives of the expert and the decision maker differ fundamentally, clarification and consideration of various outcomes reached by each group are necessary; but clarification is often impeded by the parochial requirements of those concerned—the expert's need to stay in business and the decision maker's desire to appear decisively in control. In general, expert analysts do not march to the sound of the decision maker's drum, and what results from their collaboration must be carefully scrutinized.

These differences in perspective lead to different degrees of effort, a range of plausible outcomes from analytic work, and varying standards of assessment. Scientific experts, for example, have, by and large, been dedicated to rigorous measurement and the development of theories. This approach has often produced results that are not particularly relevant for others in the decision-making process. As Max Millikan has pointed out, "The scientist is apt to have a strong conviction that applied research cannot be 'fundamental,' that there is something inherently contradictory in the advance of knowledge and the service of practical ends . . . The researcher may face a growing conviction . . . that the operator has asked the wrong questions, that the questions are too vaguely or too narrowly formulated, or that as formulated they are incapable of being clearly answered."[5] Those who promote or sell analyses, including MSGs, are understandably concerned about the maintenance of a positive cash flow to support expensive technical personnel and the institutions that support these individuals. Given this system of incentives, it is not surprising that those doing the marketing may promise results that far exceed the capabilities of the techniques and technicians. The behavior of others involved in the process of building and analyzing models is guided by other, similar incentive systems; the results are not always beneficial—either for technical progress or for the status of decision making.

General Glenn A. Kent, who was responsible for most United States Air Force studies and analyses between 1968 and 1972, has made some pointed comments about the analytic enterprise: "I am not so sure that analysis as a credible ingredient in decision-making will necessarily have a brilliant future. For a variety of reasons I believe the influence of analysis may be near its zenith and decline is in the offing. The watchword today is 'Beware.' Don't look now, but your credibility is showing." Among other complaints, Kent stressed the fact that "decision-makers are becoming increasingly annoyed that different analysts get quite different answers to the same problem . . . there must be something wrong when quantification of some particular problem produces such radically different results."[6] Kent's argument points up the issue of multiple orientations and, in doing so, exposes the blatant advocacy to which many MSGs are currently devoted in defense policymaking. In the process, the scientific utility of the MSG is so completely overlooked or obscured that it is impossible to determine whether or not the MSG corresponds significantly to any policy problem or reference system. "Significant correspondence," Mathematica reports, "means that the outcomes of policies fed into the computer, on the one hand, and of policies adopted in the real world, on the other hand, resemble each other *in all respects important to the policymaker in the real world.*"[7]

Clearly, the models and analyses known to General Kent and many other users of MSGs have not corresponded significantly to any reference system considered important for their policymaking needs. Still, for other purposes, a given model may be quite adequate. Underlying the problem of proper application is the more general tension among myriad specialists, all of whom operate in and are responsible for analyses and policymaking. We have mentioned mainly MSGs intended for policymaking; similar criteria exist for the evaluation of models intended primarily for the manipulation of data, measurement, theory building, education, advocacy, and other distinct applications.[8]

The fact that various individuals and groups approach the substantive issues at stake from different vantage points helps to clarify and characterize the actual purpose and use of a particular MSG. To the extent that the clash of purpose between expert analyst and policymaker is resolved in favor of the former, however, policy applications will be slighted.[9] To the extent that an MSG is biased toward the more purely scientific values of measurement and theory building, for example, it may lose its appropriateness as a tool for policymaking. And to the extent that an MSG is intended to support a partisan policy position, its value as an operational device subject to scientific standards and validation may be diminished.

Professional Standards

Not surprisingly, the issue of different orientations and incentives has been treated differently by various experts. Often it has been defined generally, in terms of strains among professional roles and in terms of the problems of status and identification that arise when professional norms and standards conflict with those of a specific institution (see chapter 18 for a discussion of this topic).[10] In simulation and gaming, however, the general problem has taken on special characteristics. Model building and gaming are normally not the primary source of professional identification and reward for individual practitioners. Norms of professional conduct are not well established; personal identification with the development and use of MSGs is neither widespread nor easily assessed; and, despite the field's sharing and drawing on the mystique of scientific analyses, there is scant evidence that those active in the business readily submit their work to the imperatives of the more clear-cut scientific disciplines.[11] Topics that must be confronted and resolved more satisfactorily than they have been if the profession and its products are to develop much beyond the stage of expensive curiosities are listed below (these issues are discussed in greater detail in later chapters).

Responsibility. Any operational model-building activity should start with a clear identification of the professional who takes primary responsibility for its design, construction, and use. This information should be included in any comprehensive documentation of the model.

Standards and rules. There are a few rules of conduct to guide professional model builders and gamers. In the absence of explicit norms, expectations held by professionals vary widely or are largely not articulated, a condition that has contributed to the highly fragmented body of experience in the field.

Disciplinary action. Poor performance should be assessed routinely and appropriate sanctions invoked to improve future performance. Precedents and procedures from other scientific professions should be modified and adopted in this field as well.[12]

Professional communication. The tendency toward fragmentation of experience and activity is reinforced by poor or nonexistent communication among isolated groups of professionals who labor in ignorance of each other's existence. Simply improving communication could increase the degree and extent of professionalism.

External recognition. Public understanding and recognition of the mysterious methods used by professionals in the field are currently insufficient. This unsatisfactory situation has been reinforced by the advocacy-oriented, in-house, or closed-corporate style of much building and use of MSGs. Such styles are unhealthy and have worked against efforts to present the results of the work to public or scientific scrutiny.

Validation. The slogan "Validation is a happy customer" might be embellished to read, "Ultimate validation is a follow-up contract." Although a strong relationship between client and modeler is important, others must also be satisfied if the model-building enterprise is to develop and mature. Among the participants to be included in the concept of an expanded public are co-workers, other occupational groups, employment organizations, government regulatory agencies like the General Accounting Office and the Office of Management and Budget, educational-training agencies and institutions such as universities and professional societies, and affected citizens.

The present scientific worth of an MSG is not generally questioned, especially when it is being used to demonstrate or advocate a partisan position. The naive belief that analytic experts will always behave as professionals may keep the non-expert participant in the modeling process from questioning the underlying assumptions, data, and research techniques used by the expert. Although, ideally, professional standards and sanctions would guide these activities and legitimize the results generated by the modeling process, such standards are likely to be nonexistent, in short supply, or not widely held or adhered to.[13] The problem is fundamental and still unresolved.

In-House Analysts

In the jargon of the trade, the biases and perspectives of the individual military services are often referred to by the colors of the service's uniforms—a "green" point of view for the Army; "light blue" for the Air Force; "dark blue" for the Navy; and "purple" for civilians and a select few military staff members, who have ostensibly given up their ties to their parent service, employed by the Office of the Secretary of Defense. MSGs associated with each of the services often reflect the services' points of view. It is not all that difficult to understand why modeling activities become tinted. The scientific endeavor that guides much of the in-house military analytic effort, including modeling and gaming, is inevitably subordinate to considerations of combat in fighting for a relatively larger share of the annual federal budget. In an environment where the competitors are equipped with powerful computational capabilities and employ numerous technocrats, the wonder is that top-level decision makers have not been buried by even greater stacks of computer printouts and reports measured by the foot.

Although major military operations and sophisticated weapons systems have been planned and realized in the past without the benefit of copious, usually machine-based analyses, it is impossible even to contemplate a new weapons system today without resorting to expert analysis by the technocracy. MSGs are normally used for this purpose. When trying to justify any tool of war, however, one needs to be reminded that all analyses deal with fundamental uncertainties about its performance and about the environment in which the tool might eventually be employed. The results of all such analyses are generated by a program, the workings of which are obscure and often unfathomable. The interested onlooker does not know, for instance, what the structure of the MSG is, what data are assumed to be relevant, what is omitted, what factors influence which others and how, what numerical values have been used, or how sensitive the outcome is to changes and uncertainty in the assumptions. These issues are all important, and concerted efforts need to be made to render the mechanisms of the MSG less opaque and to generate alternative MSGs based on equally plausible assumptions about the performance of weapons and the operational environment of the future. Our view, based on the results of our survey and our own analyses, is that sufficient efforts are not now being expended in either area.

This criticism becomes even stronger when the actual constraints and incentives that influence the behavior of the in-house military analytic staff are examined. A stereotypical "analysis shop" is directed by a highly trained officer, a colonel or a naval captain. Among other resources, he has bright junior officers, qualified for the job by postgraduate training in computer and analytic skills, and numerous civilian scientists and outside consultants on call. Because a military career rarely depends primarily on the strength of the analytic work produced in such a tour of duty, one potential consideration of the warrior-turned-analyst is to finish his two- or three-year assignment with an unblemished reputation for efficiency or fitness, so that he may return to active military service and resume his professional career. Furthermore, high marks are seldom earned by questioning the wisdom or feasibility of a large weapons system or by undertaking and then failing to complete an analysis, even if the technical or scientific problems turn out to be insurmountable.

The civilian scientist works within the confines of his own peculiar rationale. Often well paid and immersed in the bureaucratic life, he cannot be faulted greatly for going along with the programs undertaken by his uniformed colleagues and superiors. Playing the role of spoilsport and critic has seldom earned the occasional outside consultant an invitation to play the game again. While the precise motivations for any consultant's choice to undertake defense analyses probably cannot be determined, many are undoubtedly attracted by the opportunity to work among powerful officials and to do so while earning a great deal of respect and money. Lesser considerations have persuaded more than one person to relax his individual standards, to say nothing of his concern for the few, exceedingly weak norms of the modeling profession.

Analytic Firms

Outside firms also play a significant role in military systems analysis. Attracting highly trained and talented individuals from the best universities, these institutions exert strong influences over their clients and staffs so as to maintain a strong and steady cash flow and thus assure institutional survival. Working with strictly limited resources, where time is often in very short supply, even the best trained, best intentioned, and best motivated analyst may find himself struggling with conflicting scientific, personal, professional, and institutional demands—to the extent that one or more of these may be subordinated or overlooked. We do not disagree that research institutions must exist and survive as a means to the end of improved public welfare; what concerns us here is the situation in which the means has become an all-consuming end in itself.

The current structure of business relationships between many consulting firms and their clients in the individual services and the Office of Secretary of Defense has, as an unintended consequence, created relationships of dependency; their outcome has not been sufficiently considered. For instance, numerous "families" of MSGs consist of unbroken strings of marginal additions and improvements on some initial model; taken in the aggregate, they persist for years. Long after the original purpose for constructing the patriarch MSG has been forgotten, managers and salesmen continue to find new reasons for adding subtle refinements, additional details, or improved algorithms. The actual applications of the variations are often hard to identify or justify.

A related perversion of the institutional relationship between client and analyst occurs when funds provided for certain specified tasks are spent for quite different purposes—whether to satisfy individual analysts, to develop new or more

refined research capabilities, or to examine questions judged
to be important but actually of little or no interest to the client.
If it lacks independent sources of funds, such as endowments
or guaranteed grants with no strings attached, an institution
may find itself in an uncomfortable position when the time
comes to write the final report and tell the client what he has
bought. Indeed, this situation has led to the development of an
entirely new language, aptly christened CONGRAM (contractor grammar) by Amron Katz, a long-time, critical translator of
this exotic tongue.[14] CONGRAM is not only the language of the
slick but uninformative briefing but also of proposals intended, according to Katz, to describe the imperfect past, the
insufficient present, and the absolutely perfect future—that is,
what will happen when the proposal is accepted, funded, and
implemented.

Another manifestation of the less than satisfactory relationship between clients or users and contractors or producers of
MSGs arises when a user buys a complicated model or simulation; eventually he or the person who inherits it no longer un-
derstands the whole model, if he ever did. At some point the
user wants the model to perform a task he thought it was able
to do or now feels it should do; however, he may not have the
necessary technical competence or may lack adequate documentation, in which case he must go back to the producer,
who will offer to write a modification or an extra subroutine or
even a whole new model—for a fee. In the case of some of the
larger models, this procedure can drag on, and apparently has,
for many years. Whatever the specific details, the end results
are predictable: the user is captured by the builder, and the financial health of the producer's organization is improved by
the amount of the fee. If the sunk costs in a model are great,
the tendency for a user to try to get a little bit extra for his
money exacerbates the problem.

The proliferation of inadequate and useless MSGs is also
partly attributable to insufficient professional review. This is
not solely a problem in the case of analytic firms; instead, it
pervades the entire system. Nevertheless, it can be discussed
in the context of these firms, where expectations about scientific and professional procedures are relatively high. Most
firms have internal procedures to check the scientific accuracy

and intelligibility of their products. However well these procedures are meant, they do not necessarily accomplish their objectives, for several understandable reasons. Working under strict time constraints to develop, test, and operate a model, even the most responsible analyst may find himself hard pressed to get his work in a form suitable for detailed internal review before it is scheduled for presentation to the client. In such a situation, a project leader is in no mood to have to answer numerous, penetrating questions raised by a fussy colleague. At the same time, managers and salesmen are not eager to request more time or additional money from a client to fix up a weak piece of work. These reactions tend to ensure that friendly referees are chosen or that the review process itself is short-circuited in the interests of meeting the deadline and getting the model to the client. This tendency is further reinforced by the fact that within an individual firm, the model-building staffs themselves are usually tightly knit groups of specialists; it is hard to criticize a co-worker's work strongly, particularly when he will eventually be called on to review one's own efforts, which may themselves be hastily produced and somewhat inadequate.

External review—tough, independent, and insulated from these institutional and human foibles—seems to be the logical corrective to these deficiencies; yet more than half of the MSGs we analyzed during our survey did not have the benefit of an external professional review. And, as noted earlier, a closely related investigation conducted by the GAO to determine the current status of documentation practices in computer systems reached essentially the same conclusions.[15]

Universities

The university once played a significant role in the analytic and model-building process. More recently, however, it has been a less eager, even sometimes reluctant, participant. In fact, we were surprised to find that only a small fraction of the MSGs surveyed had been built under direct university control. Individual university-based experts do occasionally work as consultants to an in-house analytic enterprise, however, and frequently serve as consultants on specific projects undertaken by consulting firms. If institutional interest increases as universities grapple with worsening fiscal problems, the role of the university in the creation and evaluation of military MSGs will be increasingly important.

Other Major Issues

CLASSIFICATION

Although classification to protect information is not itself an institution, its effects serve as institutional constraints on the communication and development of analytic work. Proprietary factors often interfere with the modeling and decision-making processes. Contractors who have developed all or part of an MSG may decide that particular details must be protected from exploitation by competitors, particularly when it is to the contractor's longer-term advantage to develop a basic model for resale to subsequent clients or even to the new staff of the same institutional client. Proprietary interests are, needless to say, at odds with and override scientific, public, and practical demands for better and more effective products. Excessive secrecy is unworthy of those responsible for the overall development and use of MSGs. Too often, in practice, proprietary safeguards have masked unsatisfactory or even shoddy work. Some means to guarantee the interests of the model-building analyst and his firm while simultaneously ensuring that the MSG itself operates correctly and in accord with existing scientific norms and standards must be developed. Adherence to good scientific practices and responsible behavior need not be sacrificed or compromised for essentially irrelevant proprietary interests. A good empirical indicator of the pervasiveness of the problem is the generally poor documentation associated with any given MSG. Shoddy documentation often naturally follows shoddy work. Developers, for instance, may know that the various assumptions embedded in their MSG will not stand up to scientific scrutiny or that the program will not operate without "fudge factors," special allowances, mysterious mechanisms, questionable operational procedures, or some other dubious practice.

Classification of information for security reasons is not a serious constraint in the case of most operational MSGs, so long as input data have not been assigned and the MSG is not used to generate specific values. The structure, specification, and coding of the majority of MSGs surveyed are not classified; hence there is little or no reason in most cases to restrict the availability of this information. Despite this rather surprising fact, communication of technical and theoretical matters is basically nonexistent outside the circle of those directly responsible for an MSG's production. The need to classify input data is understandable and valid. We do question another prevalent practice, however—the uncritical use of input data. Builders and users of MSGs rarely investigate why data were originally collected, how they have been used in the past, what restrictions limit their explanatory power, and other questions about their validity. Data are used and reused on the assumption that they measure what is being replicated in the MSG. The fact that basic data are frequently classified only confounds the technical problems of data validation.[16]

CONTROL

Other institutional participants in the MSG business have not exerted pressure to correct or modify the current process. Investigating the reasons for this lack of action involves identifying several potential sources of influence and examining why each was not adequately performing the oversight function. Congress, at first glance, seems a likely source of extramural control. Its supporting staff is small, however, and it has failed to develop any real capacity to understand, much less use, the new problem-solving technologies. Thus Congress has proved to be a poor match for the military in a contest of technocratic politics. Moreover, Congress's tendency to give the military experts what they want, even though the results have not always justified the trust, has contributed to the problem. In the future, the Congressional Budget Office (CBO) might usefully exert some control and oversee the modeling process.

The General Accounting Office (GAO), Congress's official watchdog agency, is making staff changes that will increase its ability to examine analytic activities undertaken by the executive branch; however, its efforts are sporadic and depend on a specific congressional inquiry. A particular GAO audit may make use of a technically trained analyst, but evaluations have usually been conducted by specialists in the law and accounting, not in computer and modeling techniques. Finally, the

GAO serves congressmen, many of whom are neither able to understand nor interested in what they consider technical esoterica. Unsurprisingly, GAO reports are nearly always phrased in distinctly nontechnical terms. It is highly unlikely that congressmen would be interested in knowing that the data used to generate an index of the effectiveness of a weapon were suspect or that the procedures for estimating parameters for an MSG were highly dubious, even though some, if not all, of the conclusions reached in the analysis might therefore be invalid. Nevertheless, someone ought to be raising questions of this sort.

Even within the executive branch, technical control over modeling activities is not pursued with even a fraction of the diligence and expertise required for the task. The Office of Management and Budget (OMB) is an institution that might exercise some degree of control. OMB is small, however, staffed for the most part by budgetary analysts, and concerned with programs and problems on a far larger scale than those associated with most modeling activities. A $500,000 model-based study carried out somewhere in the Pentagon is not apt to catch the attention of an OMB analyst whose accounts are measured in billions of dollars and whose interests are focused on expenditures, rather than on the technocratic paraphernalia used to justify them.

The Joint Chiefs of Staff could, in theory, perform a controlling function. In General Glenn A. Kent's words, however, "the theory is no better than the practice: it is merely substituting one form of parochialism for another. To be more pointed, the illumination on problems by the services will predictably reflect their own color. The illumination afforded by Joint Chiefs of Staff (JCS) studies has a way of coming out black because it goes through all of the filters."[17] On rare occasions, the services themselves convene a technical review panel to assess the validity and utility of MSG construction, operation, and use. The Army, for instance, did so in 1971 in response to the initial probings of a GAO audit team sent by the House Appropriations Committee to look into war gaming in the Pentagon.[18] The report filed by this panel, the Army Models Review Committee, contained some important insights and positive recommendations for improvement; nonetheless, it is difficult to avoid the impression that their efforts were inspired by a desire to cover their bets before the GAO had a chance to do any detailed investigating, rather than by concern about the fundamental technical issue set before the panel. The glare of legislative scrutiny has now passed on to other areas of real or imagined misfeasance and the panel's work has not continued, nor have its recommendations been adopted to any significant degree.

The National Security Council might naturally take a deep interest in the quality of model-based analyses, but for a number of reasons it has provided little or no critical appraisal. Its inaction is not surprising in view of its distrust of the military's sometimes self-serving assessments and recommendations and of its own preference for a nontechnical style of analysis. Professional societies, such as the College of Gaming and Simulation of The Institute of Management Sciences (TIMS) and the Military Operations Research Society, appear to be a natural source of technical oversight and control. TIMS has undertaken little such activity, however, primarily because so few in the professional community derive their primary identification from modeling and gaming and because it does not have the power to reward extraordinarily good work or to invoke meaningful sanctions against substandard performance.

The highest-level decision makers, it seems, should exert a controlling and cleansing influence on the modeling process; it is they who are ultimately responsible for operational choices. They have not wielded this influence, however, and some basic problems appear here, as well as in other areas.

Senior officials responsible for many billions of dollars' worth of war-making machinery and many thousands or millions of lives cannot be expected to care very much about technical minutiae, and they seldom do. The communication link that exists between those who build models and those who eventually make use of their results is a tenuous one at best—how can several pounds of computer printout be translated into fifty words to inform a general on his way to the heliport? Even the more technically sophisticated general officer or high-level civil servant has little time for the fine points of most analytic activity. Communication between staff and superior is further complicated by the desire to keep the decision maker happy and not introduce sensitive issues; this attitude ensures that the rare items of information presented for a senior official's attention are carefully selected and predigested. As the results of an analysis move into the highest levels of command and decision, through successive strata of subordinates, the message—whether from a rough model or a highly sophisticated and valid analysis—tends to become more precise and less equivocal.

SYSTEMIC PATHOLOGY

Lack of consensus about the relationship of individuals, organizations, and events and the resulting confusion that pervades MSG production, operation, and use have observable consequences that can only be termed pathological. Disorganized thinking is not limited to any single individual or group, and its existence and impact can only be discerned by means of a careful examination of the overall system in which they are operating.

When several groups and individuals are responsible for the production, use, and evaluation of a complex entity, like an MSG, the process can best be understood as the result of various forces setting, modifying, and adjusting goals. Before we attempt to look at this process, five questions, drawn from the foregoing discussion, must be considered:

1. What individuals or groups are involved in ordering, building, and interpreting an MSG?
2. What are the goals of each, as well as they can be determined?
3. What priorities does each assign to his goals?
4. Are there reasonable measures that can be used to determine, describe, or characterize these goals?
5. What are the limits imposed by the chain of command and the available resources—limits of time and money— that influence the various goals?

Questions about intention, specification, control, and validation—like these—make it clear that individual perceptions are important in complex systems, even though they are extremely difficult to understand. General intentions must be translated into specific steps in order to begin to evaluate the worth and usefulness of the work. Specification must be clear and reasonable enough to be controlled. Finally, the parties involved must agree about what constitutes an answer to their operational question, so that some evaluation of the results can be performed. In this chapter we have introduced the individuals and institutions for whom these broad questions must be resolved; in the following chapter we shall continue our analysis by describing the processes at work in the military analysis system.

16 | The Decision-Making Process

> Careful empirical work can disclose the genuine complexity
> of the decision process; it can challenge dogmatic rigidities
> of view.
>
> Robert Rubenstein and Harold D. Lasswell,
> *The Sharing of Power in a Psychiatric Hospital*

ONE OF THE most difficult aspects of operational MSGs to assess is their effect on the subsequent behavior of participants. In other
words, just what differences can be ascribed to the production,
operation, and use of these sophisticated devices? What has
been learned?

Divining the impact of operational MSGs on participants,
the institutions with which they are affiliated, and the decision-making process in which they are embedded is scarcely
made easier by currently inadequate or nonexistent assessment procedures. Indeed, as we have already noted, the need
for a thorough and independent evaluation of operational activities is one of our major findings. Empirical work aimed at
clarifying the role and influence of MSGs in the overall decision-making process is severely impeded by the lack of the
basic information that would result from competent, consistent evaluations.

The importance of evaluating modeling activities must be
assessed in the context of the interactions between participants and institutions over time. The typical MSG's entire life
cycle must be considered. Tracing the interplay of various participants through the life of an MSG provides a better understanding of the whole sequence and calls attention to the
phases in which more concerted attention and action would
provide significant gains.

Our examination has discovered eight distinct and interrelated phases in the general life cycle of the MSGs used opera-

tionally within the Department of Defense. They are (1) initiation, (2) promotion, (3) prescription, (4) production, (5) operation, (6) use, (7) evaluation, and (8) termination.

Initiation is the synthesis and generation of ideas and plans in response to perceived needs. It requires intelligence in the conventional sense of gathering information about one's own and others' capabilities and weaknesses, in such forms as net-assessment and technological-forecasting studies. Viewed this way, initiation can be described as the recognition or identification of problems. Once a problem is recognized, many possible ways to alleviate or resolve it may be explored, among them the use of analytic methods. In this earliest, creative phase, numerous incomplete and inappropriate solutions to the problem are inevitably advanced; they are generally rejected during a later phase. The initiation phase also stresses redefinition of the problem, identification of a range of possible solutions and solution methods, and selection of the most practicable set within that range.

Promotion involves securing the attention and tangible support of those who control resources. It is the entrepreneur's domain and requires promotion both of one's own ability to generate solutions to the perceived problem and of the existence of and danger posed by the problem itself. Concern for presumed improvements in a capability for aircraft recognition and destruction, for example, might lead to studies of various aircraft configurations' potential for penetration and survival. Those undertaking such studies would obviously make a point of their technical virtuosity in a number of areas; it is equally important, however, to emphasize the salience of the problem itself. If penetration is not a real problem, then there is little need to study it. In the domestic arena, to cite another example, the desire to create "model cities" and the conviction that poverty can be alleviated through martial mechanisms have reflected the promotional targets of problem-solving institutions and politicians as much as they have the real needs of cities and poor people. In spite of its obvious importance, however, the impact of promotional work on the definition of problems and the various ways they might have been defined, assessed, and eventually resolved has seldom been stated.

The prescription phase concentrates on the specification of

agreements about how the identified problem is to be attacked. Contracts are drawn and tangibly represent joint decisions about the importance of the problem, the potential means of resolving it, and the selection of problem solvers who appear to be competent to achieve a solution. It is the logical bridge between promotion and the construction of a model, simulation, or game, if that technique is chosen. Basic questions about the appropriateness of alternative techniques could and should be raised at this juncture, but they seldom are. The importance of the problem compared with a host of alternative problems should also be considered seriously at this juncture, but it seldom is.

Production—the actual construction of an MSG—hinges on factors such as its purposes, the identity of the sponsor, the resources (including time, talent, and cash) to be devoted to the effort, and specific, technical matters such as the MSG's size, level of detail or aggregation, and input data requirements. Production is a process that is susceptible to scientific scrutiny and evaluation, although they have not been much in evidence.

Operation is the running and testing of an MSG or analysis, a phase during which scientific standards are applied and technical and procedural questions like the following are addressed: What tests were used to try out the MSG? Was the MSG constructed and documented so that it could be replicated in another setting by another group? Has it been replicated? What considerations were taken into account in conducting sensitivity analyses and other tests of the MSG's structural and behavioral properties? Have the input data been critically examined to ensure their validity, appropriateness, and accuracy? Have the key assumptions inherent in the MSG's structure been explicitly examined, and have their relevance and applicability to the problem at hand been checked and conveyed to the user? Has the MSG had an external, professional review, and, if not, why not? The operations phase is the special province of the technical expert. What transpires during this phase is nonetheless of more widespread interest and concern than most people would imagine—especially for those involved in the use of the MSG.

The meaning of the use phase is at once obvious and subtly

deceptive. Someone is obviously going to be using the MSG, especially if significant amounts of money have been invested in it. The problem is to determine, first, whether the actual use corresponds to the original intention of those for whom the MSG was built and, second, whether that use is appropriate, a determination that must take the MSG's strengths and weaknesses directly into account. How frequently is the MSG used, and by whom? What are the costs of its use? What are its effects and benefits? The answers to these questions will indicate whether the MSG is being misused or abused, matters that must be taken seriously. Misuse occurs for a number of complex reasons but primarily because understanding of the existing interrelationships among the production, use, and evaluation phases is lacking. The incentive structures of institutions that produce MSGs are another important cause.

In practice, evaluation is backward-looking and is often limited to asking the classic performance questions of who got what, why, and how. Complete evaluations should also ask more specific questions. Who was responsible for a given analysis throughout its existence? Who certifies professional qualifications in the business? What technical standards exist for the production, operation, and use of such MSGs? How do technical experts and decision makers or users learn about these standards? How and under what conditions are sanctions invoked against substandard performance, and who invokes these sanctions? How and when is excellent work rewarded, and by whom? That most of these questions cannot be answered readily demonstrates that evaluation scarcely exists in the process currently responsible for the majority of operational military MSGs.

Termination ends the cycle. When an MSG has fufilled its purpose, has been used to good effect, or requires considerable and expensive modifications, termination initiatives should be expected. In actual practice, however, MSGs that were or should have been terminated are often regenerated or resold, particularly when the user's institutional memory is short and spotty. The process of termination itself is also poorly organized, except for the largely irrevelant contractual matters left to the bookkeepers and lawyers. If meaningful evaluations were properly carried out, the decision to terminate would be based directly on scientific, if not pragmatic and common-sense, grounds. Instead, the decision-making process remains open-ended. MSGs are altered or revived periodically to form whole families of models the initial purposes, uses, documentation, strengths, weaknesses, and costs of which have long been forgotten.

The process or sequence of decision making is summarized in figure 16-1, which indicates the timing of the phases through which most MSGs progress and reveals areas worthy of increased attention, as well as breakdowns, discontinuities, overlooked phases, mismatches and communication problems between the individual participants and their institutions, and other factors that influence the process and its products. This is a simplified view of the dynamics of the current situation to be sure. In the following sections we shall focus on what appear to be some of the more serious deficiencies in the process and therefore in many current practices and relationships.

The life cycle of most MSGs appears to follow one of two well-worn tracks through the decision-making process, with the choice depending on whether the MSG is to be produced by an in-house group or farmed out to external model-building specialists. Each track will be examined. The blocks in figure 16-1 are labeled according to the key individuals and institutions at each phase of the process; they change size or disappear and reappear according to each individual or group's level of involvement. To keep the figure as clear as possible, routine interactions among participants have been omitted, although they are discussed. Because the predominant form of MSG in our survey was the all-machine variety, this discussion refers to that type, unless otherwise noted.

The Phases of Decision Making

INITIATION

Models, simulations, and games are born in several ways, of which two stand out prominently: in response, first, to internal demands and actions taken by in-house personnel and, second, to demands emanating from entrepreneurs in defense contract-research establishments. In the past, MSGs were routinely suggested and initiated by isolated individuals,

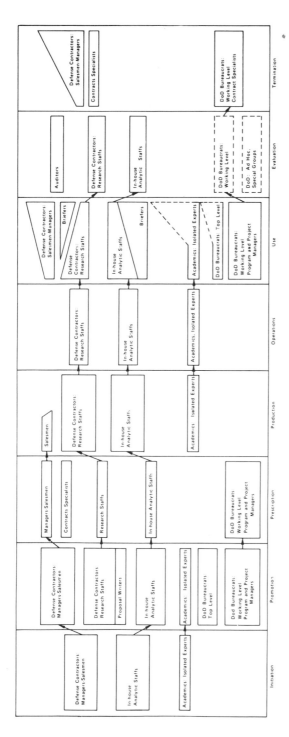

Figure 16-1. The decision-making process. In this diagram, the arrows connecting blocks indicate that the participation of the group named continues. The approximate size of each block indicates the relative degree of involvement of the individual or group it contains; an upward slope, that the involvement of the group or individual increases during the phase in question; and a broken line, that the group's participation may be sporadic or contingent on earlier events. The block labeled "Defense Contractors: Managers-Salesmen," for instance, is large during the initial stages of the process, diminishes during operation, increases in size and importance throughout the use of the MSG, drops from sight during evaluation, and builds up again during termination. DoD, Department of Defense.

usually based in universities; this practice has waned in the last decade, however, as the university's role in military research has declined, as the capability and capacity of in-house modeling groups have improved and increased, and as the number and cash-flow requirements of defense-contract institutions have increased.

How does an MSG come to life? The initiation phase starts it on either the "external" or the "internal" track (fig. 16-2). On the external track, which emphasizes the use of outside modeling groups, the process routinely begins with a periodic visit by a salesman or manager to a client agency within the military. The visitor may have been in uniform himself recently and may have been playing the role of the client on the other side of the desk. The extent and impact of this old-boy network are not reliably known. The practice probably results inevitably from the small number of knowledgeable professionals in a specialized field; as routine as it appears to be, however, this situation has not been acknowledged and assessed adequately. During the initial visits, the user's model-building requirements and available resources may be discussed, and the salesman may extol the virtues of his firm and its qualifications to meet or exceed those requirements. An

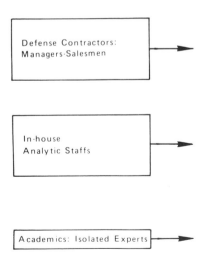

Figure 16-2. *The initiation phase.*

MSG may also be initiated when a previous modeling effort, or one of its components, has recently been phased out and the salesman is seeking new employment for his crew.

In the case of MSGs on the internal, or in-house, track, someone on the inside—a staffer, a high-level official, a supervisor several levels removed, or perhaps a civilian consultant to the study group—has an idea that may need a full-blown analysis. Whether model building is the best research approach to the problem, though a reasonable question, is seldom asked. The initiation may take the shape of a formal study-requirement document, full of references to military threats, the latest intelligence estimates, old studies, current legislative debates, and a variety of other factors. Whatever the actual source and nature of the impetus, the in-house staff responds by considering its current work load, the availability and capabilities of staff members, and limitations on resources. If the potential model-building task appears at this stage to fall within the scope and skill area of the in-house staff, promotional activities begin soon thereafter. If, because of the difficulty of the project, time pressures, the size of the undertaking, or some other factor, the in-house staff is unwilling or unable to undertake the project outside contracts or subcontracts on all or part of the job may eventually result.

PROMOTION

More participants enter the picture during the promotional phase, after the need for a modeling effort has been established (see fig. 16-3). The contractor calls in his key research people and his proposal writers, who may be entirely separate from the research staff. High-level bureaucrats in the Department of Defense and the armed forces become active during this phase, in proportion to the resources thought to be needed for the job. As already noted, a peculiar discontinuity exists between MSGs costing much less than $500,000 and those exceeding $1 million. Projects at the lower end of the scale are probably handled routinely by the working bureaucracy of program and project managers, while those at the upper end probably require higher-level support and sanction. A more detailed examination of promotional practices might shed light on this matter.

For in-house work, promotion is relatively trouble-free.

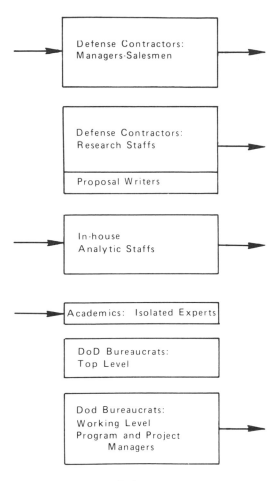

Figure 16-3. *The promotional phase.*

Competition for funds is usually restricted to internal contests for resources that have already been allocated in the group's overall annual budget. In other words, competition for the approval of a specific project, if any, arises between staff members, not between services or outside contractors. The external track offers more obvious possibilities for competition. The various outside contractors not only are competing with each other but, in a real sense, are also in competition with in-house staffs for a portion of the available resources.

(Competition in this sense occurs when total annual budgets are being set and gross divisions between in-house and outside work are determined. The contract-research business is receiving increasing competition from within the client agencies that were formally highly dependent.) It is not surprising, therefore, to see proposals for increasingly complicated, larger, and more difficult ("state-of-the-art") MSGs; this work can only be done outside the user agencies and may be so technically and theoretically specialized that only one contractor is capable of carrying it out (the "sole-source" contract). Unsurprisingly, also, such competition erects barriers to technical communication and contributes to the professional fragmentation that pervades the field. Where product differentiation is the crux of promotion and the uniqueness of the product is based on the supposed technical expertise of a firm's research staff, communication among modeling experts is not likely to be extensive. One result is that outside experts are often employed as consultants during the promotional phase, both to provide detailed technical information and to lend an aura of scientific distinction to the proposed MSG effort.

Distinctive historical relationships color the promotional phase of different types and forms of MSG. In many of the larger machine simulations represented in our survey, for example, a technical specialist provided the fundamental ideas, which were presented to the client by a highly skilled and personable entrepreneur; this mediation often effectively eliminated any interpersonal contact between the technical specialist and the client. Free-form MSGs concentrating on military, political, and diplomatic issues characteristically lacked the skilled middle man, and the technical specialist was left to sell, produce, and operate the final MSG product on his own. Game-theory and mathematical MSGs follow a similar pattern, although the entrepreneurial skills and successes of their main proponents have, if anything, been even less notable than those of their free-form counterparts.

PRESCRIPTION

Prescription includes the drafting and awarding of contracts, and it is in this phase that program and project mana-

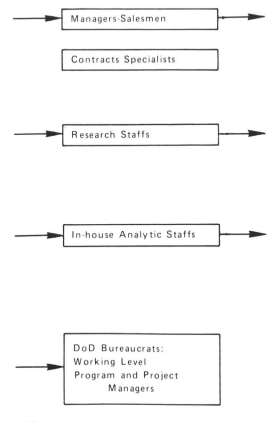

Figure 16-4. *The prescription phase.*

gers with the defense bureaucracy become active (see fig.16-4).
For MSGs that follow the external track, prescription depends
on the efforts of the contractor's salesmen and managers and
his specialists. The involvement of the research staff is generally limited to the project or group leaders, who may translate promotional language into dollars and cents, chores,
schedules, and bodies. At the client agency, the main point of
contact is the project manager, who may call on contractual
experts to execute a formal document. MSGs on the internal
track generally involve no formal contractual negotiations or
specifications; a portion of the operational budget is simply allocated, deadlines are set, and the project is identified, usually,
by the name of the MSG and the group responsible for its de-

velopment. Two groups of participants, outside experts and high-level defense bureaucrats, drop from sight during this phase. Neither is ordinarily concerned with prescription.

PRODUCTION

The MSG is actually built almost entirely by technical specialists, whether the work is produced in house or by outside contractors (see fig. 16-5). This specialization is understandable, even obvious, in view of the highly technical character of most MSGs. That the user or client rarely participates at this stage is a less obvious fact. The translation of his intentions and needs is relegated to small, select groups of technicians, far removed from the high-level councils where the results of the MSG may one day be presented, considered, and even integrated into choices affecting national security. A working model is developed in the production phase and is able to generate output values from assorted input data; it does not

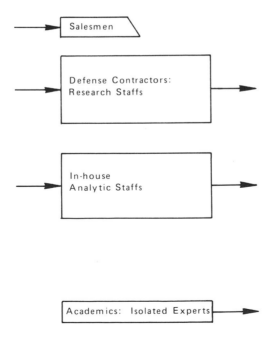

Figure 16-5. *The production phase.*

necessarily produce valid and reliable information about the processes being modeled.

For MSGs following the external track, the main concern of the Defense Department manager should be the accurate translation of the initial job specifications into a working MSG, on schedule and for the prescribed price. The importance and difficulty of this function are not ordinarily appreciated, nor is it often well performed. During production, few incentives encourage active and intelligent participation by the program or project manager, who serves as the user's agent and representative on the scene; in fact, the few incentives that can be discerned reduce the chances of faithful translation by diverting attention to bookkeeping and other contractual chores. Maintaining the mystery of an all-machine MSG's mechanism is understandable as a way of guarding proprietary interests. Nonetheless, the multiple costs of secrecy, measured less in money than in usefulness, seem unacceptably high.

In-house production has increased to the point where nearly half of all the MSGs we surveyed were internally built. Several key features of in-house production shed some light on the reasons for the poor quality and the rarity of documentation and external professional review. When a tightly knit group of military technicians is assigned to build an MSG, the pressure to produce something that works, on time and according to a budget, is greater than the pressure to be concerned about scientific niceties. Other pressures, including the need to please the boss and remain in tune with the political realities of the Pentagon, operate in numerous, subtle ways during this phase of the process. The effects of many of these pressures might be reduced if greater attention and perseverance were applied during the next phase, that of operation.

OPERATION

On the external track, some testing and technical validation of MSGs, including sensitivity testing, occurs during the phase of operation, but not much. Individual staff members may undertake validation in response to professional norms or as part of the preparation of scientific papers for presentation to other interested model builders (see fig. 16-6). Individual outside ex-

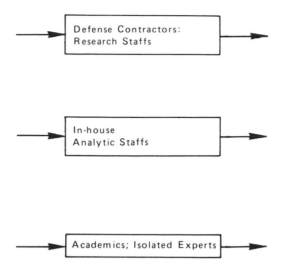

Figure 16-6. *The operations phase.*

perts also occasionally reappear at this stage to check some technical or theoretical detail of a given MSG. The Military Operations Research Society's periodic meetings offer some evidence that professional communication may result from such operational testing.

An MSG following the internal track is less likely to undergo complete operational testing, we believe, because a clear bias exists in many in-house modeling shops against research or against what is perceived as "endless" testing. Because in-house technical specialists are military men first and model-building analysts second, the demand to get an MSG built, running, and producing results is understandable. It is also dangerous and can easily lead to the misuse of a powerful and costly device.

USE

When an MSG reaches the point of generating results a large number of participants actively enter the process (see fig.16-7). If it has been developed by an outside research contractor, his salesmen and managers reappear, slowly at first and then more rapidly, to market the product. The job is easier if the product happens to be interesting to the client and if it

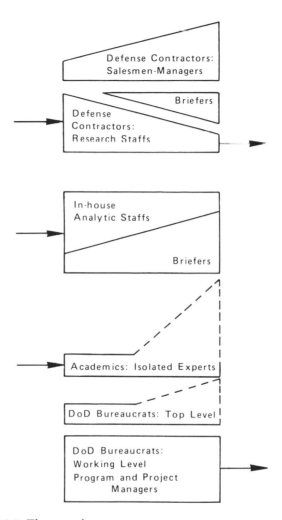

Figure 16-7. *The use phase.*

has some attractive scientific aspects. Neither feature is necessary for the contractor's salesmen to do their job during the use phase, however. If the MSG does not work—that is, if it is not yet capable of producing output values or is still under development—the salesman or manager's task differs somewhat from that of pure marketing, and he concentrates on getting additional financing and extensions of time to complete it, although his level of participation remains intense.

The contractor's research staff contributes the raw material for presentation to the client and is responsible for writing reports, documentation, and dissemination of results to other professional groups. While some modelers may actually come in contact with the client during briefings and other presentations, such communication tends to be limited and diminishes in importance as staff efforts are redirected to other modeling and research chores. The meter is always running, in a real sense, for these expensive technical specialists.

A new group, the briefers, emerges at this point. They may be select members of the model-building crew, technically inclined salesmen and managers, or even highly trained individuals whose fundamental skills are in the preparation and presentation of briefings. The polished "dog and pony show," as such briefings are sometimes called, is often the result of this group's efforts. Many of these presentations are impressive, yet we would be more impressed if equivalent time and attention had been expended during the previous phases, especially those of production and operation, to increase the likelihood that what is being formally presented is scientifically viable, if not operationally pertinent.

In-house technical staffs are normally more self-contained and self-reliant than those of consultants during the use phase. The individuals who did the work usually present the results, and the specialized briefer is not normally involved. This is not to say that the in-house briefing lacks esthetic appeal; on the contrary, the briefings based on multiple flip-charts and slide shows are highly developed as an art form both in private corporations and in the military. If the MSG is interesting and produces useful results, high-level defense bureaucrats may be active during the use phase, as the ascending broken line for this participant block in figure 16-7 indicates. Alternatively, the official may learn about an MSG's results only indirectly, when he is presented with findings and recommendations gleaned from MSGs and other kinds of analyses. If the MSG does not work, he will probably hear nothing about it unless large sums of research money or blatant misconduct is involved.

Participation by academic consultants follows an analogous pattern. If a modeling effort produces results that are likely to be of interest or use to high-level officials, a contractor or an in-house research staff may find it worthwile to enlist expert assistance to help present the results. On the other hand, if the MSG fails to operate according to plan, outside talent might be brought in to help resolve the problems.[1] The working defense bureaucrat, the program or project manager, is also active during this phase. If the effort is a positive one, his bureaucratic accounts are duly credited. If the effort is in some way deemed not to be a success, he is on the spot to try to salvage it or else to smooth over the matter to avoid a blot on his own career-performance record.

Evaluation

As we have repeatedly stressed, the evaluation phase is imperfect and underappreciated. No one participant group stands out as particularly effective, and several other likely groups do not appear at all (see fig. 16-8). The managers and salesmen are gone, and the contractor's primary response during evaluation consists of answering questions put to him by the government auditor (often housed within the research firm itself) to be sure that the funds can be accounted for and that contractual details have been satisfied. These auditors are not competent to judge the technical value of an MSG, nor are they expected to be. Research staffs, both in house and outside the agency, do very little during this phase. Few or no positive incentives encourage anyone to evaluate either the scientific merits or the practical utility of an MSG in detail, but there are many incentives not to do so.

For an external researcher, the problem is a real one. Detailed evaluation implicitly calls into question his firm's corporate wisdom and capabilities, both of which have been heavily promoted from the inception of the MSG. Such a challenge translates readily into a threat to continued business. In addition, a fact of professional life militates against external evaluation. The number of professionals involved in the modeling business is relatively limited, and attacks on the priesthood are made only at serious personal peril. In any event, no one does it regularly. Instead of rigorous, independent, routine evaluation, we find, at best, perfunctory evaluation in which A evaluates the work of B in a neighborly fashion; B returns the favor to C; and C, knowing full well that his own present and

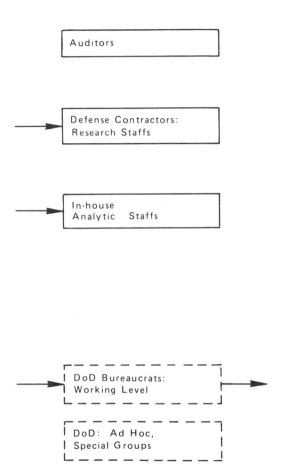

Figure 16-8. *The evaluation phase.*

future efforts could be threatened, completes the sequence with a favorable review of A's work.

In-house staffs have somewhat more incentive to carry out an occasional evaluation, especially on work hired out and produced under contract. Bureaucratic points can be made with the boss if a bright major or colonel can detect a few of an MSG's inevitable weaknesses and limitations. This is a risky game that does not consistently reward the critic, however, since such aggressive acts invite retribution in the short run and, in the long run, reduce the chances of employment on the outside, should the officer's military career be cut short.

The outside expert is rarely evident; only an occasional consultant will comment adversely on someone else's work. Beyond ego gratification and the possibility of feeling that he has raised the scientific standards of the profession, the outside expert has little incentive to undertake an evaluation. It is nearly certain that the negativistic evaluator will not soon be invited back; he may generally be perceived as a crank, as well. The high-level officials are gone; they have extracted what they were after, if there was anything to extract, in the previous phase of the process. The defense program or project manager is not especially interested in evaluations and participates only when a given MSG developed under his stewardship is called into question by someone else.

The only participants in the evaluation phase with any real influence are special groups convened to review large sets of MSGs or to assess current technology and practices. These groups usually exist for limited periods; they seldom have the necessary technical competence to do the job and hence rely on in-house specialists; and they seem to come into being mainly to head off external audits or investigations. We believe that the following additional groups, at the very least, should be integrated into the evaluation phase of the production and use of MSGs:

Legislative bodies
U.S. General Accounting Office
Congressional Budget Office
Office of Technology Assessment
Congressional staffs

Executive bodies
National Science Foundation
Office of Management and Budget
Joint Chiefs of Staff
National Security Council
National Bureau of Standards

Professional groups
Military Operations Research Society
The Institute of Management Sciences
Operations Research Society of America

Independent institutions and individuals
Universities
Skilled and interested professionals
Analytic firms specializing in evaluation

There are two basic reasons for adding these participants: first, to improve and strengthen all previous phases by providing realistic and honest information about technical and operational performance at each stage, thereby restructuring the incentive systems that apparently motivate and underlie much current behavior, and, second, to add a deterrent to substandard individual performance throughout the current system. Since no one seems to care about or be responsible for rigorous evaluation of MSGs, the fact that little is performed should not be surprising. It is clearly in the interest of many existing groups and institutions, however, to respond to the challenge presented by poor or nonexistent evaluation procedures.

TERMINATION

When it is time to end a modeling effort, the contractor's salesman or manager reenters the picture and tries, increasingly hard, to find alternative employment for his modeling crew (see fig. 16-9). The firm's contract specialists play a minor role in tidying up details—a task they share with the responsible working-level defense bureaucrat or his own contract representative. Neither external nor in-house researchers are directly involved. Final documentation of a modeling effort should occur at this stage, but it seldom does.

We expect stern and even outraged reactions to this characterization of the decision-making process as it now exists. Although we have undoubtedly misrepresented the actual life cycle of any particular MSG, we have great confidence in the overall accuracy of this summary. As in medicine, the first step to cure of the problems in the modeling community is an honest and thorough examination and diagnosis. A next step in trying to improve the health of the system producing and using operational military MSGs is to use a case history to pinpoint the probable sources of troublesome ailments. This

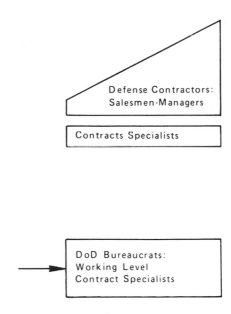

Figure 16-9. *The termination phase.*

chapter and those that precede it represent an attempt to accomplish this task; the next step—prescribing a remedy—is the focus of the next part of this book.

PART SIX

Recommendations

17 | Improving Standards

> In contemporary terms those who combine skill with en-
> lightenment are *professionals,* while those who are in com-
> mand of a specific skill are members of an *occupational* or
> hobby group . . . The true professional can manipulate an
> armory of skills with awareness of *aggregate* consequences
> in mind.
>
> Harold D. Lasswell, *A Pre-View of Policy Sciences*

MAKING RECOMMENDATIONS is a hazardous occupation. The practitioner who puts
forth his suggestions may be accused of a lack
of objectivity, while the nonpractitioner who dares to speak
out may be accused of not knowing enough. Nevertheless, we
sincerely believe that the use of military models, simulations,
and games is extensive enough and the potential value of work
in this area is great enough that many separate, interrelated
changes must be considered in professional standards and
practices, in managerial stewardship, and in the performance
of the entire system responsible for these devices. We begin by
considering professionalism.

Professionalism

Webster's New Collegiate Dictionary defines the word *profession* as "a calling requiring specialized knowledge and often
long and intensive academic preparation," "a principal calling,
vocation, or employment," or "the whole body of persons engaged in a calling." This definition leads to several questions:
What might be the guiding standards and rules of conduct of
the profession? How is the profession recognized by those
committed to it and those for whom it functions? How does
one prepare for entry into the profession? We contend that the
modeling and gaming profession has not been sufficiently delineated or developed to allow its participants to identify and
associate freely with it, nor has it been able to establish and

enforce an ethic, which Webster defines as "principles of conduct governing an individual or a group."

So far, the profession of modeling and gaming is loosely defined as those individuals with highly diversified and specialized skills who happen to find themselves in organizations that conduct modeling and gaming, as well as many other functional tasks. Without an unambiguous primary identification (as an analyst? a soldier, sailor, airman? an economist or mathematician? a computer programmer?), the would-be professional is confronted with conflicts and problems of status that are difficult indeed to resolve.[1] These problems are compounded by the lack of a clear statement of the MSG professional's responsibility, like that which exists for some of the better established professions.[2] The establishment of general, recognized norms might begin to resolve the modeler's role conflicts. Without such norms, many individuals cope with the problem by aligning themselves more closely with the host organization than with their professional peers.

In at least one view (others, of course, are possible) the basic elements of a profession include identification, or individuals' expectations about themselves in a social setting; quality control, the procedures by which those identified as professionals assure adherence to group expectations about performance; maintenance and continuity, the ways the profession sustains itself and evolves in response to changing contextual demands; and sanctions, the procedures used to reward or punish those who either conform to or deviate from group expectations about behavior.[3]

Professional identification appears to be very weak both in the modeling and gaming profession and in the broader research-and-development community.[4] Computer programming is an identifiable function in many analysis groups, but programmers perform a wide variety of tasks, many of which are more properly labeled as modeling, data-base management, documentation, dissemination, and librarianship. Creating differential job descriptions, and hence establishing clearer expectations about what the job is and how it should be done, would enhance professional development considerably. Military careerists know that the path to advancement and flag rank is more certain if one maintains one's identity as a troop commander, ship captain, or pilot than if one becomes labeled primarily as an analyst or modeler.[5] The nonmilitary modeling and gaming specialist also faces problems of identification. The issue has been summarized by John K. Walker, Jr.:

> On the one hand there is the analyst as scientist—pure in heart with the objective of gaining insight, discovering and revealing truth. On the other hand, there is the analyst as advocate—no longer disinterested and above the battle, but deeply involved in extolling the virtues of a particular policy or decision in seeking to persuade an executive or decision-maker or even engaged in adversary proceedings where he seeks to discredit some rival analyst or to demolish some competing argument.
>
> In actual practice, of course, the analyst is often in some intermediate situation where he is part scientist and part advocate. Not only may he have varying roles, but he may also typically have a multiplicity of relationships with a wide range of people in different organizations and at different levels in the hierarchies. Some may expect the analyst to be an advocate whereas others may expect him only to reveal the absolute truth.[6]

This schizophrenic character is not unique to the modeling and gaming profession but has confronted scientists in all fields as they have moved from relatively contemplative to more partisan or public roles.[7]

Formal concern with the quality of work produced in a profession is one proven way to clarify status and reduce individual problems about identity and roles.[8] We would like to see master modeler qualifications created for those entrusted with responsibility for the production, operation, and use of large or important MSGs. Comparable certification for other MSG specialists would similarly improve the quality of work that could be expected. Improved evaluation, discussed earlier, could have some of the same desirable consequences. Maintenance of the profession involves the selection, training, and promotion of those who identify themselves as modelers and gamers; in this area, too, procedures and practices could be developed that would improve the present situation.[9]

Sanctions may take many forms. It may even be appropriate, as a last resort, to rely on legal action to resolve the worst cases of professional misconduct.[10] Litigation to recover damages from a modeler and his sponsoring institution for demonstrably negligent or harmful performance might produce interesting results. Certainly it would not take many such cases to convince the profession that it should take itself and its responsibilities more seriously.

PROFESSIONAL RULES OF CONDUCT

There are few definable rules of conduct in the modeling and gaming profession, and there is a great deal of equivocation and uncertainty about appropriate professional behavior; the results for research in general and for the profession specifically have not always been salutary.[11] What is required, in essence, is the creation, publication, and enforcement of a consistent set of norms that the majority of the profession could accept and follow. The current fragmentation of modeling and gaming and the lack of intergroup communication prevent the development of a shared body of experience from which norms and expectations might be derived.

Bernie Rosenman has framed several pertinent questions about the related issue of technical performance: Have some fundamental precepts of operations research been forgotten? Were they imperfectly appreciated? Were they ever known in the first place?[12] In addressing these questions, Rosenman has developed five situational categories that represent questionable technical practices prevalent in the profession. The first, "the expected value found to equal the mean," refers to simulation results that could have been produced by a straight analytic model; the practice, he comments, is of no serious consequence, "assuming, of course, that the simulations were correctly done . . . but why does this kind of thing occur so often?"[13] In the case of "the one-shot experiment," only a few plays of a game or a few runs of a large simulation are used as the basis for decisions about problems that are in fact too complex for simple analytic models. Rosenman writes: "I have seen the outputs of simulations where it was clear that a steady state had not been reached yet where that was what the results purported to be. In some cases this somehow hadn't been realized by the analysts. In other cases where this defect was known, the point was made that time or funds or both didn't permit doing enough plays or runs to get statistically significant results. Yet results that might be close to nonsense were being presented as a basis for decisions for some honest-to-goodness problems.''[14]

The third case—"the 'best' model is indeed 'best' ''—uses empirical data to determine parameters, then uses this information against the same data base to test the models. Building and using an MSG in this fashion is permissible only if sensitivity testing has determined whether or not the underlying structures and distributions can in fact be carried over intact from previous to future cases. Often they cannot. Rosenman's fourth case is labeled "when is a Poisson not a Poisson?" In this case, the analyst is confronted with a Poisson distribution function (a specialized measure of the probability of unlikely events) based on acceptable statistical analyses but that, in actual operation, produces numbers that are simply not believable. "For some reason, it doesn't always occur to the analyst to divide the empirical data into at least two time frames, using one for hypothesis development and the other for hypothesis testing" (the so-called split halves technique).[15]

Rosenman's entire commentary on the final case, "your guess is as good as mine," is worth quoting.

> We have had occasions when results obtained from our own simulation experiments seem to be different from results obtained by others and we can't find out why. The program documentation can't be found and the analyst is either no longer there or can't remember what he did two years ago. Thus, we can't find out how their starting positions were developed, what was done with ending positions, how costs or performance were calculated, and so on. That is indeed a disquieting situation, for now you can't even be sure of your own results.[16]

In the situation where two independent analysts working with the same problem and using the same body of data derive quite different results, essential questions are raised about the profession itself and its scientific foundations and credibility.

The need for professionally sanctioned and sponsored review is quite clear in these cases. At a minimum, an impartial external review board should assess the scientific merits of each analysis, isolate the significant issues, and establish a common ground for evaluation of assumptions, scenarios, input information, and other factors.[17] Such a group does not currently exist, nor do the incentives, resources, and demands that would be likely to create one.

PROFESSIONAL EVALUATION

A comprehensive examination of the quality and uses of military analyses performed in the last two decades now seems warranted. Such an effort would be expensive, but not when compared with the total resources that have been spent for the work under examination. If performed authoritatively and well, it could contribute enormously to professional development.[18] In addition to this one-time, full-scale effort, routine postmortems should be conducted whenever a generation of an MSG family is being set aside in the interests of a newer and more promising group, whenever a given MSG is used with great frequency and is in danger of unexamined or inappropriate use, and whenever an MSG (or, for that matter, a facility or gaming laboratory) is facing serious trials. Only through such cumulative endeavors will the profession begin to achieve sufficient credibility.

Because of the secretive style of much current activity and its tendency to be used for advocacy, the scientific worth of an MSG is not generally questioned. The assumption seems to be that professional standards underlie the message being advocated, but these are not evident. If the validity of an MSG is demonstrated by "a happy customer," then the definition of who is the customer or client must be expanded to include professional colleagues, professional societies concerned about modeling and gaming, government regulatory agencies and controlling authorities, educational and training agencies, and the public itself.[19]

PROFESSIONAL DEVELOPMENT AND EDUCATION

Modeling and gaming activities lack continuity. Even though they are in fact ongoing and open-ended, the necessity to time them according to the demands of contracts and project deadlines has created the appearance of individual, discontinuous, and often totally disparate activity. This fragmentation is reflected in the way professionals are educated. Experience is obtained on the job and is very uneven in quality. Where does one go to learn the business? How are professional expectations, as well as professional skills, imparted? Who is responsible for seeing that successive generations of modelers and gamers are adequately prepared and knowledgeable about the experiences, trials, successes, and failures of those who have preceded them? What institutional mechanism exists to gather together various professionals' experience for the purpose of improving current practice and performance? Until these questions can be answered—and they cannot at the moment—the profession is not likely to progress much beyond its current status of an expensive hobby.

Ideally, actual research needs and personnel requirements should be communicated to educational institutions so that the training of the next generation of military analytic specialists could take into account the needs and potentials of the current and future national-security environment. Because universities have virtually no exposure to work in military modeling or the personnel responsible for it, few programs specifically prepare upcoming generations of military analysts. Programs are needed that would emphasize the substantive issues treated in most military MSGs, in addition to more focused technical courses of study in the traditional disciplines of operations research and computer science. The goals of these programs should be, first, to train aspiring analysts to understand better than they presently do the substantive issues involved in military analyses and, second, to encourage those with substantive preferences to become more knowledgeable than they usually are about the methodological requirements of this kind of work.

We have repeatedly noted the disjunction between research and operational activities. Because model builders are insufficiently in contact with those in research and training institutions, the flow of operational questions and problems into the research setting is inadequate, and the counterflow of promising research findings is likewise much weaker than it should be. We believe that improved connections between training institutions and operational agencies, in the form of more and better-prepared analysts, would help to offset this deficiency.

JOURNALS

Professional journals have both technical and substantive responsibilities that have not been thoroughly exploited and discharged. On the technical side, military analyses are seldom found in the *Journal of the Operations Research Society of America*, although this has not always been the case. The Military Operations Research Society conducts periodic meetings and publishes proceedings. The published information is usually classified, however, and does not circulate far beyond the society's restricted membership. An unclassified, widely circulated version of these proceedings would add significantly to the available body of knowledge and would do much to improve communication between insiders and concerned outsiders. The Institute of Management Sciences could publish military management analyses, including MSG-based studies, in *Management Science*, but it rarely does. Perhaps a special section devoted entirely to military studies could be created within this journal. *Simulation & Games*, a journal mainly concerned with educational MSGs, has occasionally published articles on free-form, political, diplomatic, and military games; this tendency could be encouraged.

On the substantive side, the journals *Survival, World Politics, International Security*, and *Comparative Strategy* and the *Journal of Conflict Resolution* emphasize, in varying degrees, research on national-security issues. None, however, appears to have succeeded in tapping the main body of work represented by the MSGs discussed in this book. Because the aims of these and other, related professional publications have been defined over the years to exclude, for the most part, active participation by the military-analysis community, there is ample reason to establish a high-quality professional journal devoted to substantive military analyses.

We have made an effort to review and evaluate some of the professional literature in the field of modeling and gaming.[20] This effort, we believe, could easily be institutionalized and would do much to create needed standards and the expectation that written work might be appraised by professional colleagues and peers. The National Science Foundation might sponsor this sort of appraisal and dissemination; the existing Rand-sponsored effort might serve at least as a point of departure for a fuller, continuing effort.

Standards

In the interests of professional development, operational MSGs might be appraised according to several distinct dimensions, such as their theoretical bases and content, their technical worth, the ethical possibilities built into the formulations, and their pragmatic or utilitarian aspects. Each of these important topics is worth extended discussion, and any good evaluation of an MSG should treat them in some detail. Of the few evaluations that are made, many are inadequate. Not only do they contribute little to professional development, but they also jeopardize the productive development of methodologies because of the indiscriminate and often unfounded claims made on behalf of the work.

The objective of the profession should be nothing less than the implementation of comprehensive, thorough, and consistent standards of evaluation for substantive contributions; we are presently far from approaching that goal. Rigorous and systematic evaluations of operational military MSGs are seriously needed. Individual initiative has not been adequate to date, nor has it been institutionalized to the point where evaluation is carried out with "comprehensiveness, competence, reliability, independence, promptitude, and economy."[21] This point has been stressed by a panel of the National Academy of Sciences: "Even when the proponents of a technology (whether in the government or in the private sector) seek financial support from public revenues, their own assessments still provide the basic inputs into the political system.[22]

Evaluating an MSG is a difficult task. While it may, in principle, be checked by anyone who acquires the necessary skills, such evaluations are sporadic. It has been suggested that checks are not routinely made because of a "conspiratorial silence of experts."[23] Whatever the reasons, the fact remains that no generally acceptable standards exist by which an MSG's technical merits may be judged.

Wherever the fundamental perspectives of the modeler and

the policymaker or other user differ, evaluation is needed. The need is greatest in terms of the variables and parameters selected for inclusion in an MSG. The ways in which these items are arranged form a concrete theoretical statement, the implications of which must be evaluated individually.

Wherever multiple representations of complex phenomena, such as the structure and process of war, are not developed and considered, evaluation is also needed. As Robert P. Bush and Frederick Mosteller note, "Almost any sensible model with two or three free parameters . . . can closely fit the curve, and so other criteria must be invoked when one is comparing several models," a point that leads them to recommend developing multiple models to explain the context being modeled.[24] Wherever an MSG has been seriously at odds with reality, evaluation is needed. That is to say, "the appropriateness of the operational indices" must be determined, and an evaluator must ensure that they remain "chronologically pertinent to the ordering of . . . events as the future unfolds."[25]

Wherever the ethical ramifications and limitations of an MSG are not explicitly considered, evaluation is needed. This issue has been raised by Robert A. Dahl and Charles E. Lindblom in the context of determining and weighting preferences; it is equally applicable to the modeling field. They contend that it is impossible to quantify everything of importance, particularly preferences, which are always numerous and conflicting and are often unknown, particularly if they have not been experienced. Much factual knowledge is poorly articulated. Finally, they note, mathematics and machine calculations cannot replace human decision makers. "Someone must control those who run the calculations and machines. Someone must control these controllers, etc. At every point there would be opportunities for attempting to feed into the calculator one's own preferences. Doubtless, pressure groups would organize for just such a purpose."[26] To us, these fears seem realistic.

Wherever an MSG's purpose and use cannot be determined and correctly matched, evaluation is needed. Whether an MSG is intended for operational, training, experimental, entertainment, or some other purposes has fundamental implications for the criteria of evaluation. The question "Is the

MSG good?" should be rephrased as "Is the MSG feasible in the context of a specific application?"

No single type of evaluation is most important; determining an MSG's suitability to its potential operational applications merits detailed consideration, however. Operational MSGs might be expected to reflect the biases of decision makers who use them. But, as noted earlier, to the extent that the model builder wins out in the "clash of interest and utility," operational applications will be slighted.[27] To the extent that an MSG is biased toward "pure" scientific characteristics—measurement and theory building, for instance—its appropriateness as a tool for decision making may be diminished. Strong statistical assumptions may have been made, for instance, or the common assumption that all but one of the relevant factors remain unaltered may have been invoked to clarify and make tractable a difficult problem; these and other technical procedures may bias and limit an MSG's operational utility.

A CHECKLIST

When an MSG is being constructed for operational purposes, concern for the practical or substantive problem has rightly been considered to be fundamental. "Experience suggests," writes Robert K. Merton, "that the policymaker seldom formulates his practical problem in terms sufficiently precise to permit the researcher to design an appropriate investigation . . . This initial clarification of the practical problem, therefore, is the first crucial step."[28] The question that is actually addressed depends to a large extent on the researcher's skill, interest, and sensitivity in understanding the decision maker's practical problem. After the question has been agreed upon, subject to marginal reformulation as the work progresses, its importance for the decision maker should be determined. Its usefulness may be assessed in terms of the decision maker's control over the variables included in the question, or in terms of other suitable criteria. If there is some agreement that an answer to the question would be useful and that the decision maker does indeed have a measure of control, then more specific, evaluative questions can be asked.

Although no set of questions or criteria for the feasibility or

desirability of producing an operational MSG will be definitive, the following should serve to initiate discussion:

Are the variables related to the practical problem accessible,
accurate, appropriate, or measurable at acceptable cost?

Does a good data bank containing these variables already
exist? Is it accessible? Are the variables in it flexible, usable,
and documented?

Is there sufficient, reliable theory concerning the problem to
allow the construction of an MSG affording good representation? Are the phenomena that are encompassed well
understood?

Will it be necessary to consider alternative theoretical possibilities and to construct different models of the phenomena? If so, are data available or are the prospects for
obtaining them acceptable, relative to their cost?

To the extent that these questions cannot be answered constructing operational MSGs may be a waste of time and other
scarce resources. Alternative approaches, including collecting
the necessary data, conducting further research, or doing more
thinking about the problem, may be more appropriate and potentially more productive.

The evaluation of existing operational MSGs requires a different set of questions:

Is the disparity between the output of the MSG and the decision maker's requirements so great that the MSG is rejected out of hand? Can this disparity be reduced at a
reasonable cost in time, effort, and money?

Are the output and input of the MSG generally intelligible?
Are they in a form that is intelligible to the decision maker?

Do the results of the MSG offend common sense?

Are elements of the identified problem excluded in the interests of generalization or precision? If so, how are accommo-
dations made in moving from the model results to formal
and substantive conclusions?

Do the modeled assumptions lend themselves to critical analysis by those with real information from the system being modeled? Are these assumptions examined?

Can the logical implications of the MSG be traced and assessed as to their likely impact on output?

Has the MSG been made static and descriptive in the interest of simplification? If so, how are adjustments made to account for the complex and dynamic properties of the problem?

Is the MSG able to predict, through reconstruction, the time series upon which it is formulated? Has it been able to predict time series from the reference system developed subsequent to the MSG's formulation?

Does the MSG reproduce the behavior of the system being modeled?

Does the MSG reproduce the behavior of its constituent subsystems and elements, or does it yield only accurate total output measures?

Is it possible to include submodels or to change individual behavioral relationships or parameter values that appear to have a bearing on the problem without destroying the processing, logical, or qualitative behavior of the MSG? Can this be done without significantly increasing its operating costs?

Have relevant and important variables, as determined empirically and by sensitivity testing, been omitted in the interests of precision or economy?

If there are known structural changes in the empirical context, are provisions made in the MSG to capture these? Or, are these changes assumed or ignored?

If these questions are not satisfactorily answered or are not even raised, it is unlikely that the MSG in question will ever be useful as an operational device.

THE PROFESSIONAL STAKES

Decision makers and the general public have often been led to expect far too much from operational MSG activities that are concerned with difficult, basically political questions, such as what the goals of the nation should be in terms of its national security and defense, what decision makers and the public should do about realizing these goals, and how policies should be framed and executed to accomplish them. Unrealistic expectations may arise if the limits and possibilities of present-day MSGs are not clearly understood. Predictions are expected, for example, before even the crudest understanding of a problem has been achieved. Absolute certainty about the capabilities of extraordinarily complex weapons systems is expected even when no one has any idea under what circumstances or even whether they will be called on to perform. Precise cost specifications are demanded as a matter of course in areas where technological miracles will have to be performed. At best, MSGs can help to answer questions about large-scale structures and gross interactions in a moderately well defined setting. As important as these functions are to a developing profession and discipline, by themselves they are generally unsatisfactory as guides to public decisions and policy.[29]

The tragic fact about many innovations, including some of the modeling and gaming techniques considered here, is that as the innovation diffuses, it is distorted, abused, or exploited for private gain. Quite typically, early claims of miracle cures achieved with MSGs have led to bitter disillusionment.[30] Even partial incorporation based on a more realistic assessment of the true worth of an innovation can proceed, if at all, only after much careful matching of need and capability. This chapter, and indeed this entire book, is directed largely to the difficult task of generating criteria for the realistic measurement of a promising collection of innovations. The many tasks in professional development that remain to be accomplished are formidable obstacles to achieving this goal.[31]

The profession and the field have grown up rapidly and without clear guidance, but professionalization has finally begun. Coordination, standards, communication, independent evaluation, review, and accounting activities are healthy indicators of a new awareness that will eventually advance the collective and individual interests of the profession.

The Dimensions of the Problem

Far more than talk is needed, however. Since the late 1960s, the Military Operations Research Society and the Operations Research Society of America have convened panels to discuss professional development. The proceedings of each of these meetings have been published and provide accounts of debates on the various issues, but professional practice continues much as before.[32] In 1971, the General Accounting Office (GAO) stated flatly that there were "no Government-wide ADP documentation standards."[33] In 1973, the GAO recommended that the Department of Defense "formally adopt guidelines for reporting of study results similar to those of the Operations Research Society of America,"[34] which developed its guidelines in 1971 in the wake of the celebrated controversy among analysts over the antiballistic missile. Also in 1973, the GAO recommended the establishment of a "requirement for periodic, independent technical reviews of computer models to insure continued improvement in their development and employment as well as in the studies in which they are used."[35] As far as we can determine, no such reviews have been undertaken. In 1974, the GAO was still able to conclude, "Our current study showed that the documentation guidelines at Federal agencies were still inadequate."[36] In 1975, a study sponsored by the National Science Foundation determined that only about 20 percent of the nonmilitary models funded by the federal government could pass a minimal standard for documentation.[37] And, finally, in 1976, the GAO, evidently even more impatient with the lack of progress in these areas, stated that "many model development efforts experienced large cost overruns, prolonged delays in completion, and total user dissatisfaction with the information obtained from the model." Its report recommended that the General Services Administration and the Department of Commerce undertake "prompt and positive action . . . on our recommendations to provide the needed guidance and standards. The findings in this and previous GAO reports show that much of the money spent by the Government for model development is wasted."[38]

Unfortunately, the importance of these problems is by no means generally appreciated throughout the Department of Defense, as a letter from the Acting Assistant Secretary of Defense to James H. Hammond, the official in charge of the GAO's 1973 inquiry, indicates: "As to the recommendation for establishment of more formal guidelines, it is the opinion of the [Department of Defense] that adequate guidelines are present in existing directives and manuals, and that extension of reporting requirements is unnecessary."[39]

As much as anything else, the issue of professionalism is one of will. Modelers and gamers must exhibit their willingness to follow the guidelines of their profession. Model buyers must demonstrate their willingness to impose sanctions against substandard individual and institutional performance and to pay for evaluation. Individual analysts must be willing to adhere to scientific principles of conduct to a far greater extent than they presently do. Unless these actions are accomplished—and in the near future—the modeling professional may shortly have to spend more time defending his models than developing and using them.

18 | Improving Stewardship

> To the extent that the bureaucrats can keep the facts that
> underlie their decisions to themselves, their power is en-
> hanced. Conversely, to the extent that the public is in-
> formed, *their* power is enhanced.
>
> Martin H. Seiden, *Who Controls the Mass Media?*

THE GENERAL DISCIPLINE of modeling, gaming, and simulation is highly diverse and encompasses at least four different subject areas, each
of which has its own criteria for validation and its own measures for cost and effectiveness. It is thus a difficult entity to
grasp analytically. Nevertheless, we shall venture our opinions on the significance of the results of our survey in the sections that follow.

The Significance of the Survey Results

PURPOSES

Evaluations of weapons systems, performed primarily by
the individual military services for their own use, are the predominant application of MSGs, in terms of both the absolute
level of activity and total expenditures. Ironically, expenditures and public knowledge about gaming and simulation are
inversely proportional. Free-form gaming has achieved continuing publicity, but expenditures are trifling compared with
those for all-machine, technical evaluations. Many models,
simulations, and games are literally unknown outside a small
coterie of users and producers.

The degree of knowledge that anyone even in this group
may have about a particular MSG is evidently limited. Many
incomplete replies, in which the respondents had little confidence, were obtained on questionnaires from responsible and
knowledgeable professionals. The fact that several respon-

275

dents took more than seventy hours to complete the question-naire reinforces this impression. Moreover, a large amount of what is essentially research money is being spent in the absence of rigorous and accepted research standards. As a result, basic knowledge about both substantive and procedural matters is neglected. Very little is being spent on validation or on basic research about MSG methods, data, and uses; as a result, the credibility of gaming and simulation remains limited.

In our opinion, in-house technical-evaluation models are being produced in large numbers without sufficient attention to quality and scientific rigor. We found that, in many cases, in-house work has ignored scientific standards of data collection, management, and validation; that documentation of in-house work is often very poor, a failing that is frequently rationalized on the grounds that the work is not meant to get outside the builder's shop; and that about half the sampled MSGs were not externally reviewed, with most respondents rejecting the need for such reviews on bureaucratic rather than scientific grounds.

PRODUCTION

The evident preference among builders and users for large, all-machine models and simulations is questionable on several grounds. Large-scale, finely detailed MSGs that try to address problems containing significant uncertainties may serve only to generate errors and clarify nothing.[1] Given what appear to be poor data, extremely fine temporal and spatial levels of model resolution, and low levels of demonstrated concern for supporting research, the reliability of the MSGs produced may be doubtful. Large models are usually complicated and expensive to build and use, require extended periods of time to operate and interpret, and are the least defensible types scientifically. They are affected very quickly by changes in purpose and personnel, bad documentation, gaps in logic, and problems in preparing, maintaining, and validating data.

If large models must be produced, the key to control seems to be in continuity of personnel. Staff changes decrease use of an MSG because new personnel do not know what a model is supposed to do, how it does it, or why. Where sunk costs are great, the large and expensive model tends to be used anyway, even though none of its caretakers can determine its validity for new applications. Documentation should ameliorate this problem, but it seldom does.

OPERATIONS

We believe that difficulties with documentation are more basic than the questionnaire replies indicate. The cost of documentation standards—that is, of requiring documentation to meet certain specific criteria—is very low, considering their significant contribution to better management control. The need for standards is particularly great in the case of very large simulations. When generations of programmers modify programs without updating the documentation carefully, simulations can become useless.

Many capabilities built into MSGs have never been subjected to validation. Not only is their empirical basis dubious or lacking, but few efforts are being made to collect missing or questionable input data or to execute sensitivity analyses according to an appropriate experimental design. The lack of sensitivity analysis is related to deficiencies in estimating the validity of input parameters. Neither of these matters is currently taken seriously. Over all, there is less than a fifty-fifty chance that a sensitivity test will be performed; when it is, the outcome frequently goes unrecorded.

Most of the MSGs we surveyed had not been subjected to any external review, with the result that many contain implicit and intangible input the existence of and rationale for which have not been documented in any way. The institutional memory in the general system is not extensive. Even for MSGs of fairly recent vintage, respondents seemed unable to answer technical and cost questions with much confidence. A comprehensive review of data-validity problems is needed, and some strong corrective measures should be instituted.[2]

USE

The present level of professional communication, in our opinion, is dangerously low. Better coordination, documentation, and examination of use are needed at the operational, experimental, and administrative interfaces. It is not enough that a study be finished according to formal contract specifications; what becomes of the study and how it is used are far more important. What is learned from the model, and how much, must be evaluated so that future resources can be expended more rationally. Perhaps a moratorium on expenditures for new studies should be declared until existing ones have been properly evaluated. Technical evaluations of weapons that are used very little or not at all, or that are misused, for example, may be worse than no studies at all. Management policies such as the frequent turnover of key personnel in some military activities, coupled with uneven documentation, account in large measure for the ineffective use of models. If no one remembers why or for whom a particular model was built or how it operates, it is unlikely to be used correctly; even worse, a new model that will do the same job may have to be built from scratch. If documentation is scanty or completely absent, the waste becomes virtually certain.

It is difficult to determine the influence of the MSGs we surveyed; half of them did not even result directly in a briefing. Written comments suggest that they "did the job," but little information was provided on the importance of the task or of the policy decisions that depended on it. Documentation accompanying any MSG should indicate clearly what it has been used for, who has used it, and when it was used. The dearth of written scenarios and the lack of explicit consideration of intangible and uncertain elements are matters of concern to us. Well-specified numerical models can be misused all too easily by changing the problem context or interpretation. A model that is impressive in one context may be inappropriate in another, even if specific data for the hard numbers are adequate. The value of a model depends on skillful interaction among those who know its original uses, those who determine its new purposes and applications, those who set the soft numbers, and those who provide the background interpretations. Little evidence is available on how these tasks are currently being performed, if they are being done at all. The bias of most of the builders and caretakers we surveyed toward engineering and applied science appears likely to make replication of their MSGs risky.

What all of these findings mean, stated briefly, is that there is no substitute for people who know their business. One of the real dangers that we perceive lies in the poverty of scientific interaction between those who know their business and those who are trying to generate business. The Department of Defense has nurtured a group of specialists who are doing some competent and useful work, but there are few ways for them to communicate their knowledge to those in the broader civilian sector.

The tenuous nature of much of the data being used, the immaturity of validation procedures, and the relative neglect of important scientific and operational procedures like sensitivity analysis and scrutiny of the appropriateness of particular methods to specific issues indicate that advocacy, rather than scientific preference, prevails in decision making. Can scientific content be improved and unfounded advocacy be reduced? Generally, the answer is yes, although the problem is difficult.

One desirable innovation would be to make the advocacy process two-sided rather than one-sided, as it is now.[3] The quality of the debate on weapons procurement would be improved, for example, if legislators as well as Defense Department proponents had the benefit of professional advice and assistance. Existing procedures for challenging the assumptions and quality of work done in support of any one position, system, or decision are simply not adequate. Lawyers and accountants may be able to win debating points from the engineers, generals, and mathematicians, but the process is still far from a rational, let alone an ideal, one.

COSTS

Cost accounting for current MSG activities has serious deficiencies, even allowing for its difficulty. Better management control requires that some record of cost be kept on the initiation, production, operation, and evaluation of every MSG. Even crude figures accurate to within 100 percent of the actual costs would be an improvement over current information.

Whose responsibility is cost control, and in whose interest? Developers have little reason to be interested in costs except as they contribute to their own revenues. Questions about alternatives to modeling and simulation are seldom explored in the operational setting, and current procedures do not seem to include formal consideration of whether there is a cheaper, easier way to proceed. Consideration of alternative techniques should be a managerial concern; the choice of the most appropriate method should be dealt with at the technical level.

More than one-third of the respondents to our questionnaire either did not or could not reply consistently to the most elementary cost questions. Moreover, those who did respond had a low level of confidence in their answers. That responsible people were unable to supply even rudimentary cost data suggests that cost accounting has been neglected. It is evident that cost data, perhaps conceived primarily as relating to investment, quickly become separated from the work itself. As a result, users, caretakers, and even builders have only vague notions of cost a year or so after a project has been undertaken.

Projects budgeted at between $200,000 and $300,000 appear to be relatively easy to fund. Judging from our survey data, it is far easier to obtain two separate budgets for two different models in this range than it is to obtain one for a single model at $400,000 to $600,000. Families of MSGs have been maintained for years with separately labeled components funded separately and used and evaluated independently. Many appear to build on the same basic work and should be considered as such. Most money seems to be spent where professional visibility and active participation by higher-echelon personnel are minimal. This finding raises an important question about the effectiveness of expenditures. Are we trying to compare items that cannot be compared?

Machine models and simulations appear to favor so-called value-free engineering work and are primarily produced by bright lieutenants, captains, majors, or possibly colonels, in cooperation with civilian contractors. Such work can easily lead to larger studies that generate briefings for colonels and generals and their civilian counterparts. The context, including verbal descriptions and scenarios, and details about the purposes and limitations of a model are seldom spelled out. Man-machine exercises, in contrast, are frequently used for teaching or training in the staff colleges. As a result, there is some chance that a two- or three-star general or admiral might have learned something as a result of a man-machine exercise he participated in. Such activities may also be used in an experimental laboratory where the staff are not necessarily military and where the purpose is altogether different. As noted, the least expensive activities are the political and military exercises that may have commanded the attention of the highest-level personnel at one time or another. The real value of free-form military games, however, is a question that deserves further study.

Little attention has been paid to the nature of claims that a certain study has influenced policy. An imaginative briefing by someone like Herman Kahn or a political and military exercise run by someone like Albert Wohlstetter and including high-level participants may have had more influence on policy than most multimillion-dollar models and simulations. On the other hand, neither may have made any difference. Much depends on the timeliness of an exercise and its relevance to current problems. Questions like those just listed must be made explicit. It may then be possible to take a more objective look at the routine expenditure of millions of dollars for middle-level, engineering-type MSGs.

Areas of Ignorance

Total experience in modeling and gaming is unnecessarily and harmfully fragmented. Groups of defense managers are often unaware of the existence of others doing fundamentally the same work elsewhere. The solution to the problem has two basic dimensions: the creation of information about the collective experience and the subsequent retention of this information and its transmission to others involved in the production and use of military MSGs. The first part of the solution responds to the pressing needs for documentation, library efforts, and a host of management-control procedures that would together generate much needed information about current processes and practices; the second, to the need to understand the current variety of impediments to communication and of related design elements to overcome these impediments.

As we mentioned in chapter 11, no one has a complete enough overview of the whole context; without it, the system responsible for military MSGs drifts aimlessly. Who keeps tabs on individual conditions and standards and on industry norms? Who evaluates the effects of deficient documentation practices on the entire enterprise and the impact of the high turnover of military users and producers on the quality and effectiveness of MSGs? Who studies the implications of the apparent trend toward increased capacity and willingness to build and use MSGs in house? Who is responsible for searching the overall context for cues to research that is likely to have payoffs not only for the military but for the profession as a whole? Who initiates transfers of knowledge from one operational or analytic setting to others? Virtually no one.

Detailed investigation of the obstacles to the creation and transmission of knowledge is needed to determine the effects of proprietary motivations on the accurate representation of MSG production and use; the extent to which entrepreneurial incentives and impulses override scientific incentives that might otherwise produce effective and efficient analyses; the results of individuals' desires to advance the state of the art rather than to merely solve the client's problems; the effect of classification on external review and scrutiny; and the extent to which classification is invoked to obscure the failures of questionable work. The results of such investigation would go a long way toward resolving the broader issue of who has power in the military analysis system. Our own analyses of the decision-making process, described in the following section, attempts to provide some insight into these and other important considerations relating to communication, professionalism, MSG standards and use, and power.

Communications and the Decision-Making Process

Our earlier analysis of the decision-making process focused on the connections among universities, the formal intelligence community, weapons developers, defense-research contractors, and the military decision-making bureaucracy. At present, the academic community is not well integrated into the process at any time during the life of the average MSG; participation is limited to the isolated scholar who acts as a consultant for brief periods. This state of affairs has been brought about jointly by the academic experts, who have eschewed responsibility for participating in military analyses, and by the military analysts, who have been reluctant to expose their analytic work to outside scrutiny. The formal intelligence community has traditionally provided early warnings of potential threats to the national security but has done so with scant technical expertise or capability in model building. Furthermore, competition among the various intelligence agencies has tended to block communication when MSGs are initiated. By default and by choice, their initiation has fallen mainly to the defense-research contractors and the in-house analytic staffs, both of which groups receive periodic stimulation from manufacturers of weapons as they pursue their own promotional activities.

One logical link in the flow of information occurs during initiation. Because those who produce MSGs tend to be insulated from the initiation phase, demands for new information to structure their MSGs do not regularly flow back to the intelligence community or to the outside. Hence, we see model builders using data that are outmoded and of questionable validity rather than making their needs known to those who could provide better raw information. If they are not told what the analytic needs are, intelligence specialists cannot be blamed for being unresponsive to the modeler's requirements.[4] Communication may also be distorted by too much concern with portrayals of enormous enemy threats and our own deficient capabilities. The approach of the "worst-case analysis" can produce results that are either erroneous or never fully disclosed. The impact of salesmen during the promotional phase has added to the general confusion about what areas need analysis and what kinds of analytic techniques should be used. Mechanisms should be established to monitor sales activities and to identify and correct misperceptions.

Because communication and information are limited during the earliest phases of the decision-making process, it is little wonder that prescriptive actions are applied only to mundane contractual matters, with no serious concern for assessing the importance of the problem, determining the appropriateness of those who have been selected to work on it, or deciding whether the research resources might not be spent in more productive ways than those being negotiated in the contract. As indicated earlier, the decision maker or user of the MSG is not usually an active participant during the prescriptive phase;

he has virtually no contact with the outside world of scholarship or with the public; and, in many cases, those about to be charged with building a model do not have access to prescriptive discussions. Communication between the research salesman, the research team, and the client is critical at this juncture. What is being promised in hopes of securing the contract and what can realistically be expected to be delivered must be specified. The relationship between what the decision maker needs and what he can use, on the one hand, and what his bureaucratic agent imagines these needs to be, on the other, must also be made clear.

Communication among groups of participants during the production phase also tends to be fragmented. The decision maker and his representatives hire the model builders as experts, with the result that the builders are rarely questioned about the assumptions they bring to the analysis, about the appropriateness of the techniques they use to analyze the problem, or about their adherence to recognized professional and technical standards. There is likewise little input from the decision-making side; the user's real, stated, and unstated purposes for conducting the work, his resource capabilities, whether they are reflected in the work, and the usefulness of the various elements in the MSG in assessing items of direct interest to that user are rarely stated explicitly. Without participation by and communication between these key groups, these factors will remain obscure.[5]

The isolation of the operations phase from the rest of the process and its restriction to a handful of highly skilled technicians have identifiable costs, as well. In the absence of communication among groups of experts, how does any given MSG receive the scientific scrutiny that is required to ensure that its technical details are defensible? What media exist to report on tests and other validation efforts undertaken to ensure the scientific merits of the work? Since the decision maker or user is not involved directly during the operations phase, what assurance is there that the MSG is pertinent to the real problems at issue?

Actual use of the MSG should turn information back into the process; much of this information, however, derives from participants who have had little or nothing to do with the production and operation of the MSG. For instance, the salesman reappears and intervenes to protect proprietary, not scientific, interests. Briefers have been known to include findings and conclusions that were never even considered in the formal analysis. Outside academic experts are seldom included in the efforts to generate an MSG that works in some rudimentary sense, yet they may bring information into the context that bears on the broader problem under consideration, even though it has no relationship to the particular analytic instrument. Communication requirements during the actual use of the MSG might be called "utility analyses." Information on how the MSG was used and how these uses accord with the purposes delineated at the beginning of the project, how often the MSG has been used, by whom, at what cost, and with what results would clearly help those involved in the evaluation of the results.

Many important questions arise in the evaluative phase as well: What technical standards have been used or developed in the process of building and using an MSG? Have they been communicated to other current and potential participants in the process? Did outside professionals have a hand in the evaluation of the MSG, and were the model builders certified as a result of their performance? What about the interface between the builders and decision makers in the military and in Congress? Have the latter been apprised of extraordinarily commendable or reprehensible performances related to any given piece of analysis? What kinds of lessons have been learned, and how are they communicated to other users, builders, or funders? Have technical lessons been shared with those responsible for the training of future generations of model builders and users?

Finally, a number of issues must be addressed in the termination phase of an MSG: What rationales were employed in the decision to terminate the MSG? Who decided to cut off its use, to terminate the services of participating outside or inhouse groups, or to modify, store, or scrap an MSG? How are these choices communicated? If new research or operational questions or requirements are discovered while an ongoing activity is being terminated, how are they communicated to those most likely to be able to answer or satisfy them? What safeguards exist to prevent the needless and costly resale and regeneration of an old MSG to unsuspecting users?

This summary stresses the need for continuity of participation among key personnel throughout the life of an MSG; currently, no single identifiable group participates in the process from start to finish. It also stresses the need for a variety of information about the MSG and the communication of that information to diverse individuals involved both directly and indirectly in the modeling enterprise. Professional review and oversight are crucial elements in both of these points.

PROFESSIONAL REVIEW

At present, MSGs are not routinely or systematically subjected to outside professional evaluation. Part of the problem results from failures of communication, and part from deficient professional expectations and demands about performance. Operational models should receive the most stringent appraisal possible. In view of the large amounts of cash involved, it is surprising that thorough, detailed, and accessible evaluations have not already been forthcoming. The lack of any institutional provision for effective review is a serious structural weakness in the profession and discipline. Pluralism seems to be called for to avoid premature limitations on creativity in this area; sets of questions and general areas of investigation might be standardized, however, for the use of those responsible for model assessment.

The few responsible critiques that are made receive only limited dissemination. They occasionally appear in specialized journals or tightly controlled technical memoranda or are spread by word of mouth in limited technical circles, but this process is no more satisfactory than the procedure by which individuals take it upon themselves to comment on the MSGs in the first place. Proper institutions are needed to oversee appraisal of MSGs. Agencies that already exist at several levels of government might serve this purpose, or a national board of review might be established, composed of distinguished model builders, social scientists, military analysts, and decision makers. The Institute of Management Sciences, the Operations Research Society of America, or other professional bodies, if properly supported and chartered, might serve as effective prototypes. Panels of the National Academy of Sciences are another possibility.

Some new method of reviewing professional and technical publication is also needed. Professional associations might retain a review panel of ten or twelve scholars to review MSG documentation continuously and to consider detailed technical issues and questions related to the purposes and uses of MSGs. All members of the panel would review the same information but would work independently to avoid developing group biases. Their opinions could be polled by any of several available methods to obtain unbiased group evaluations. The composite review would then be published in an appropriate journal. For some models, a numerical evaluation might suffice; for others, such as those on which reviewers strongly disagreed, more than one interpretive review might be warranted.

CREATING BETTER INFORMATION

Documentation is an important element of improved communications and a significant focus for some of the managerial improvements discussed above. At present, however, it is largely uneven, inaccessible, or nonexistent. Although the problem has not gone unnoticed by responsible officials in the federal government, their initiatives to improve the situation have yet to be implemented widely or authoritatively.[6]

The character and extent of the problem are reflected in our survey findings. As indicated earlier, those farthest removed from actual use of MSGs provided the most glowing assessments of the quality of documentation, while those directly responsible for the MSGs overwhelmingly assessed the quality of documentation as either average or poor. This state of affairs was also found in the companion nonmilitary survey: "Reviewing the documentation available for many of the models included in the survey makes us doubt that as many as 20–26 percent of the models funded by the federal agencies would meet such a standard [of excellence] in practice."[7]

We believe that adequate standards exist to begin the long overdue task of documentation. In 1974, in fact, the National Bureau of Standards established a task force on documentation, which developed a standard form for recording and reporting summary information about software, including MSGs. Both the Office of Management and Budget and the General Services Administration, under different auspices, have a responsibility to see that these standards are met. Nonetheless, we are unaware of any concerted effort to implement and enforce these standards.

In our view, the minimal documentation necessary for any operational MSG that is to be run elsewhere or be reviewed by outside professionals comprises the following elements:[8]

- A program listing
- A listing of variables with definitions
- Flow charts
- A verbal description of the program
- An operator's manual
- A programmer's manual
- A summary of the theoretical bases of the MSG
- Data-reduction methods and techniques used to specify relationships and to assign input values to the parameters
- Cost data related to production, operation, and use
- A listing of personnel involved in all phases of the MSG's life cycle
- A statement of the existence and history of external professional review, including findings and remedial steps taken
- A utility analysis, with details on types of use, frequency of use, cost, and assessments of outcome

Insistence on even this much documentation will undoubtedly provoke charges that professionals' time is being unnecessarily wasted.[9] We view the matter differently and contend that the lack of documentation is perhaps the most glaring single deficiency in the entire system responsible for operational MSGs.

Increased documentation and inspection of MSGs may have some unexpected and unfortunate consequences, however. As evaluators and auditors try to penetrate more deeply into the activities of operating agencies, the operators may respond by manipulating or withholding detailed information. One result might be that the breakdown of communication would be intensified.[10]

IMPEDIMENTS TO COMMUNICATION

The orientation and purposes of the model builder and the decision maker are more often conflicting than complementary. Within many agencies, a wide gulf between modelers and nonmodelers results in a reduction of the already limited interchange between them. In addressing a modeling problem, modelers, in general, have great self-confidence, technical optimism, and a strong predilection to view the world as orderly and usually quantifiable. Nonmodelers frequently resent this self-confidence, feel they know better than to be overly optimistic about many of the problems confronting them, and can seldom reduce the complexity of their everyday world to orderly, numerical dimensions. Modelers use a specialized jargon that does not lend itself to clear exposition or to easy communication with nonspecialists. In addition, modelers seldom see the importance of explaining their work either to fellow professionals or to the decision maker who will use the MSG.

Interpersonal communication is unduly obstructed by these factors; the likelihood of communication with others outside the modeling group is further minimized by the lack of attention to documentation. Up to now, the model builder's job has been the production of MSGs, not documentation and dissemination. In part, this state of affairs has resulted from the educational process that has taught model builders to view their roles rather narrowly. For the most part, however, it derives from the fact that projects are often behind schedule or problems more·difficult than they were expected to be and that they often produce results their creators are not especially anxious to disseminate.[11]

Other impediments to communication also exist, and their impact on the overall decision-making process must be determined separately in each case. First, MSGs are complex and confusing to the nonspecialist; hence they engender suspicion and distrust more often than acceptance and confidence. Second, the strong reliance on quantification needed to specify and operate an MSG leads many decision makers to reject all results because they do not conform to their detailed understanding of the actual situation being modeled. Third, modelers often fail to learn the sometimes subtle, but always important, details of the real context; such partial and superficial understanding leads to MSGs that are easily dismissed.

Strategies to Improve Management

We sampled opinion on various mechanisms that could, in principle, help to resolve current communication difficulties; the results indicate the extent of those problems and suggest several ways in which resolution might be sought.

We asked the respondents to our questionnaire for their professional opinions about a number of issues, including the potential usefulness of clearinghouses, regional centers, and external professional review boards. On the question of establishing a clearinghouse to coordinate information about all MSG activities within the Department of Defense (a function the Defense Documentation Center does not adequately perform), respondents were generally quite favorable. More than half thought it would be useful or highly useful (see figure 18-1).

The issue of standardization was raised twice. The first time, we asked about the advisability of increasing the standardization of gaming and simulation activity within the Department of Defense. The second time we asked, "Is it premature to try to form a professional standards committee for models, games, and simulations? Is it needed? Would it

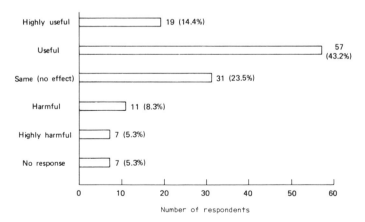

Figure 18-1. *Respondents' opinions of MSG clearinghouses.*

probably do good or harm?" The respondents' comments gave us some insight into the reasons for the pronounced opposition to standardization, which is evident in figure 18-2.

We also asked for opinions on regional centers to coordinate production, operation, and use. About 60 percent of the respondents thought such centers would be harmful or highly harmful. Another question asked whether the creation of external review boards would be an improvement; 57 percent opposed the idea, which they considered harmful or highly harmful, and said it would be impossible to staff them adequately. We asked respondents to comment further on each question. The prevailing attitude of those opposed to clearinghouses was that such facilities would add an unnecessary layer to the existing bureaucracy. Most said something like "In theory it sounds fine, but in practice it just won't work." We were struck by the extent of some of the respondents' concern about standardization of many kinds—of languages, data formats, or documentation. Many professionals considered these

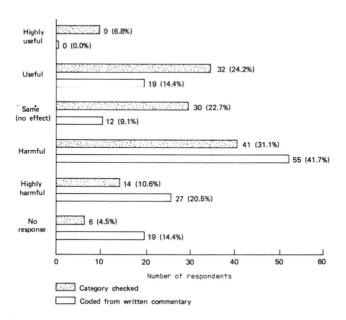

Figure 18-2. *Respondents' opinions of standardization.*

attempts premature and feared they would stifle creativity. (The few respondents who favored standardization were mainly users with little or only recent experience.) The relatively negative reaction to regional centers was also based on worry about new bureaucratic problems and the separation of models from those who understand, need, and use them. Those who could see some merit in regional centers argued that they would save money on personnel and computer resources; benefits from coordinating data-processing and computer-software systems were mentioned only occasionally.

In one of the most interesting sets of replies, 17.4 percent of the respondents indicated that an external review board would be highly harmful; 39.4 percent, that it would be harmful; and only one respondent, that it would be highly useful. The argument against the review board was that it would be impossible to assemble a panel qualified to review specific models in sufficient depth to justify the time and effort. Many respondents clearly felt that they were perfectly capable of providing all the review needed. Judging from the results of this survey and informal, supplementary interviews, however, we doubt that they are right.

All responses to opinion questions were tabulated against the respondent's own role in order to determine whether place in the decision-making process had any noticeable effect and against the service responsible for each MSG in order to judge whether organizations had systematic preferences. While no significant relationships were revealed between the respondent's role and his opinions about clearinghouses, external review, or technical coordination, other correlations were significant. Correlation of the respondent's role with his opinions about standardization, for instance, showed that funders and sponsors were most in favor of the creation of standards, with caretakers almost equally in favor; designers and builders favored them least; and users were somewhere in between (see table 18-1). The correlation of the respondent's role with his opinions about regional centers revealed that funders and sponsors were again most in favor, although less so than for standards; again, designers and builders were least in favor, but they too were less strongly committed on this issue than on standardization. (see table 18-2).

Table 18-1. Cross-tabulation of respondent's role and opinion on standardization.[a]

	OPINION							
ROLE	HIGHLY USEFUL	USEFUL	SAME	HARMFUL	HIGHLY HARMFUL	NO RESPONSE	TOTAL	PERCENT OF TOTAL
Funder or sponsor	2	10	3	3	1	0	19	(14.4)
User	2	10	10	17	2	1	42	(31.8)
Designer or builder	2	4	14	14	5	2	41	(31.1)
Caretaker	3	7	2	5	1	0	18	(13.6)
Control	0	0	0	1	1	0	2	(1.5)
Other	0	1	1	1	4	3	10	(7.6)
Total	9	32	30	41	14	6	132	—
Percent of total	(6.8)	(24.2)	(22.7)	(31.1)	(10.6)	(4.5)	—	(100.0)

a. $\chi^2 = 56.45$, with 25 degrees of freedom; $p < 0.0003$.

Table 18-2. Cross-tabulation of respondent's role and opinion on regional centers.[a]

| | OPINION | | | | | | | |
ROLE	HIGHLY USEFUL	USEFUL	SAME	HARMFUL	HIGHLY HARMFUL	NO RESPONSE	TOTAL	PERCENT OF TOTAL
Funder or sponsor	0	5	1	8	4	1	19	(14.4)
User	1	4	5	21	5	6	42	(31.8)
Designer or builder	0	6	3	18	9	5	41	(31.1)
Caretaker	0	2	0	12	0	4	18	(13.6)
Control	0	0	1	1	0	0	2	(1.5)
Other	0	0	1	1	1	7	10	(7.6)
Total	1	17	11	61	19	23	132	—
Percent of total	(0.8)	(12.9)	(8.3)	(46.2)	(14.4)	(17.4)	—	(100.0)

a. $\chi^2 = 42.53$, with 25 degrees of freedom; $p < 0.0157$.

Tabulations of service against opinions on the creation of clearinghouses are shown in table 18-3; against opinions on standardization, in table 18-4; and against opinions on technical coordination, in table 18-5.

The problems facing managers in the field of modeling and gaming are so pervasive and severe that no single strategy will suffice to deal with them. Some of the more straightforward of the multiple strategies that are called for are counteradvocacy systems, increased use of surveys and questionnaires, and greater availability of catalogs of MSGs.

Two-sided advocacy should be cultivated as balance for the lop-sided system that currently dominates the flow of information about weapons and national security. Open, regular, and more rigorous review of the millions of dollars' worth of studies and analyses, including MSGs, done annually by the Department of Defense and its various agencies is sorely needed. Defense-research contractors and in-house analytic groups have provided the department and the armed forces with a high level of professional analytic support, but Congress has little countervailing power when proposed Defense Department expenditures must be evaluated. The creation of an independent consulting group would provide legislators with the technical information and support they need to judge the merits of complex budget requests. The Defense Department's requests are based on studies and analyses with a large technical component; thus Congress and the general public would benefit from having technical expertise available to provide reasonably objective and independent assessments of those requests.

Congress's current grave misgivings about any or all arguments presented by the military has led some legislators to reject those arguments as a matter of course. The converse situation, which is equally unsatisfactory, has recently developed; legislators abdicate spending decisions to the military out of fear of being stigmatized politically. The creation and active participation of a technical analytic institution outside the Department of Defense could improve the quality of the budgetary debate by allowing the facts to emerge and be judged more directly on their merits than is currently the case.

Table 18-3. Cross-tabulation of military service and opinion on clearinghouses.[a]

	OPINION					NO		PERCENT
ROLE	HIGHLY USEFUL	USEFUL	SAME	HARMFUL	HIGHLY HARMFUL	RESPONSE	TOTAL	OF TOTAL
USA	11	25	14	6	1	2	59	(44.7)
USAF	3	8	8	1	1	5	26	(19.7)
USN	3	23	2	4	4	0	36	(27.3)
Other Defense Department	2	1	7	0	1	0	11	(8.3)
Total	19	57	31	11	7	7	132	—
Percent of total	(14.4)	(43.2)	(23.5)	(8.3)	(5.3)	(5.3)	—	(100.0)

a. χ^2 = 41.12, with 15 degrees of freedom; $p < 0.0003$.

Table 18-4. Cross-tabulation of military service and opinion on standardization.[a]

	OPINION							
ROLE	HIGHLY USEFUL	USEFUL	SAME	HARMFUL	HIGHLY HARMFUL	NO RESPONSE	TOTAL	PERCENT OF TOTAL
USA	4	19	10	20	5	1	59	(44.7)
USAF	3	3	9	4	2	5	26	(19.7)
USN	0	9	7	13	7	0	36	(27.3)
Other Defense Department	2	1	4	4	0	0	11	(8.3)
Total	9	32	30	41	14	6	132	—
Percent of total	(6.8)	(24.2)	(22.7)	(31.1)	(10.6)	(4.5)	—	(100.0)

a. $\chi^2 = 35.67$, with 15 degrees of freedom; $p < 0.0020$.

Table 18-5. Cross-tabulation of military service and opinion on technical coordination.[a]

	OPINION							
SERVICE	HIGHLY UNDESIRABLE	UNDESIRABLE	INDIFFERENT	DESIRABLE	HIGHLY DESIRABLE	NO RESPONSE	TOTAL	PERCENT OF TOTAL
USA	9	8	7	15	19	1	59	(44.7)
USAF	2	3	9	2	2	8	26	(19.7)
USN	5	7	6	11	6	1	36	(27.3)
Other Defense Department	1	0	6	2	2	0	11	(8.3)
Total	17	18	28	30	29	10	132	—
Percent of total	(12.9)	(13.6)	(21.2)	(22.7)	(22.0)	(7.6)	—	(100.0)

a. $\chi^3 = 46.85$, with 15 degrees of freedom; $p < 0.0001$.

Such an institution should not meet with disapproval in the more thoughtful quarters of the military establishment, if the congressional reaction noted previously is as prevalent as it appears to be.

The development and initial testing of our survey instrument represents at least seven or eight man-months of professional effort. The fact that another research group could use the instrument to probe nonmilitary MSGs encourages us to recommend that comparable work be undertaken periodically on a routine basis. This kind of mapping could logically be the responsibility of the National Science Foundation and the Defense Advanced Research Projects Agency; a joint venture undertaken by these two agencies might include the task of reviewing and evaluating the literature (described earlier in this book).

Some of the armed forces currently produce catalogs of active MSGs, but these listings are far from complete, are not routinely published, and suffer from limited or closely controlled distribution. The leadership demonstrated by the Studies, Analysis and Gaming Agency of the Joint Chiefs of Staff in its recent publication of a descriptive catalog of its own MSGs is commendable and should be extended to all Defense Department work.

The foregoing discussion has been aimed specifically at those who are most responsible for and able to make the changes needed in the military analysis system—program and project managers and those with whom they interact. Fundamental communication among these individuals is lacking; our survey findings and analysis consistently underscored severe deficiencies in the areas of documentation, external review, and communication between those who build and those who use military MSGs. Besides providing an understanding of possible reasons why stewardship is poorly developed, this chapter has set forth several strategies that would, if implemented authoritatively, do much to resolve many nagging problems impeding effective management. The changes we propose will not come about easily, nor will they be carried out well until those in charge realize that current practices are shortsighted and cannot continue; furthermore, they must realize that the recommended changes will, over time, work to their credit and improve the overall performance of the system in which they serve. In our final chapter, we shall summarize and integrate our many individual professional and managerial insights, findings, and recommendations to determine when, how, and with what resources specific changes can be enacted to bring total performance up to an acceptable level.

19 | Improving Performance

In this, a roughneck type of sport,
One fellow of the bolder sort
Prepares to deal some mighty smashes.
He'll get a soaking, like as not,
And what is worse, the broken pot
Could crack his head when down it crashes.

Jacques Stella, *Games and Pastimes of Childhood*

IN PREVIOUS CHAPTERS we have attempted to diagnose the multiple ailments afflicting the construction and use of operational models, simulations, and games by the military. In many cases, we have either implied or directly suggested remedial and corrective actions. In this chapter we shall attempt to collect the individual and partial recommendations made earlier and to summarize what has to be done, how much effort will be required, and who might logically assume responsibility for the changes. Much important detail is not reconstructed here; readers may wish to consult earlier discussions before deciding what they, as individuals or as members of an institution, might be willing and able to accomplish.

A number of fundamental questions underlie our recommendations for the improvement of the overall performance of the system. To what extent, for instance, can the outcomes of military models, simulations, and games be used to describe operations and systems in the real world? How well are MSGs being used to inform and improve decision making? How might these devices be made more effective, persuasive, and useful? What organizational structures and procedures might improve their usefulness? What is the current state of the art of evaluation, that is, of asking and answering hard, pertinent questions about MSGs? What is the level of professionalism in the area? How well and by what means are these devices managed by and for the Department of Defense and, by ex-

tension, the nation as a whole? We do not pretend to have answers to all of these questions; throughout this book, however,
we have tried to formulate them well enough to encourage
productive discussion and to focus attention on what appear
to us to be the major issues.

Some may view our efforts to be highly presumptuous;
others may dislike the thought of having to live with new and
possibly unnecessary controls and sanctions; still others may
not even acknowledge that the issues discussed here affect
their lives in so many critical ways. Our recommendations are
made, however, because we believe the stakes are simply too
high to allow the system to continue operating as it now does.

Before considering detailed recommendations for change, it
may be useful to restate several key facts about the system responsible for military MSGs. First, the use of MSGs is well established within the Department of Defense. Although it is
difficult to establish precise expenditures, a sum of roughly
$30–40 million is allocated to new construction each year.
About half of the MSGs built are analytic models; about 35
percent are simulations; about 10 percent, man-machine or
manual games; and the remainder, other related analytic
approaches.

Most of the MSGs (about 45 percent) are intended to perform technical evaluations. Doctrinal evaluations account for
about 20 percent, and force structure analysis, for about 30
percent. Fewer than 1 percent are devoted to political, diplomatic, and military problems and international relations, and
the proportion dedicated to research and improvement in
methodology is about 1.5 percent. By far the major use of
MSGs is for the evaluation of weapons or weapons systems;
this work is usually categorized as technical evaluation. The
least frequent, and in many ways the least expensive, application is free-form gaming of the historical variety and political
and military exercises sponsored by the Studies, Analysis, and
Gaming Agency of the Joint Chiefs of Staff. Free-form gaming
is the least tightly controlled of the various types; it receives
the most publicity, and it tends to be associated with the highest policymaking levels of the government. It also has the
greatest popular appeal, mainly because it can be understood
by the layman, has few good practitioners, and provides a

product the value of which is extremely difficult to measure.

The community of those interested in the application of MSGs is diverse, including politicians and bureaucrats who are concerned with budgeting problems but not involved substantively or directly with technical problems and military institutions directly concerned with operational problems, such as obtaining evaluations and assessments to further their immediate plans and policies, but far less concerned with technical, theoretical, or methodological issues. Those who are most closely concerned with the actual production of MSGs and the improvement of technical methods and substantive understanding split into two camps: the technocrats (engineers and mathematicians) and the behaviorists (social or behavioral scientists). The former prefer large-scale simulations or pure mathematical models, while the latter are more interested in man-machine systems and gaming exercises. The diversity of focus and training among users has made the development of professional standards for gaming and simulation a difficult task. Very different approaches have developed, with the engineering approaches, mathematical approaches, and behavioral approaches, in particular, having very little in common and suffering as a consequence. Work on game-theory and pure mathematical models has tended to be too abstract and too far removed from applications to problems to be of much practical value. Work on gaming exercises, including free-form gaming, has tended to be too far detached from rigorous and scientific norms and practices. Communication among groups concerned with operations, those working on the development of new methods, and those interested in developing standards and theory has been minimal, to the detriment of all concerned. The split between technical and behavioral approaches is marked and has limited the value of the work produced.

In spite of these negative findings, the United States is the world's most advanced nation in the uses of military models, simulations, and games. Developments in the Soviet Union appear to be ten to fifteen years behind those in the United States, and the Soviets seem to be committing many of the same errors that were made as modeling, simulation, and gaming activities evolved in the United States during the past thirty years.[1] That our primary adversary shows clear signs of inferiority in this particular arena is no cause for satisfaction; indeed, whatever edge we may possess in the general area of specifying, understanding, and managing problems needs to be increased. It is to this general objective that this book has been directed.

Specific Recommendations

Individual recommendations for change are arranged in table 19-1 according to what we judge to be the level of effort, in money, manpower, and diligence, necessary to effect the change. The three gross classifications of effort are "minimal," which should require little more than administrative or managerial attention; "moderate," the expenditure of resources for which will probably require the approval of higher authorities within the Department of Defense and other institutions; and "maximal," which includes actions that, if taken, would achieve most of the professional, managerial, and social objectives we consider worthwhile. This list is not exhaustive; other analysts and professionals might generate similar specialized lists. Ours is intended simply to respond, insofar as possible, to the needs of the current system.

Accomplishing the changes that require less effort will often make it easier to carry out related, more difficult recommendations. The publication of more military studies and analyses in the open public literture, for instance, would prepare the way for an open, public journal devoted entirely to these topics, at least in principle, by identifying goals and nurturing an audience for this kind of scholarship. If these two goals, of "minimal" and "moderate" difficulty, were achieved, "two-sided advocacy" publications, a "maximally" difficult goal, would be considerably more likely.

MINIMALLY DIFFICULT RECOMMENDATIONS

The intention of each of the recommendations requiring a minimal level of effort will be discussed briefly below. Where appropriate, likely agents or agencies are suggested (these suggestions should not be considered as directives or as defining the only way to accomplish the job at hand).

First of all, the creation of sanctions that would both reward

Table 19-1. Summary of recommendations.

GENERAL ISSUE AREA	SLIGHT LEVEL OF DIFFICULTY	MODERATE LEVEL OF DIFFICULTY	MAXIMAL LEVEL OF DIFFICULTY
Professionalism	Creation of rewards and sanctions for excellent and deficient professional practice.	Authoritative imposition of sanctions.	Exploration of legal and economic sanctions available to routinize imposition.
		Retrospective assessment of use, including quality, of military MSGs in last decade.	Continuation of assessment for subsequent efforts.
	External professional review of all military MSGs in current operation to ascertain scientific merit of each.	External professional review of all frequently used military MSGs in current inventory.	
	Professional society sponsorship of panels and seminars related to military MSG standards, ethics, and practices.		Creation of additional, in-house technical billets for master modelers and support staffs.

Table 19-1—*continued.*

GENERAL ISSUE AREA	SLIGHT LEVEL OF DIFFICULTY	MODERATE LEVEL OF DIFFICULTY	MAXIMAL LEVEL OF DIFFICULTY
Professionalism	Publication of more military MSG summaries in open literature.	Support of university and advanced service-school technical-training programs.	Creation of service academy and advanced professional-school programs in modeling and gaming.
		Development of open, public journal devoted entirely to military operational MSGs.	Two-sided advocacy publications for contentious weapon and national-security debates and issues.
Stewardship	In-service training for Defense Department managers of MSG-based work.	Designation and funding of an overall Defense Department agency to catalog and control all MSGs in inventory.	Publication of annual summary of current and proposed MSG-based work, including sponsor, designer, institutional connections, costs, research questions, operational questions, users, and outcomes.
	Implementation of National Bureau of Standards guidelines and procedures for documentation.	Imposition of NBS standards on entire inventory of current MSGs.	Creation of a special library and cataloging archive related entirely to military MSGs within Defense Documentation Center.

Table 19-1—*continued.*

GENERAL ISSUE AREA	SLIGHT LEVEL OF DIFFICULTY	MODERATE LEVEL OF DIFFICULTY	MAXIMAL LEVEL OF DIFFICULTY
Stewardship	Selection of most frequently used MSGs in current inventory; submission of work to outside review for assessment of operational utility of each.		External assessment of validity of all large-scale and frequently used military MSGs.
	Attempt to assign costs to MSGs in the current inventory.	Development of consistent, department-wide cost-accounting procedures and practices for MSGs.	Implementation of consistent, department-wide cost-accounting procedures.
	Development of users' guide to MSG practitioners, including institutional affiliations.	Extension of this guide to include all federally funded MSG-based research and analysis activity.	

Table 19-1—*continued*.

GENERAL ISSUE AREA	SLIGHT LEVEL OF DIFFICULTY	MODERATE LEVEL OF DIFFICULTY	MAXIMAL LEVEL OF DIFFICULTY
Stewardship	Routine, periodic symposia in intelligence community to discuss basic data requirements for MSGs and analyses.	Department-wide assessment of current operational data sets to determine purpose, quality, appropriateness, and uses.	Generation of new data in areas found to require them.
	Development of utility analyses of current MSGs.	Maintenance of utility-analysis profiles on all currently used MSGs.	
	Consideration of studies and analysis career alternative for uniformed services.	Stabilization of studies and analysis billets to five years to improve continuity.	
Research	Provision of support for validation of basic data, including methods.	Increase in support for free-form gaming with attention to diplomatic, economic, and political topics central to issue of national security.	

Table 19-1—*continued.*

GENERAL ISSUE AREA	SLIGHT LEVEL OF DIFFICULTY	MODERATE LEVEL OF DIFFICULTY	MAXIMAL LEVEL OF DIFFICULTY
Research	Increase in support for analytic modeling, including mathematical programming, game theory, and closely related techniques.		
	Development of standardized methods of sensitivity analysis.	Improvement of methods for data-base management systems.	Increase in man-machine gaming generally and in facility support specifically.

excellent and punish substandard performance is well within the reach of the professional, military modeling and gaming community. Not only could the Operations Research Society of America and The Institute of Management Science share part of the burden, but the individual armed services and the Department of Defense are likely to have an interest in this goal as well. Various specific mechanisms can be imagined, including cash prizes for distinguished work, citations for the best work at annual professional meetings, and warnings or censure for deficient practices.

There is no justification for the fact that over half of all operational models are not presently scrutinized by anyone beside those directly responsible for their production and use. Particularly because in-house analytic work is increasingly prevalent, the need for careful and continuous examination of these MSGs cannot be overstressed. The Army Models Review Committee is one possible prototype for an organization that could accomplish at least part of the task. Such review groups should be permanently constituted, however, and should have adequate resources. An additional review by qualified outsiders seems appropriate in some cases, especially for large, expensive, or extensively used MSGs. The National Academy of Sciences, the National Science Foundation, and the Defense Science Board all have at least partial mandates for oversight and review; at best, they have a social responsibility to carry them out.

In recent years, professional societies have made efforts on an ad hoc basis to consider at least general questions of standards, practices, and ethics for military operational modeling, gaming, and simulation. Such activities are important and require more than the occasional panel or a partially informed discussion. The numbers of professionals involved, the resources expended, and the seriousness of the topics together point to a substantial need, one that is now satisfied only casually, at best.

Journal editors and editorial review boards need to be made aware of the extent and importance of the analytic work that undergirds many of the articles and reports they now publish. Professional journals have a responsibility to demand more than an author's assurance that an analysis has been conducted; they should require proof that data and models support the points of view being summarized in any given presentation.[2]

Uniformed officers with managerial responsibilities for studies within the Department of Defense would benefit from a two-to three-month course designed to acquaint them with the realities of modeling and gaming. We were generally impressed with the integrity of most of the defense managers encountered in the course of our study; the problem is that many of them came to their jobs with only a smattering of technical preparation and virtually no sensitivity to the facts of bureaucratic and political life. On-the-job training is ineffective in preparing many of these managers for the extensive responsibilities they are being asked to assume. Individual services might create a couse of study and preparation for them; alternatively, the job might be hired out to university-based groups.

The General Accounting Office has repeatedly recommended that the National Bureau of Standards, among other agencies, should play a key role in creating and maintaining standards for all federally funded models, simulations, and games. As a result the bureau has begun to develop guidelines and procedures, especially with respect to documentation. The problem, as noted in earlier discussions, is that an effective means to enforce these standards has yet to be devised. Many defense managers simply hope that the currently increasing demands for standard procedures will disappear if they are ignored. It may be technically accurate to claim that adequate standards already exist, but the real problem of nonenforcement and noncompliance remains to be solved. Enforcing standards for documentation may eventually require even firmer and more authoritative actions on the part of agencies like the General Accounting Office; how much better it would be for everyone concerned if those for whom the standards are intended would comply willingly and responsibly.

External professional review is a multifaceted process. In addition to general reviews of the scientific validity of MSGs, the utility of the more active MSGs in the current inventory should be assessed to discover how and by whom these models are being used and with what results. Such utility analyses would do much to help determine the overall impact of any given MSG, or of general methodologies, on ultimate policy decisions. Information of this sort, together with an assessment of the scientific merits or each MSG, would make up an essential part of its total documentation. Another form of record keeping, cost accounting for MSGs, has been markedly inadequate. Chapter 14 represents a preliminary effort at least to identify classes and categories of costs important in the construction and use of MSGs; a full account of costs is a monumental intellectual and practical task that remains to be undertaken.

One relatively inexpensive encouragement to the development of an institutional memory among key model-building groups and professionals might be a users' guide to MSG practitioners. To ensure coverage, responsibility for the creation and maintenance of this useful guide might naturally fall within the scope of either the Defense Advanced Research Projects Agency or the Studies, Analysis, and Gaming Agency of the Joint Chiefs of Staff. The current tendency to reuse data collected for earlier MSGs increases the importance of forging communication links between the analytic shops and the intelligence community; such links are now tenuous and depend for their existence on the personalities or acumen of key managers. Regularly scheduled opportunities to exchange data requirements and to determine the availability and reliability of data seem essential as a step in the direction of efficiency and greater productivity.

We believe that many uniformed members of the study bureaucracy approach their responsibilities with trepidation and with the hope that no event during their stewardship will endanger the overall pattern of advancement in their careers. The importance of studies and analysis to the military's performance of its mission is now great and may increase. The creation of a well-defined defense-management career path, in recognition of this fact, would enhance the possibilities for careful management within the military. It is therefore an option that merits the attention of personnel planners in the individual services.

Our survey indicated that a serious emphasis on research is nearly absent in the military modeling community. As a result, many, if not most, of the MSGs in the current inventory are based on very little solid research. One looks in vain for inquiries into the validity of much of the primary empirical data on the basis of which multimillion-dollar MSGs have been constructed.[3] Much needs to be done in this area by all who buy and use operational MSGs. Another improvement that would require only small amounts of effort is an increase in research expenditures for analytic modeling, with the proviso that such efforts be more firmly grounded in realistic problems than in even the recent past.

A final, relatively inexpensive means to improve research practices is the performance of sensitivity analyses. Not only is there little apparent awareness of the importance of testing the sensitivity of models today, but there is even less clarity about what a good sensitivity test is or how it might be able to increase users' understanding of an MSG's strengths and weaknesses. A certain amount of effort should be expended to popularize the concept of this kind of technical appraisal and testing and to demonstrate the need for it.

MODERATELY DIFFICULT RECOMMENDATIONS

Once specific sanctions have been devised and accepted by a significant proportion of the professional community, mechanisms will have to be created to impose them in an authoritative manner. Procedures for appeal, restitution, and redress should be considered as well. The importance of external professional review has already been stressed. At a moderate level of effort, we urge defense managers to allocate the necessary resources to ensure that all extensively used MSGs in their charge are subjected to careful and thorough scrutiny.

A great deal could be learned from the postmortem examination of a carefully selected set of operational models. The investment in retrospective assessments of strategic models need not exceed a few man-months, a modest expenditure considering the probable benefits. The process should involve collecting the documentation, thinking about the game, and then defining the lessons learned from the overall experience. Such an assessment could be specified at the very beginning of funding any new MSG; some proportion of the total resources should be earmarked for this purpose. We are concerned that no body of cumulative experience and knowledge exists in the field at present. No large-scale, important system can survive long or well if no attempt is made to learn from the past.

Many participants in the current system are poorly prepared, both technically and professionally. We recommend the creation and support of both university-based and service school-based centers where potential builders, managers, and users of military MSGs could learn their trades. At some point a clearinghouse for all defense modeling activity should also be created. Such an institution ought not, however, to be set up too quickly or without a great deal of planning and thought. Among other activities, such an institution might be responsible for publishing both an open, professional, high-quality journal devoted to modeling and classified summaries of equally high quality, intended for the internal use of those actively engaged in the development and use of models.

The imposition of guidelines for documenting the entire active inventory of MSGs, devised by the National Bureau of Standards or another agency, will require at least a moderate level of effort. Most MSGs are not now well documented, and provisions for documentation have been assigned a low priority or have not been addressed at all; thus much work remains to be done in this area.

Once some effort has been made to reconstruct the costs associated with MSGs in the current inventory, the next important step might be for someone with cost-accounting expertise to assemble this information in an effort to devise and promulgate consistent, meaningful cost-accounting procedures and practices for the use of the entire Department of Defense. Supervision of this effort, which would require a moderate commitment of resources, could be delegated to one of the research agencies located within the individual services, such as the Office of Naval Research; the authority for the project must reside at the highest levels of the Defense bureaucracy, however, perhaps within the comptroller's office or in the office of the Director, Defense Research and Engineering.

Because the Department of Defense is the largest buyer and user of MSGs within the federal government, its leadership in the creation of a users' guide to MSG practitioners would ensure coverage of a large proportion of the total professional community. The extension of this listing to include all federally funded, MSG-based research and analysis would be yet another step in the direction of improved performance and control in the system as a whole. This recommendation is consistent with the spirit of numerous suggestions for better practice made by the General Accounting Office. Because the National Science Foundation has already indicated its willingness to become involved in surveys and assessments of nonmilitary MSGs through its Research Applied to National Needs division, it is a likely candidate for this particular task.

Regular symposia for officials in the intelligence and study bureaucracy might be extended to include the assessment of all current operational data sets being used by MSG groups within the Department of Defense. The task would be a formidable one; it is essential, however, since carrying it out inadequately or not at all poses an obvious threat to the entire modeling enterprise. The importance of this task requires an agency to assume overall responsibility for its fulfillment. The National Security Council itself, perhaps through one of its working or task groups, might be the logical institutional authority for this task.

Once a working consensus is reached about what ought to be contained in a utility analysis, the next step is to require this form of documentation on all MSGs in the active inventory. The magnitude of the job will require moderate effort initially; maximal diligence will be necessary, however, to ensure that utility analyses are routinely applied to all current and future MSGs, with a consequent improvement in overall standards.

In line with the trend toward stabilization of tours of duty for uniformed officers in the Department of Defense, we recommend that study and analysis assignments be made for five years (not including the special training needed to prepare officers for these assignments). These longer tours of duty would increase managerial continuity, now seriously deficient, and might have the additional effect of altering professional expectations and bureaucratic incentives in desirable ways.

Two separate but related aspects of free-form gaming require additional attention and resources. First, the range of topics for study by these methods should be expanded to include diplomatic, military, economic, and closely allied topics; second, scientific investigations should be undertaken to establish the underlying validity of these techniques and to test the accuracy and utility of the insights generated through game play. Specifically, much attention needs to be paid to the writing of scenarios and to the design, leadership and use of games. Federal sponsors of research both within and outside of the official Defense Department structure, might encourage the necessary scientific investigation; one logical source of the demand might well be the Studies, Analysis and Gaming Agency of the Joint Chiefs of Staff.

Although we have not addressed the issue at length in this book, the data used and generated by MSGs needs to be better controlled. Data-base management systems, archiving, and library functions are currently poorly organized and do not function nearly as well as one would expect from the magnitude of the overall system. At the very least, a task group needs to be convened to study the nature and extent of the problem. At best, their recommendations for improvement should be vigorously acted on.

MAXIMALLY DIFFICULT RECOMMENDATIONS

In presenting these specific recommendations, we presume that most, if not all, recommendations requiring a slight or moderate level of effort will be considered, if not implemented, before those that require maximal effort, since the recommendations build on one another. Thus severe legal and economic sanctions should not be imposed until such sanctions have been devised, discussed, and implemented in several other ways. Only after gradual and thoughtful progression through the two earlier steps would the necessary groundwork exist to allow serious, formal sanctions to achieve the desired effects.

Extending a demand for retrospective assessments of MSGs to include all future work, rather than selected previous work, will enhance its effects in similar ways. Until the appropriate personnel for this task are identified and learn to do it well and efficiently, there is little reason to believe that wholesale assessments will work at all or very well. In-house technical assignments for master modelers and related professional support staffs will not be easy to set up and will depend on both the development of professional training programs and the stabilization of tours of duty for defense managers. The difficulty of the task and the time that will be required to perform it, however, should not prevent the necessary effort from being made.

If they are currently taught at all, technical and management courses in modeling, simulation, and gaming are not emphasized in the curricula of any of the established service academies or advanced professional schools. Some individual programs, such as those at the Naval War College and the Industrial College of the Armed Forces do exist, however, and might be expanded. In any case, the extent of training programs must be expanded to accommodate the needs of the field and profession.

The need to increase the amount of available information and to broaden the discussion of national-security matters is discussed later in this chapter. One specific means to accomplish this goal, however, is to develop two-sided advocacy publications for both specialized and popular consumption. An annual summary of the documentation of current and proposed MSGs, with the concept of documentation greatly expanded to include information about sponsorship, individuals responsible for construction and use, costs, the nature of research questions, the operational issues considered, users, and outcome, will require a truly maximal effort. We have no idea what such a document would ultimately cost; if, however, less difficult recommendations about documentation, cataloguing, archiving, and control were implemented, it would become possible to gauge the feasibility of this particular task. Similar thinking underlies our recommendation for the establishment of library and cataloguing practices and procedures within the Defense Documentation Center. Action on earlier recommendations would, at least in principle, make this goal easier to achieve.

Another major task is the careful professional examination of the scientific worth of large-scale, extensively used military MSGs. If a particular model is heavily relied on to analyse selected national-security issues, its validity must be established beyond any reasonable doubt. If an MSG is scientifically invalid or otherwise deficient in significant ways, its continuing use must be questioned seriously. Once cost-accounting procedures have been devised, they must be implemented on a wholesale basis—not a simple or an inexpensive task. Ideally, related efforts will already have made full-scale implementation at least a real possibility.

The generation of new empirical information to support and inform operational MSGs is a crucial long-term objective. It will not be achieved, however, either in the absence of improved communication between those who are best equipped to produce those data and those who need to use them or in the absence of detailed and systematic investigations into the adequacy of data currently relied on.

Finally, what we consider the neglect of man-machine gaming facilities and research requires attention and correction. The present reliance on all-machine, engineering-based MSGs ignores the indisputable fact that weapons systems depend in subtle ways on human beings for their most effective employment. Increased support for man-machine gaming would recognize this fact and would do much to put the human being back into the equation.

General Recommendations

The variety of changes needed to improve the performance of the system might be viewed in terms of clusters of general problems to be resolved one by one. This approach, though useful, is not without pitfalls. A general perspective may prevent one from seeing how more specific issues may affect the overall outcome. In addition, there is a danger that some general problem areas may receive a great deal of attention while others, equally important, remain too long on the agenda. Nonetheless, we have sorted out what appear to be several of the more important general issues that deserve time, attention, and consideration for discussion here.

Resource levels. We recommend that consideration be given to greatly increased expenditures on research into the uses of models, simulations, and games by the Defense Department. This increase should be contemplated, however, only in conjunction with a change in current practices and a shift in the emphasis of much of the work. So far, expenditures have been low relative to the potential value of the work; relative to its current value, however, expenditures have been too high.

Advocacy versus scientific validation. The process of building and using MSGs illustrates the clash between science and advocacy. As long as model builders do not question the environment set for them by those who solicit the work, the selection of appropriate estimates can cause virtually any point of view to be supported. Accordingly, open, regular, and more rigorous review of the MSGs that are being built and used is necessary. Procedures should be instituted to challenge the validity of data that are now used routinely and unquestioningly.

Communication between civilian and military groups within the profession must be improved. A professional advisory group at the level of Congress or the General Accounting Office might enhance the quality of the dialogue between Congress and the Department of Defense, in particular. In the last thirty years a multitude of consulting and advisory groups has sprung up, many of them used extensively by the Department of Defense or by the specific armed services. They have provided a high level of professional analytic support for the defense establishment. Unfortunately, the technical resources available to Congress are not so numerous, nor have they been relied on so extensively to unravel the numbers provided when highly technical issues, such as those treated in this book, are at stake.

We believe that an independent consulting group should provide legislators with the technical support they need to judge the merits of complex budget requests. Because the Defense Department's requests for funding are based on largely technical studies, legislators, the military, and ultimately, the general public would benefit if technical expertise were available to help Congress obtain a reasonably objective, balanced, and independent assessment of those requests. The Congressional Budget Office has begun to fill this need on a limited basis, but further technical efforts are required.[4]

Cost accounting. There is now no institutional memory about the cost of building, running, updating, and evaluating

MSGs; thus any effort would represent an improvement over present cost-accounting procedures. The definitions and categories we were forced to create for our survey might serve as a useful point of departure. As a minimal requirement, a brief cost dossier on each MSG should be kept throughout its life cycle.

External review and standards. Professional reviewing is a critical mechanism of quality control and one that is too much neglected. In response to those who claim it merely adds another bureaucratic impediment to getting the job done, we cite the competent, efficient efforts of the Army Models Review Committee.[5] That committee was set up on an ad hoc basis and its work was temporary, however; ongoing support for evaluation procedures is called for as well. The Joint Chiefs of Staff might assume the function of reviewing MSGs for all the services. This task would require qualified professionals to serve on a long-term, continuing basis, as well as strong incentives to ensure adherence to scientific standards of evaluation. The group responsible for overseeing the review process should also deal with questions about standards, including when sensitivity analyses are needed and what constitutes data validation.

Documentation. Documentation of MSGs today is largely uneven, unavailable, or nonexistent. At a minimum, the documentation of an MSG should include the program listing; flow charts; listings, definitions, and sources of variables; the program deck with comments and caveats about operating quirks and special library and input or output routines; the operator's manual; the programmer's manual; the player's manual for man-machine or free-form MSGs; the analysis routines used to reduce data and estimate input parameters; appropriate data on the costs of constructing, updating, and running the MSG; the register of critical personnel involved in its initiation; the production personnel and the validation procedures they used; the history of its operations; and a record of the MSG's use. Many will complain that assembling so much material would impede the work at hand. We believe, however, that conscientious and consistent attempts to provide such documentation will improve existing management practices and may in time open the way to increased knowledge and improved technology.

We find no evidence of excessive redundancy in the production or use of MSGs (such as would occur if too many models were built to study the same problems). Communication among MSG builders is poor and needs improvement; even if it were good, however, a certain amount of redundancy would be desirable. Standardization of efforts should not be confused with adherence to professional standards. We recommend strongly against instituting the first, which is premature; efforts should be made, however, to promote the second.

A central clearinghouse. In the next five to seven years, the creation of an additional bureaucratic operation for the clearing of work on MSGs is unlikely to be productive. At present, however, a legitimate need exists for a professional focal point, which might be provided by a professional review board of the sort described above, at least as an interim measure. Work in gaming and simulation is fragmented to an unnecessary and unhealthy extent. The joint usage of MSGs—that is, the sharing of MSG construction and use among the military services and government agencies—is one possible remedy. Others are the scientific replication of MSGs; collective attempts to account for and reduce costs; and the sharing of special overhead charges for large-scale, general-purpose computational systems, to a greater extent than is now done through the National Military Command Systems Support Center. Joint usage promises the more efficient use of scarce professional talent and the diffusion of professional standards. The creation of a models review committee under the Joint Chiefs of Staff and based on the Army prototype would be another step in the right direction.

Research. Basic research in the field is seriously lacking. The majority of the MSGs we sampled depend on a limited intellectual investment in fundamental knowledge. Although this is probably not the time to expect much funding for basic research, the need to investigate topics like simulation methods, data validation, sensitivity analysis, and statistical tests for simulation outputs is serious. In the area of analysis, study is needed on formal models of combat, such as allocation and search game theory. In the "softer" subjects that bear directly on applied MSGs, there is a need for studies of panic behavior, threat and confrontation, and, in particular, human factors and motivation. At another level, work is required on basic questions of use, both for particular MSGs and for whole families and classes of MSGs.

The image of research among funders and builders in the professional community needs refurbishment. Research now appears to be so stigmatized that one can scarcely acknowledge sponsorship of a pure research project without bracing for criticism. Nevertheless, the need for basic research is so critical that if no other funding were available we would favor a plan to reduce all current expenditures for MSGs by a significant proportion and to use the saving for basic research.

All indications are that the larger MSGs have been of little value. The size, length of time under development, and generality of an MSG all appear to be directly related to the difficulty of controlling, validating, and using it. Undesirable outcomes resulting from changes in personnel, bad documentation, poor conceptualization, and poor professional communication and review are exaggerated with large MSGs. We recommend that standards for approving the construction of large-scale MSGs be much more stringent than those for smaller projects. We believe that large-scale MSGs tend to be unable to handle scenarios and other elements that are hard to quantify. Funds might better be spent on the basic research needed to acquire that capability than on the premature construction of large programs.

Free-form and man-machine gaming. It is time for an assessment of the worth of free-form and man-machine gaming in defense work compared with that of all-machine simulations. Ideally, this evaluation should be made by a combined team of military and nonmilitary personnel. We suspect that free-form gaming should be more widely used. Man-machine gaming for operational purposes appears to be relatively expensive and is not used extensively. Both man-machine and free-form gaming for training and teaching have received too little support. In addition, an investigation of the relationships among the multiple uses of MSGs should be undertaken. Especially in light of the projected size of the new Naval War College gaming facility, the relationships among training, evaluation, operational, and research uses must be better understood.

Gaming in the civilian sector. In spite of some negative findings, our survey revealed distinct advances in the state of the art and the emergence of professional standards. We are troubled, however, by the lack of professional communication between the specialized, in-house model-building shops and those outside them. Many of the mistakes made in applying simulation and gaming to Defense Department problems are probably being made once again in the civilian sector.[6] Given the present lack of communication, it may be fortunate that funding for MSGs from the Departments of Health, Education, and Welfare, Housing and Urban Development, and Energy, along with that from similar agencies, remains so much smaller than that from the Department of Defense.[7] Serious efforts should be made to find ways of sharing some of the hard-won wisdom of the military areas with those applying modeling and gaming to nonmilitary problems.

The Decision-Making Process

A third way to order our recommendations is by means of a consideration of the decision-making process responsible for the overall performance of the system of military analysis. This approach is potentially fruitful insofar as it calls attention to structural weaknesses and suggests areas in which relatively small investments of time, attention, and resources could significantly improve performance. The evaluation phase of the decision-making process appears to us to be particularly in need of development and appreciation. In our view, this phase is the key to improving overall performance. Some specific suggestions for strengthening evaluation procedures are presented below. Incentives for individuals or groups to assume reponsibility for evaluation seem inadequate in the current professional environment. Those that can be identified tend to work against the performance of thorough, professional evaluations. Professionals employed by contract-research firms are usually not paid to evaluate their own work or that of competitors and colleagues. Contracts are available for building and operating models but not for evaluating them. The disincentives to questioning the competence of one's firm far outweigh any conceivable incentives. At the individual level, the reasons for not being too harsh on one's peers are obvious; the community of MSG professionals is small, and retribution for a strongly unfavorable critique is highly likely.

In the military, in-house technical professionals, the majority of whom are uniformed officers, appear to have somewhat different incentive systems, but the outcome, in terms of evaluation, is about the same. If the basic idea embodied in an MSG was handed down by higher authority, persistently questioning the idea and the analysis that supports it will not advance one's career nearly as much as going along with the program. Individuals generally, and understandably, consider their own careers more important than their identity as modeling professionals.

Restructured incentive systems might result in better and more routinely performed evaluations. They might also result in the assignment of responsibility and the imposition of rewards or sanctions for commendable or dubious performance, in a better appreciation of the fact that not all modeling succeeds, and in an increased willingness to spend cash on research and on the collection and validation of basic information.

Evaluation is presently left primarily to auditors, whose efforts, according to the GAO, are often thwarted by poor documentation, the high turnover of research personnel, and insufficient technical training.[8] Members of research staffs occasionally take the risk of criticizing work produced in their own shops or by professional colleagues; working-level defense bureaucrats may from time to time inspect the work that they hire out and manage; ad hoc groups are occasionally convened for the purpose of examining specific collections of operational MSGs or those that have proven to be particularly troublesome or useless.

If the profession is to grow and develop in productive and positive ways, many more individuals and institutions must participate in the decision-making process. Increased participation could result in better communication; contribute to a realignment of incentives and priorities for those who buy and produce MSGs; and serve as a deterrent to those who might otherwise be tempted or allowed to produce MSGs that do not meet technical and professional standards. For instance, if professional societies, such as the Operations Research Society of America and The Institute of Management Sciences, were to select a sample of operational military MSGs; commission skilled, independent, expert reviewers to evaluate this sample; and then make their findings known to buyers, users, and the professional community at large, overall MSG quality would be likely to be improved. Such an initiative would require funding, since the talent required is not inexpensive and the time investment would be considerable. A fixed override of as little as 5 percent on current contracting and production costs could generate sufficient resources to pay for this type of outside professional review. It would produce about $10 million, or 5 percent of an estimated total investment for MSG production of between $150 and $200 million.

On the legislative front, the participation of the constituent agencies of Congress that are most closely concerned with the use of MSGs could be increased and sustained by a simple tithing arrangement. That is, for every ten dollars of new MSG construction, one dollar might be appropriated to evaluation and dispensed to the GAO, the Congressional Budget Office, and the Office of Technology Assessment.[9] Creating such a funding authority would in and of itself produce an incentive to improve cost accounting. This plan is based on the assumptions that the burden of assigning monetary values to new MSG construction would be shared by legislative and executive technical groups and that the allocation of funds would be open to discussion between those seeking resources for evaluating MSGs and those seeking resources for building them. One attractive possibility might be for competing evaluation groups to submit proposals bidding on individual jobs or classes of models. The proposals could then be judged by an expert panel convened by the National Academy of Sciences or a similar agency. Universities and other independent bodies might be enlisted to participate in the communication of lessons learned from the external evaluations—lessons about techniques, applications, and decision-making practices. The creation of training programs in the university setting, suggested above, would also build a market for this kind of instructional material and lead to the longer-range goal of improved professional development.

Democratic values have always been important in the United States; our analysis indicates that the time is ripe for the creation of independent sources of information and technical proficiency to assist in shaping and sharing these values as they relate to national-security matters. A more general proposal to establish networks of global monitoring intended to inform both citizens and authorities about the wisdom and implications of policy choices is at least one comprehensive institutional design to accomplish the broader goal of increased and informed participation.[10] It is not going to be easy to include the citizenry in the policymaking process, but continuing to operate in isolation from them has so many unacceptable costs to government and society that the matter must be confronted seriously.[11] Efforts to develop the modeling profession must include consideration of new methods and procedures to involve and educate citizens, to create information networks, and to inform the public about the problems and possibilities inherent in the complex substantive issues dealt with by military analysts.[12]

Appendixes
Notes
Glossary
Index

APPENDIX A

The Evaluation of Models, Simulations, and Games

MANY OPERATIONAL CONCEPTS could be incorporated into a summary of appropriate criteria for evaluating MSGs. We find the list proposed by the Army Models Review Committee to be concise and useful.[1] The first six descriptive items apply to characteristics of an MSG; the final eight, its utility. They are (1) consistency; (2) enrichment potential; (3) experimental validity; (4) military realism; (5) physical reasonableness; (6) visibility to the analyst; (7) credibility; (8) flexibility; (9) interface potential; (10) resources required; (11) responsiveness; (12) sensitivity of the model; (13) technical user capability; and (14) visibility to the user. Many of these criteria have already been discussed extensively; however, several others are less familiar and merit additional comment.

Military realism and physical reasonableness are certainly desirable qualities for any model, but realism and relevance are not equivalent. By their very nature, models are unrealistic, and it is important to make and use "correctly" unrealistic models. A skilled officer, experienced in the realities of a military situation, can provide accurate information yet give poor advice to model builders trying to capture that reality selectively in their model. If he lacks appreciation of the model-building art, the military adviser or other expert consultant may supply inappropriate information, too much or too little detail, or particular rather than general features of the situation being modeled. If the model builder himself is not sufficiently versed in the empirical realities, this communication barrier may have serious consequences for the overall effort. In addition to the dangers of inaccurate specification, an inappropriate demand for realistic models may mean that expensive, unnecessary work is done to capture particular details. A technically unsophisticated user might even find himself in the position of requesting additional work to accomplish this goal. A contractor will do the work for a fee, but the results may not have much bearing on the basic research problem. Realism for its own sake should be guarded against in many situations.

This point provides a strong rationale for having all modeling performed in house by highly trained, uniformed experts. In principle, it is desirable for the empirical specification, the construction of the model, and final use tasks to be performed by a single individual or group; however, many factors mitigate against the simple application of this principle. They arise from the dominant incentive systems, the motivations of the various participants, and the general need for more, rather than less, exposure of the decision-making process.

Visibility to the analyst—that is, the ease with which a model can be checked, reviewed, altered, and investigated—depends very much on the model's documentation and on the dissemination of detailed information about it to technically capable individuals who understand and care about what is going on. Because documentation is generally poor, because dissemination is almost nonexistent, because many key participants move on to other assignments in less time than it takes even to build many MSGs, because a large proportion of the data used by military MSGs is secret, and because many MSGs are operated by people who know little about the model's history or limitations, the importance of visibility to outside analysts is great.

Credibility poses another problem. Most anomalous results are wrong, and life is too short to treat seriously even a fraction of the clearly unreasonable suggestions that may result directly from a model or indirectly from its use. "Crank" claims—that the tank would be critical in World War I, for instance, that air power would be a serious factor after 1935, or that the Russians might be mad enough to try to place strategic missiles in Cuba—rarely surface or are taken seriously by those involved in the modeling business. Even if a naval game at Newport had suggested the Japanese would use kamikaze pilots in World War II or if anyone had dreamed that they might be foolish enough to attack Pearl Harbor, these possibilities would probably not have been noticed; they would simply have been too "incredible" to consider. These examples call attention to the fact that an unexpected or apparently incredible result requires justification and effort that go beyond merely pointing out that it was derived from a model, simulation, or game, if it is to be taken seriously. Using MSGs is usually a mundane enough activity for credibility to be a good criterion. It should not be invoked so single-mindedly, however, as to prevent someone from occasionally taking a result that looks impossible seriously.

The criterion of flexibility is two-edged. Certainly, flexibility is desirable in itself, but attempts continually to increase a model's flexibility may lead builders and users seriously astray; the quest for spurious generality has distorted the model in a number of specific cases. Closely related is interface potential, which modeling professionals discuss in terms of how all modules will ultimately fit together with all others; it is flexibility carried to an extreme. While it makes sense to construct as many compatible models as is economically feasible, there must be a clearly defined need to do so. Making an abstract debating point or an inflated claim in a proposal about the need for modules that can work together is easier and cheaper than actually making several models consistent and compatible. Unless there are important and well-defined questions and plenty of cash to finance the quest for answers, we doubt that the interface of models for its own sake will be worth a significant amount of attention. The technical problems alone are usually insurmountable, or nearly so.

Technical user capability and visibility to the user are both important criteria, but they should not be overemphasized. Both underscore key organizational problems within the bureaucracies that must use MSGs. It is important to stress the difference between an attractive briefing with fancy graphs and displays, on the one hand, and solid, technically verifiable model results, on the other. Promotional efforts aimed at high-level officials must relate on substance rather than mere style.

APPENDIX B

The Questionnaire

MUCH OF THE information presented in this book was obtained through the analysis of the responses to a lengthy and detailed survey questionnaire. During its construction, this instrument was revised several times in response to valuable suggestions made by many experienced professionals in the field. Because the final version, which was distributed to the military modeling community, is more than seventy pages long, we shall not reproduce it here. Instead, we shall list the general topics covered by the questions; they indicate some of the major technical distinctions we feel are important for analyzing and improving MSGs intended for both military and nonmilitary purposes.

Our confidence in the utility of this instrument was increased when other researchers obtained the support of the National Science Foundation to apply it, in modified form, to nondefense MSGs.[1] We would be more encouraged, however, if this kind of investigation were institutionalized and replicated on a regular basis. The following is a summary listing of questionnaire topics:[2]

PREFACE

PURPOSES OF THE QUESTIONNAIRE

INTRODUCTION. TERMINOLOGY

Labels/Administration (For Office Use Only)
  Internal ID Tag
  Publication ID Number
  Abstracted

Instructions
  Models and Simulations
  Builders and Users

Part I. Basic Information on Purposes, Use,
  Benefits, and Costs
    Questionnaire Time
    Simulation/Study/Model Name, Designer Building
      Agency, Author Name, Agency or Authority, Spon-
      sor or Work Name
    Category
    Respondent's Role
    Length of Time Acquainted with this Work
    List Last Two Assignments
    Respondent's Information: Name, Rank, Title, and
      Position
    General Purpose of Model, Game, or Simulation
    Specific Purposes
    Purpose
    Classification (Without Inputs)
    Classification (Input Data, Other Information)
    Professional Review
    MSG Parent or Antecedents, Direct
    Name Direct Parents
    Name Indirect Antecedents
    Development Initiation Date
    Use Initiation Date
    MSG Spinoff
    Names of One or Two Spinoffs
  Model/Simulation/Game Production and Purpose
    Funding Source
    MSG Production
    MSG Initiation
    Initiator Purpose
    Specificity of Purpose of Funding Source

Best Alternative Procedures
Major Use of MSG
Analysis Procedures
Judged Effectiveness of Best Alternative Procedure
Number of Briefings
Level of Briefing
Purpose of Briefing
Importance of MSG to Decision
Measure of Benefits
MSG Production Costs
  Direct Costs to Build
  Direct Funding to Build
  Amount of Funding to Build
  Total Costs to Build: Direct, Indirect, Imputed, Un-imputed
Model/Simulation/Game Operating Costs and Operations
  Annual Cost to Operate, Gross
  Cost to Operate, Single Use
  Annual Update Costs
  Operational Life Span (To Date)
  Still Active?
  Model Users
  Operational Use: Annual Frequency
  Experimental Use
  Experimental Example
  Experimental Purpose, Initial
  Educational Use
  Educational Example
  Educational Purpose, Initial
  Transferability of MSG Use
  Transferability: Costs to Operate
  Obsolescence
  Related MSG
  Duplication of Use
  Clearing House
  Standardization
  Regional Centers
  External Review Board
  External Review Board, Specification

Notes

1. Models, Simulations, and Games

1. MSG is an abbreviation we have created for convenience and ease of reference.

2. The Scope of Operational Gaming and Simulation

1. For a more detailed breakdown of gaming activities, see Martin Shubik, "On the Scope of Gaming," *Management Science* 18, no. 5 (January 1972), pt. 2, pp. P-20–P-36.

2. Alfred H. Hausrath, *Venture Simulation in War, Business and Politics* (New York: McGraw-Hill, 1971), pp. 30–32; Roberta Wohlstetter, *Pearl Harbor: Warning and Decision* (Stanford, Calif.: Stanford University Press, 1962), pp. 371–373, 381; Mitsuo Fuchida and Okumiya Mastake, *Midway: The Battle That Doomed Japan* (Annapolis: U.S. Naval Institute Publications, 1955), pp. 20–25, 52, 94–97.

3. Olaf Helmer, *Analysis of the Future: The Delphi Method* (Santa Monica, Calif.: The Rand Corporation, P-3558, March 1967). Norman C. Dalkey, *Delphi* (Santa Monica, Calif.: The Rand Corporation, P-3704, October 1967).

4. Norman C. Dalkey, *The Delphi Method: An Experimental Study of Group Opinion* (Santa Monica, Calif.: The Rand Corporation, RM-5888-PR, June 1969).

5. Some of the problems and opportunities are discussed in greater detail in Garry D. Brewer, "Gaming: Prospective for Forecasting," in *Forecasting in International Relations*, ed. Thomas Robinson and Nazli Choucri (San Francisco: Freeman, 1978), chap. 14.

6. See William Ascher, *Forecasting* (Baltimore: Johns Hopkins University Press, 1978).

3. Methods of Modeling and Simulation

1. F. Y. Edgeworth, *Mathematical Psychics* (London: Kegan Paul, 1881).

2. L. S. Shapley and Martin Shubik, *Game Theory in Economics* (Santa Monica, Calif.: The Rand Corporation, R-904/3-NSF, October 1972).

3. Ralph Strauch treats this issue skillfully and in detail in " 'Squishy' Problems and Quantitative Methods," *Policy Sciences* 6, no. 2 (June 1975) : 175–184.

4. Harvey A. De Weerd, *Political-Military Scenarios* (Santa Monica, Calif.: The Rand Corporation, P-3535, February 1967), is an excellent, short lesson in scenario writing, data organizing, and gaming.

4. Trends and Expenditures

1. U.S., Bureau of the Census, *Statistical Abstract of the United States* (Washington, D.C.: U.S., Department of Commerce, 1974), pp. 109, 306, 308 (hereafter cited as *Statistical Abstract, 1974*).

2. R. S. Bower, *Market Changes in the Computer Service Industry*, reprint no. 294 (Washington, D.C.: The Brookings Institution, 1974), table 2.

3. Gary Fromm, William L. Hamilton, and Diane E. Hamilton, *Federally Supported Mathematical Models: Survey and Analysis* (Washington, D.C.: National Science Foundation, Research Applied to National Needs, 1975), p. 4. While the majority of the MSGs surveyed cost less than $50,000, several cost more than $3 million.

4. A partial list of early gamers is given in Hausrath, *Venture Simulation*, pp. 390–394.

5. There is, however, some literature on the topic. See Harvey A. De Weerd, "A Contextual Approach to Scenario Construction," *Simulation & Games* 5, no. 4 (December 1974) : 403–414; Peter deLeon, "Scenario Designs: An Overview," *ibid.* 6, no. 1 (March 1975) : 39–60.

6. Fromm et al., *Federally Supported Mathematical Models*, is a good source of information on this activity.

7. See Garry D. Brewer, *Politicians, Bureaucrats and the Consultant* (New York: Basic Books, 1973), for an appraisal of the first two examples.

8. Jay Forrester, *Industrial Dynamics* (Cambridge, Mass.: M.I.T. Press, 1961).

9. See Alan G. Feldt, "Operational Gaming in Planning Education," *Journal of the American Institute of Planners* 32, no. 1 (June 1966) : 17–23, for examples and a handy summary. The work is re-

ported in full in idem, *CLUG: Community Land Use Game* (New York: Free Press, 1972).

10. Jean Piaget, *Play, Dreams, and Imitation in Childhood,* trans. C. Gattegno and F. M. Hodgson (1951; reprint ed., London: Routledge & Kegan Paul, 1962).

11. See P. A. Twelker, *Instructional Simulation Systems* (Corvallis, Oreg.: Continuing Education Publications, 1969), for the range of this activity. See also Sarane S. Boocock and E. O. Schild, eds., *Simulation Games in Learning* (Beverly Hills, Calif.: Sage Publications, 1968).

12. Joel M. Kibbee, Clifford J. Craft, and Burt Nanus, *Management Games: A New Technique for Executive Development* (New York: Reinhold, 1961); P. S. Greenlaw, L. W. Herron, and R. H. Rawdon, *Business Simulation in Industrial and University Education* (Englewood Cliffs, N.J.: Prentice-Hall, 1962). The latter provides examples covering a variety of different games.

13. See *Statistical Abstract, 1971,* pp. 200–201, for the 1969 estimate; *Statistical Abstract, 1974,* pp. 728–729, for the 1972 estimate.

14. *Statistical Abstract, 1971,* p. 211.

15. According to an official of Simulations Publications, SINAI, which was introduced at about the time of the 1973 Yom Kippur War, has sold over 7,000 copies at $8.00 each; MECH-WAR '77, a more recent game, has already sold 2,900 copies, also at $8.00 each.

16. *New York Times,* November 26, 1972, p. 1.

17. *Statistical Abstract, 1974,* p. 211.

18. Fromm et al., *Federally Supported Mathematical Models,* identified "over 650 models involving some aspect of social decisionmaking" (p. 3). Of this total, questionnaires were sent to 310 project monitors and directors.

19. This increase has already begun; see G. K. Chacko, ed., *Systems Approach to Environmental Pollution* (Arlington, Va.: Operations Research Society of America, 1972).

5. A History of War Games

1. A summary historical sketch is included in Hausrath, *Venture Simulation,* chap. 1. One of the definitive works on board games is H. J. R. Murray, *A History of Board Games Other Than Chess* (New York: Oxford University Press, 1952). See also idem, *A History of Chess* (Oxford: Clarendon Press, 1913). For Oriental board games, see Arthur Smith, *The Game of Go* (New York: Moffat, Yard, 1908).

2. Among the many excellent general historical sources available are John P. Young, *A Survey of Historical Developments in War Games* (Bethesda, Md.: Johns Hopkins University, Operations Re-

search Office, 1959); Rudolf Hofmann, *War Games* (Washington, D.C.: U.S., Department of the Army, Office of the Chief of Military History, 1952); "The War Game and How It Is Played," *Scientific American,* December 5, 1914, pp. 470–471; Clayton J. Thomas and Walter L. Deemer, Jr., "The Role of Operational Gaming in Operations Research," *Operations Research* 5, No. 1 (February 1957): 1–27; Henri de Jomini, *The Art of War,* trans. G. H. Mendell and W. P. Craighill (Philadelphia: Lippincott, 1892); W. R. Livermore, *The American Kreigsspiel* (Boston: Clarke, 1898); Paul S. Deems, "War Gaming and Exercises," *Air University Review* 8 (Winter 1956–57): 98–126; Thomas R. Philips, ed., *The Roots of Strategy* (Harrisburg, Pa.: Military Service, 1940); R. A. Raymond and Harry W. Baer, Jr., "A History of War Games," *The Reserve Officer,* October 1939, pp. 19–20.

3. Karl Groos, quoted in Murray, *History of Board Games,* p. 234.

4. Murray, *History of Chess,* chap. 1. A four-player antecedent of chess, *Chaturanga,* had this property.

5. Brian Sutton-Smith, "Strategy in Games and Folk Tales," *Journal of Social Psychology* 61 (1963): 185–199.

6. E. S. Quade contributed this insight in conversation.

7. This pattern is noted in the introduction to Farrand Sayre, *Map Maneuvers and Tactical Rides,* 3rd ed. (Fort Leavenworth, Kans.: Army Service Schools Press, 1910).

8. *Ibid.*

9. Murray, *History of Board Games.*

10. Jomini, in *Art of War,* discusses the French contribution.

11. Sayre, *Map Maneuvers,* pp. 5–6.

12. See Young, *Historical Developments in War Games,* pp. 7, 9–11. The author notes that one popular game, invented by Helwig of the court of Brunswick, was used to teach young noblemen the military sciences; it involved over 1,600 separate movement squares and featured terrain distinctions, differential movement rates for the forces, a game director, and increasingly detailed rules of play.

13. Francis J. McHugh, *Fundamentals of War Gaming,* 3rd ed. (Newport, R.I.: U.S. Naval War College, 1966), p. 2–6. There were in fact two von Reisswitzes, father and son, but the son is most often given credit for the invention.

14. Hausrath, *Venture Simulation,* p. 6; Young, *Historical Developments in War Games,* pp. 11–13.

15. Young, *Historical Developments in War Games,* pp. 13–15. See also, Friedrich Immanuel, *The Regimental War Game,* trans. Walter Krueger (Kansas City, Mo.: Hudson Press, 1907).

16. Hofmann, *War Games,* chap. 8.

17. See McHugh, *Fundamentals of War Gaming,* chap. 2, for extensive and detailed coverage of this period.

18. A fascinating account of German war games is given in Walter Goerlitz, *History of the German General Staff: 1657–1945,* trans. Brian Battershaw (New York: Praeger, 1963). See also Hausrath, *Venture Simulation,* pp. 23–37, which covers this period thoroughly.

19. Barton Whalley, *Codeword BARBAROSSA* (Cambridge, Mass.: M.I.T. Press, 1973).

20. Wohlstetter, *Pearl Harbor,* pp. 371–373, 381. Hausrath also treats this involvement in *Venture Simulation,* pp. 30–32.

21. McHugh, *Fundamentals of War Gaming,* pp. 2-18, 2-19.

22. Historical Evaluation and Research Organization, *Historical Trends Related to Weapons Lethality: Basic Historical Studies* (Washington, D.C., 1964), annex 1; J. A. Stockfisch, "Operational Testing," *Military Review,* May 1971, pp. 68–82.

23. Robert V. Bruce, *Lincoln and the Tools of War* (Indianapolis: Bobbs-Merrill, 1956), chaps. 6, 8. Goerlitz, *German General Staff,* chap. 3; James A. Houston, *The Sinews of War: Army Logistics 1775–1953* (Washington, D.C.: U.S., Department of the Army, Office of the Chief of Military History, 1966), chap. 4.

24. McHugh, *Fundamentals of War Gaming,* chap. 2; P. H. Colomb, *Naval Warfare: Its Ruling Principles and Practice Historically Treated* (London: W. G. Allen, 1895); E. M. L. Beale, *The Role of Gaming in Military Operational Research,* memo no. 190 (London: Admiralty, Department of Operational Research, 1971), introduction; Michael Lewis, "Armed Forces and the Art of War: Navies," in *The Zenith of European Power, 1830–1870,* ed. J. T. B. Bury, New Cambridge Modern History, vol. 10 (Cambridge: Cambridge University Press, 1967), pp. 274–301.

25. The cross-cultural characteristics of game play, including that related to war, are discussed in detail in Johan Huizinga, *Homo Ludens: A Study of the Play Element in Culture* (Boston: Beacon Press, 1950); see also Roger Callois, *Of Man, Play and Games,* trans. Barash Meyer (New York: Free Press, 1961). R. C. Bell, *Board and Table Games from Many Civilizations* (London: Oxford University Press, 1960); Murray, *A History of Board Games;* idem, *History of Chess.*

26. Scott A. Boorman, *The Protracted Game* (New York: Oxford University Press, 1969).

27. H. O. Yardley, *The Education of a Poker Player* (New York: Simon & Schuster, 1957); E. Bergler, *The Psychology of Gambling* (New York: Hill and Wang, 1957).

28. Callois, *Man, Play and Games,* chap. 1, contains a statement of this argument.

29. Hausrath, *Venture Simulation,* p. 34.

30. This issue has great importance but has not been properly re-

searched. See Viola Spolin, *Improvisation for the Theater* (Evanston: Northwestern University Press, 1963), chap. 2, for a basic theoretical overview of role playing.

31. Paul Bracken, "Unintended Consequences of Strategic Gaming," *Simulation & Games* 8, no. 3 (September 1977): 283–318.

32. Richard Titmuss, *Problems of Social Policy* (London: HMSO, 1950), pp. 12–13, 21.

33. Bracken, "Unintended Consequences," p. 307.

34. John Erickson, *The Road to Stalingrad* (London: Weidenfeld and Nicholson, 1975), chap. 1. Walter Goerlitz, *Paulus and Stalingrad* (London: Methuen, 1963), pp. 97–120.

35. Wohlstetter, *Pearl Harbor;* McHugh, *Fundamentals of War Gaming,* p. 2–19.

36. Andrew Wilson, *The Bomb and the Computer* (New York: Delacorte, 1968), is one popular example of the myth.

37. See Gerhard Ritter, *The Schlieffen Plan: Critique of a Myth* (London: Oswald Wolff, 1958).

38. Michael Howard, *The Franco-Prussian War* (New York: Macmillan, 1968), pp. 35–36.

39. Simply counting opposing forces and gaming the various Arab-Israeli wars, for instance, would consistently have produced Arab victories; the human element, in a general sense, was a decisive factor in the actual outcome. It is well known that a few pilots and ship commanders always account for a disproportionate share of the total hits or kills in combat, but this individual performance factor is washed out of gamed considerations. See, for example, Theodore Roscoe, *United States Submarine Operations in World War II* (Annapolis: U.S. Naval Institute, 1949), pp. 527–563.

40. A fine effort to this end has been made by M. G. Weiner, *War Gaming Methodology* (Santa Monica, Calif.: The Rand Corporation, RM-2413-PR, July 1959).

6. The Recent Development of War Gaming

1. The great difficulty we encountered in carrying out this task emphasizes the need for improved professional communication and management control; this kind of overview should be routinely produced and readily available.

2. Edward Girard, *A Non-Agonizing Reappraisal of War Gaming* (McLean, Va.: Research Analysis Corporation, 1972), p. 2.

3. Charles F. Hermann, "Simulation: Political Processes," in *International Encyclopedia of the Social Sciences* (New York: Macmillan, 1968), p. 275.

4. Herbert Goldhamer and Hans Speier, "Some Observations on Political Gaming," *World Politics* 12, no. 1 (October 1959): 71–83.

5. These questions and purposes were suggested by Joseph Gold-sen in a postmortem critique of the entire enterprise conducted in May 1956.

6. The work of Graham Allison and Richard Neustadt of the John F. Kennedy School of Government at Harvard University is a notable exception to this general point. See, for example, Richard Neustadt, *Presidential Power* (New York: Science Editions, 1962).

7. Harvey Averch and Marvin M. Lavin, *Simulation of Decision-making in Crises: Three Manual Gaming Experiments* (Santa Monica, Calif.: The Rand Corporation, RM-4202-PR, August 1964), is the main source for the following discussion.

8. Idem, *Dilemmas in the Politico-Military Conduct of Escalating Crises* (Santa Monica, Calif.: The Rand Corporation, P-3205, August 1965), p. 11. This game form also has its overenthusiastic and unrealistic exponents, including S. F. Giffen, *Simulating International Conflict* (New York: Doubleday, 1965).

9. The family of models comprising STRIP, STRAP, and STROP is perhaps of most interest today. See Norman C. Dalkey, *Families of Models* (Santa Monica, Calif.: The Rand Corporation, P-3198, August 1965); idem, "Solvable Nuclear War Models," *Management Science* 11, no. 9 (July 1965): 783–791.

10. John D. Williams, *The Compleat Strategyst: Being a Primer on the Theory of Games of Strategy* (New York: McGraw-Hill, 1966).

11. Melvin Dresher, *Some Military Applications of the Theory of Games* (Santa Monica, Calif.: The Rand Corporation, P-1849, December 1959); idem, *Games of Strategy: Theory and Applications* (Englewood Cliffs, N.J.: Prentice-Hall, 1961).

12. See Lloyd S. Shapley and Martin Shubik, *Concepts and Theories of Pure Competition* (Santa Monica, Calif.: The Rand Corporation, RM-3553-PR, May 1963); idem, *Some Topics in Two-Person Games* (Santa Monica, Calif.: The Rand Corporation, RM-3672-1-PR, October 1963).

13. Hausrath, *Venture Simulation*.

14. Research Analysis Corporation, "Gaming and Simulations: A Department of the Research Analysis Corporation" (McLean, Va., n.d.). Additional information about RAC was provided by Dondero and his staff in November 1970 and by Dondero on April 27, 1978.

15. Research Analysis Corporation, *Theater Battle Model* (McLean, Va., RAC-R-36, January 1968).

16. Research Analysis Corporation, *CARMONETTE III Documentation* (McLean, Va., RAC-R-28, October 1967).

17. In fairness to Research Analysis Corporation and to others interested in this type of MSG, we must note that individual pro-

fessionals have on occasion stressed the need for more systematic development and analysis of data to improve this state of affairs; apparently, however, no such data-base development has ever taken place.

18. U.S., General Accounting Office, Task Group on War Games Evaluation, working document, May 20, 1971.

19. Documentation of these MSGs is scarce, but some general reference is made to ARPA/COIN in Clark Abt, "War Gaming," *International Science and Technology*, August 1964, pp. 29-37.

20. Good game playing usually requires a focus on the critical aspects of the game; the player who manages these few aspects best is the winner. This kind of simplification requires further study.

21. Ralph E. Strauch, *A Critical Assessment of Quantitative Methodology as a Policy Analysis Tool* (Santa Monica, Calif.: The Rand Corporation, P-5282, August 1974), is one rare exception to the apparently general lack of interest in this issue.

22. Paul Doty, "Can Investigations Improve Scientific Advice? The Case of the ABM," *Minerva* 10, no. 2 (April 1967) : 280-294.

7. Mathematical and Game-Theory Models

1. Frederick W. Lanchester, *Aircraft in Warfare: The Dawn of the Fourth Air Arm* (London: Constable, 1916); chapters 5, 6, and 18 contain the essential exposition; chapter 5 formulates the N-Square law; chapter 6 discusses applications, especially Napoleon's plans for the Battle of Trafalgar; and chapter 18 describes problems of the partial concentration of forces, the use of aircraft in joint operations with naval gunnery, and the tactical use of aircraft. See also T. Von Karman, "Lanchester's Contribution to the Theory of Flight Operational Research," *Journal of the Royal Aeronautical Society* 62 (February 1958) : 80-93; this first Lanchester Memorial Lecture contains a biographical sketch of Lanchester and a summary of his contributions.

2. Lanchester, *Aircraft in Warfare*, chap. 5.

3. M. Hammerton, "A Case of an Inappropriate Model," *Nature* 203, no. 4940 (July 1964): 63-64, states, on this point, "All mathematical models must simplify: that is their strength. They may, in oversimplifying, distort: that is their danger."

4. A significant example is D. W. Willard, *Lanchester as a Force in History: An Analysis of Land Battles of the Years 1618-1905* (Washington, D.C.: Research Analysis Corporation, RAC-TP-74, November 1962).

5. J. H. Engel, "A Verification of Lanchester's Law," *Operations Research* 2, no. 2 (May 1954) : 163-171.

6. This is not to say that no one has tried to use Lanchester's

equations to analyze guerrilla operations; some applications have been more thoughtful than others. See M. B. Schaffer, *Lanchester Models of Guerrilla Engagements* (Santa Monica, Calif.: The Rand Corporation, RM-5053-ARPA, January 1967), for a well-qualified example; Seymour J. Deitchman, "A Lanchester Model of Guerrilla Warfare," *Operations Research* 10, no. 6 (November–December 1962): 818–827, presents a distinctly unqualified point of view.

7. Willard, in *Lanchester as a Force in History*, adds a further caution, based on his extensive empirical work with Lanchester equations, to the effect that they are not valid in large-scale situations and lack predictive power.

8. Ivan Driggs, "A Monte Carlo Model of Lanchester's Square Law," *Operations Research* 4, no. 2 (April 1965) : 148–151.

9. N. H. Lundquist, "The Functions of Operations Analysis," *Artilleri Tidskrift* 84, no. 3 (1955), stresses the fact that mathematical analyses must be limited to logical mechanics and cannot be used as a substitute for evaluation and judgment. See also P. M. Morse and G. Kimball, *Methods of Operations Research* (New York: Wiley, 1950), pp. 63–77, for a thorough treatment of this issue with respect to Lanchester equations.

10. Lewis F. Richardson, *Statistics of Deadly Quarrels* (Chicago: Quadrangle Press, 1960), is a general source; for a summary of Richardson's contributions to war gaming, see Anatol Rapoport, "Lewis Richardson's Mathematical Theory of War," *Journal of Conflict Resolution* 1 (1957) : 249–299; for a very sophisticated application of his model, see Michael Intriligator, "Strategic Arms in a Richardson Model of Arms Races," mimeographed (Los Angeles: University of California, Department of Economics, 1968).

11. See Hammerton, "Inappropriate Model."

12. A clear statement of the intellectual form of much of this work is contained in Seth Bonder, *A Generalized Lanchester Model to Predict Weapon Performance in Dynamic Combat* (Columbus: Ohio State University, Department of Industrial Engineering, Systems Research Group, RF 573 TR 65–1, June 30, 1965).

13. The standard sources are John von Neumann and Oskar Morgenstern, *Theory of Games and Economic Behavior* (Princeton: Princeton University Press, 1944); Martin Shubik, ed., *Game Theory and Related Approaches to Social Behavior* (New York: Wiley, 1964); R. Duncan Luce and Howard Raiffa, *Games and Decisions* (New York: Wiley, 1957).

14. See Trevor Williams and Cling J. Ancker, Jr., "Stochastic Duels," *Operations Research* 11, no. 5 (October 1963) : 803–817, for a representative survey of the applications area.

15. See for example, Lloyd S. Shapley, *The Silent Duel, One Bul-*

let Versus Two, Equal Accuracy (Santa Monica, Calif.: The Rand Corporation, RM-445, September 9, 1950), for one rigorous illustration of the type. See also John D. Harsanyi, "A General Theory of Rational Behavior in Game Situations," *Econometrica* 34, no. 3 (July 1966): 613–634.

16. J. R. Isbell and W. H. Marlow, "Attrition Games," *Naval Logistics Quarterly* 3 (March–June 1956) : 71–94; this article summarizes many mathematical and game-theory models in application.

17. See L. D. Berkovitz and Melvin Dresher, "A Game Theory Analysis of Tactical Air War," *Operations Research* 7, no. 5 (September 1959) : 599–620. A more general treatment of the basic problem is contained in Melvin Dresher, *Some Military Applications of the Theory of Games* (Santa Monica, Calif.: The Rand Corporation, P-1849, December 1959). Other applications are described in Martin Shubik, *On the Uses and Methods of Gaming* (New York: Elsevier, 1975), chap. 11.

18. The terms *b* and *e*, used in equations 7.6, 7.7, 7.8, and 7.9, are constants of proportionality.

19. Rufus Isaacs has detailed the state of the art in confronting search problems. See *Differential Games* (New York: Wiley, 1965).

20. See Martin Shubik, *Games for Society, Business, and War* (New York: Elsevier, 1975), for examples.

21. Martin Shubik, Garry D. Brewer, and E. Savage, *The Literature of Gaming, Simulation, and Model-Building* (Santa Monica, Calif.: The Rand Corporation, R-620-ARPA, June 1972), contains a sampling of these and related models classified and evaluated in several ways.

22. See John Cross, *The Economics of Bargaining* (New York: Basic Books, 1969); Fred Charles Iklé, *How Nations Negotiate* (New York: Harper & Row, 1964); idem, *Every War Must End* (New York: Columbia University Press, 1971). Iklé's strongly logical treatment of important bargaining and negotiation situations could easily be modeled, in part mathematically; he does not do so, however.

8. Manual Games

1. Goldhamer and Speier, "Some Observations," is a seminal work; see Lincoln P. Bloomfield and Barton Whaley, "The Political Military Exercise," *Orbis* 7 (Winter 1965) : 854–870 for an extension and development of Goldhamer and Speier's innovation; many other sources have developed this work further.

2. See Martin Shubik and Garry D. Brewer, "Methodological Advances in Gaming," *Simulation & Games* 3, no. 3 (September 1972): 329–348.

3. E. W. Paxson, *War Gaming* (Santa Monica, Calif.: The Rand Corporation, RM-3489-PR, February 1963).

4. Ibid., p. 22.

5. For example, volumes of material were generated in the course of four plays of Goldhamer and Speier's original political and military exercise, but they were circulated outside of Rand only in one or two highly summarized forms. Because of the high rank of the participants, the Studies, Analysis and Gaming Agency of the Joint Chiefs of Staff has filmed postgame sessions reconstructing game events for later showings at the convenience of busy officials.

6. The issue can be examined, however; Robert Mandel has made an excellent start in "Political Gaming and Crisis Foreign Policy-making" (Ph.D. diss., Yale University, 1975).

7. The art of scenario construction and application is surveyed in Peter deLeon, "Scenario Designs: An Overview," *Simulation & Games* 6, no. 1 (March 1975) : 39–60; Harvey A. De Weerd, "A Contextual Approach to Scenario Construction," ibid. 5, no. 4 (December 1975) : 403–414. The importance of the scenario in political and military MSGs is detailed in Harvey A. De Weerd, *Political Military Scenarios* (Santa Monica, Calif.: The Rand Corporation, P-3535, February 1967). De Weerd, *An Israeli Scenario for a Laboratory Simulation* (Santa Monica, Calif.: System Development Corporation, SP-3139, March 1968), presents a five-year forecast of events in the Middle East from 1968 through 1973 that is striking for both its plausibility and the extent of its accuracy. For other examples of scenarios, see Lincoln P. Bloomfield, *Western Europe to the Mid-Seventies: Five Scenarios* (Cambridge, Mass.: M.I.T., Center for International Studies, A/68-3, 1968), pp. 14–16; Herman Kahn, *Alternative World Futures,* paper HI-342 (Croton-on-Hudson, N.Y.: Hudson Institute, April 1964); idem, *On Escalation, Metaphors, and Scenarios* (New York: Praeger, 1965); C. K. Ogden, *Bentham's Theory of Fictions* (London: Kegan Paul, 1932).

8. Seyom Brown, "Scenarios in Systems Analysis," in *Systems Analysis and Policy Planning: Applications in Defense,* ed. E. S. Quade and W. I. Boucher (New York: Elsevier, 1968), p. 300.

9. This definition is derived from Harvey A. De Weerd, "Scenario Methodology," mimeographed (Santa Monica, Calif.: The Rand Corporation, August 10, 1972).

10. De Weerd, "Contextual Approach," pp. 403–405.

11. Jacques Durand has begun this task, however, and stresses the need for the development of detailed information about likely conflict situations, or contexts; see "A New Method for Constructing Scenarios," *Futures* 4, no. 4 (December 1972) : 326–335.

12. This is the message contained in Harold Lasswell's formula-

tion and use of the "developmental construct," which stresses the primacy of contextual detail. See "The Garrison State," *American Journal of Sociology* 46 (1941) : 455–468.

13. De Weerd, "Contextual Approach," pp. 403–404.

14. This process is described in deLeon, "Scenario Designs," pp. 50–51.

15. See H. Stuart Hughes, *History as Art and Science* (New York: Harper & Row, 1964).

16. Patrick Gardiner, *The Nature of Historical Explanation* (London: Oxford University Press, 1952), pp. 96–97.

17. John Diebold, "The World and Doomsday Fads," *New York Times*, February 25, 1973, p. E-3.

18. One attempt at performing these tasks is described by Garry D. Brewer in "Existing in a World of Institutionalized Danger," *Yale Studies in World Public Order* 3, no. 2 (Spring 1977) : 339–378, a study done for the trustees of the Ford Foundation. See also James L. Foster, "The Future of Conventional Arms Control," *Policy Sciences* 8, no. 1 (March 1977): 1–19, for a more specific effort.

19. See Robert Mandel, "Political Gaming and Foreign Policy Making During Crises," *World Politics* 29, no. 4 (July 1977): 610–625, for some refreshing views on these and related matters.

20. George Quester, "The Shah and the Bomb," *Policy Sciences* 8, no. 1 (March 1977) : 21–32, contains many "gamable" propositions. See also Mason Willrich and T. B. Taylor, *Nuclear Theft: Risks and Safeguards* (Cambridge, Mass.: Ballinger, 1974); Bruce G. Blair and Garry D. Brewer, "The Terrorist Threat to World Nuclear Programs," *Journal of Conflict Resolution* 21, no. 3 (September 1977) : 379–403; Barton Whalley, *Codeword BARBAROSSA* (Cambridge, Mass.: M.I.T. Press, 1973). Whalley's *Strategem: Deception and Surprise in War* (Cambridge, Mass.: M.I.T., Center for International Studies, CIS-S/69-9, 1969), is a gold mine for the would-be gamer. William R. Harris, *On Countering Strategic Deception* (Santa Monica, Calif.: The Rand Corporation, R-1230, forthcoming), is a compendium of research questions and policy issues that deserve concerted attention. Ole R. Holsti, "Crisis, Stress, and Decisionmaking," *International Social Science Journal* 23, no. 1 (1971) : 53–67, is representative; Fred Iklé, *How Nations Negotiate* (New York: Harper & Row, 1964), is a benchmark effort.

21. See Trevor Cliffe, "Military Technology and the European Balance," in *Adelphi Papers* (London: International Institute for Strategic Studies, August 1972); James L. Foster, "The Future of Conventional Arms Control," *Policy Sciences* 8, no. 1 (March 1977): 1–19; both are excellent sources.

22. Termination has not received a fraction of the attention it

warrants; see James L. Foster and Garry D. Brewer, "And the Clocks Were Striking Thirteen: The Termination of War," *Policy Sciences* 7, no. 2 (June 1976) : 225–243. Iklé, *Every War Must End;* and Paul Kecskemeti, *Strategic Surrender: The Politics of Victory and Defeat* (Stanford : Stanford University Press, 1958), provide historical insight and information. Prevention is treated in Fred Iklé, "The Prevention of Nuclear War in a World of Uncertainty," *Policy Sciences* 7, no. 2 (June 1976) : 245–250.

23. Goldhamer and Speier, "Some Observations," is the primary source for this discussion.

24. Ibid., pp. 72–73.

25. Ibid., pp. 77–78. The players who participated in the original game included Andrew Marshall, Nathan Leites, Harvey De Weerd and Paul Kecskemeti.

26. Herbert Goldhamer, private communication, August 1973.

27. Lincoln P. Boomfield and Norman T. Padleford, "Three Experiments in Political Gaming," *American Political Science Review* 53 (December 1959) : 1105–1115; W. Phillips Davison, "A Public Opinion Game," *Public Opinion Quarterly* 25 (Summer 1961) : 219–220.

28. Lincoln P. Boomfield and Barton Whaley, "POLEX: Political-Military Exercise," *Military Review* 45 (November 1965) : 65–71. Lincoln P. Bloomfield with Cornelius J. Gearin and James L. Foster, *Anticipating Conflict-Control Policies, the "CONEX" Games as a Planning Tool* (Cambridge, Mass.: M.I.T., Center for International Studies, C/70-10, February 1970), is one example.

29. Lincoln P Bloomfield and Cornelius J. Cearin, "Games Foreign Policy Experts Play: The Political Exercise Comes of Age," *Orbis* 16 (Winter 1973) : 1012.

30. O. Helmer and T. A. Brown, *SAFE: A Strategy-and-Force-Evaluation Game* (Santa Monica, Calif.: The Rand Corporation, RM-3287-PR, October 1962); O. Helmer, *Gaming the Strategic Planning Process* (Santa Monica, Calif.: The Rand Corporation, RM-2905-PR, November 1961). T. A. Brown and E. W. Paxson, *A Retrospective Look at Some Strategy and Force Evaluation Games* (Santa Monica, Calif.: The Rand Corporation, R-1619-PR, September 1975); our description of the SAFE games relies heavily on this work.

31. Brown and Paxson, *Retrospective Look*, p. 2.

32. Ibid.

33. Ibid., p. 5. Fred Hoffman, the project leader, became deputy comptroller in 1965 and later became deputy assistant secretary of defense for systems analysis.

34. Ibid., p. 35.

35. Ibid., p. 40. The Air Force bias of the players, who were working under Air Force Project Rand auspices, is worth noting. It is interesting to speculate about the outcome of SAFE if Navy and civilian players had been used. The possible outcome of games played by actual Soviet players is even more interesting to contemplate.

36. These political games attract the highest-level officials, who play themselves in the hypothetical or projected setting. See Hausrath, *Venture Simulation*, pp. 264-265, for commentary.

37. David Halberstam, *The Best and the Brightest* (New York: Random House, 1969), p. 460.

38. In conversation in August 1970, Jones observed that during the heyday of McNamara's Whiz Kids, interpersonal communication between civilian and military defense officials reached an all-time low and the game environment became virtually the only opportunity for interagency and even intra-agency discussion; he termed these early games "the damnedest salesmen's conventions you ever saw."

39. Frank Kapper, *Examples of Politico-Military Simulation Scenarios* (Washington, D.C.: SAGA, May 1973), pp. 1–2.

9. Man-Machine Games

1. Harry J. Walther, *Catalog of War Gaming and Military Simulation Models* (Washington, D.C.: Studies, Analysis and Gaming Agency, SAGA-236-75, June 1975).

2. J. A. Stockfisch, *Models, Data, and War: A Critique of the Study of Conventional Forces* (Santa Monica, Calif.: The Rand Corporation, R-1526-PR, March 1975), contains valuable insights about these changes in fashion and their consequences.

3. R. L. Chapman, W. C. Biel, J. L. Kennedy, and A. Newell, *The Systems Research Laboratory and Its Program* (Santa Monica, Calif.: The Rand Corporation, RM-890, January 7, 1952).

4. R. L. Chapman, John L. Kennedy, Allen Newell, and William C. Biel, "The Systems Research Laboratory's Air Defense Experiments," *Management Science* 5, no. 3 (April 1959) : 250–269.

5. This finding appears to have been lost on several generations of university-based gamers, many of whom persist in using students in experimental roles for which they are poorly suited.

6. B. Rome and S. Rome, *Communication and Large Organizations* (Santa Monica, Calif.: System Development Corporation, SP-1690/000/00, September 1964); idem, *Organizational Growth through Decisionmaking: A Computer-Based Experiment in Eductive Method* (New York: Elsevier, 1971).

7. General details about the Logistics Systems Laboratory are given in Murray A. Geisler, "The Simulation of a Large-Scale Military Activity," *Management Science* 5 (July 1959) : 359–368.

8. The experience has been relatively well reported in the open literature. See the following representative examples: Murray A. Geisler and Wilbur Steger, *The Use of Manned Simulation in the Design of an Operational Control System* (Santa Monica, Calif.: The Rand Corporation, P-2322, May 1961); W. W. Haythorn, *The Use of Simulation in Logistics Policy Research* (Santa Monica, Calif.: The Rand Corporation, P-1791, September 1959); W. H. McGlothlin, *The Simulation Laboratory as a Developmental Tool* (Santa Monica, Calif.: The Rand Corporation, P-1454, August 1958).

9. Reports on Laboratory Problem II are not as numerous as for others in the sequence; however, E. E. Bean and W. H. McGlothlin, *A Model for Assessing the Effect of Maintenance on Missile Launch Probability* (Santa Monica, Calif.: The Rand Corporation, RM-2451, September 1959), suggests the nature of the work undertaken in LP-II.

10. For details, see I. K. Cohen and R. L. Van Horn, "A Laboratory Exercise for Information System Evaluation," in *Information System Sciences,* ed. J. Spiegel and D. Walker (Washington, D.C.: Spartan Books, 1965).

11. See Murray A. Geisler, W. W. Haythorn, and Wilbur Steger, *Simulation and the Logistics Systems Laboratory* (Santa Monica, Calif.: The Rand Corporation, RM-3281-PR, September 1962), pp. 6, 9.

12. See J. R. Renshaw and A. Heuston, *The Game Monopologs* (Santa Monica, Calif.: The Rand Corporation, RM-1917-1-PR, March 1960); L. Gainen, R. A. Levine, and W. McGlothlin, *Baselogs: A Base Logistics Management Game* (Santa Monica, Calif.: The Rand Corporation, RM-2086, January 1958).

13. B. J. Voosen and D. Corona, *Misslogs: A Game of Missile Logistics* (Santa Monica, Calif.: The Rand Corporation, RM-2455, September 1959), p. iii.

14. Stephen B. Luce, "The U.S. Naval War College," *U.S. Naval Institute Proceedings,* September 1910, p. 684. See also William McCarty Little, "The Strategic Naval War Game or Chart Maneuver," ibid., December 1912, pp. 1213–33.

15. McHugh, *Fundamentals of War Gaming,* pp. 4–10, 4–11.

16. Idem, "Gaming at the Naval War College," *U.S. Naval Institute Proceedings,* March 1960, p. 52.

17. McHugh, *Fundamentals of War Gaming,* pp. 5–37, 5–39.

18. Staff of War Gaming Department, U.S. Naval War College, interview, July 1975.

19. McHugh, *Fundamentals of War Gaming*, p. 5–3.

20. Abe Greenberg, "War Gaming: Third Generation," *Naval War College Review* 27, no. 5 (March–April 1975) : 71–75.

21. Ibid., pp. 73–74.

22. U.S., General Accounting Office, *Report B-163074* (Washington, D.C.: Government Printing Office, 1971) : 26.

23. U.S., Naval War College, *Naval Warfare Gaming System Statement of Requirements* (Newport, R.I., April 1974), vols. 1–2; these documents were updated in 1975.

24. Interview, July 29, 1975.

25. Among other uses, WARS is currently being employed to evaluate weapons systems such as the HARPOON and PHOENIX systems; to study projected techniques, technology, and tactics at sea in the 1980s; to study man-machine interactions in so-called decision-point analyses; to run both simple and complex fleet games; and to cooperate in research games with naval facilities at the Naval Underwater Center in China Lake, Calif., and the Naval Electronics Laboratory in San Diego.

26. Regrettably, XRAY has not been adequately documented in the open literature, although it is reasonably well known within the military gaming community. See Edwin W. Paxson, "Computers and National Security," in *Computers and the Problems of Society*, ed. H. Sackman and H. Borko (Montvale, N.J.: American Federation of Information Processing Societies Press, 1972), pp. 65–92.

27. In this case, the venerable JOSS time-sharing system, designed by Rand, was used; modern time-shared systems and networks would multiply the basic power several times.

28. Harold Guetzkow, Richard Snyder, Robert Noel, Chadwick Alger, and Richard Brody, *Simulation in International Relations: Developments for Research and Teaching* (Englewood Cliffs, N.J.: Prentice-Hall, 1963); Harold Guetzkow, "The Use of Simulation in the Study of International Relations," *Behavioral Science* 4, no. 3 (July 1959): 183–191; Richard A. Brody, "Some Systemic Effects of the Spread of Nuclear Weapons Technology: A Study through Simulation of a Multinuclear Future," *Journal of Conflict Resolution* 7, no. 4 (December 1963) : 1–126; Robert C. Noel, *The POLIS Network* (Santa Barbara, Calif.: University of California, Political Institutions Simulation Laboratory, March 1971). The work is extensive and varied; that of Austin C. Hoggatt, his colleagues, and students is illustrative. See, for example, Austin C. Hoggatt, "Measuring the Cooperativeness of Behavior in Quantity Variation Duopoly Games," *Behavioral Science* 12, no. 2 (March 1967); idem, *A Time-Sharing Methodology for Constructing Social Simulations*, working paper no. 306 (Berkeley: Center for Research in Management Science, 1970).

10. Machine Simulations

1. See Walther, *Catalog of War Gaming*, appendix C.

2. R. H. Adams and J. L. Jenkins, "Simulation of Air Operations with the Air-Battle Model," *Operations Research* 8 (September–October 1960): 600–615.

3. These problems are treated in detail in Stockfisch, *Models, Data, and War*.

4. Documentation was voluminous, in the form of technical manuals, flow diagrams, causal networks, data descriptions, and so forth. Reporting in the professional literature was sketchy by comparison; see Clark C. Abt, "War Gaming," *International Science and Technology*, no. 32 (August 1964) : 29–37; Morten Gorden, *International Relations Theory in the TEMPER Simulation* (Cambridge, Mass.: Abt Associates, September 1965). The latter was not, strictly speaking, in the professional literature, although it was circulated in the social-science community.

5. Iklé, "Prevention of War."

6. A modest example of this application is contained in Ronald D. Brunner and Garry D. Brewer, *Organized Complexity: Empirical Theories of Political Development* (New York: Free Press, 1971).

7. *TEMPER as a Model of International Relations: An Evaluation for the Joint War Games Agency, DoD* (New York: Simulmatics Corporation, AD-653-606, December 1966); Mathematica, "Final Report: Review of TEMPER Model" (Washington, D.C.: Defense Communication Agency, Contract #DCA 100-66-C-0083, September 1966).

8. Simulmatics, *TEMPER*.

9. TIN SOLDIER was built between 1950 and 1952 by George Gamow of the Operations Research Office of Johns Hopkins University; it was a two-sided tank battle, represented on a board by small tokens. See Richard E. Zimmerman, "Simulation of Tactical War Games," in *Operations Research and System Engineering*, ed. Charles D. Flagle, William H. Huggins, and Robert H. Roy (Baltimore: Johns Hopkins University Press, 1960); idem, "The Application of Electronic Computers to Monte Carlo War Game Problems," *Mathematical Ground Combat* (Chevy Chase, Md.: Johns Hopkins University, Operations Research Office, ORO-SP-11, April 1957).

10. Walther, *Catalog of War Gaming*, pp. 53–54.

11. J. R. Lind, *FAST-VAL: A Model for Forward Air Strike Evaluation* (Santa Monica, Calif.: The Rand Corporation, P-3076, March 1965), presents a concise overview of the model.

12. SUBDUEL's documentation is complete, and the model listing itself is unclassified; it is reportedly used at least monthly by the Center for Naval Analysis (CNA), Ketron, Inc., and the Weapons

Systems Evaluation Group (WSEG), from anyone of which documentation should be obtainable.

13. Iklé, "Prevention of War," p. 246.

14. See Paul Bracken, "Urban Sprawl and NATO Defense," *Survival* 18, no. 6 (November–December 1976) : 254–260, for a critique of "contextless" MSGs.

11. The Contextual Map

1. This topic is discussed in Ilene H. Bernstein and Howard E. Freeman, *Academic and Entrepreneurial Research: The Consequences of Diversity in Federal Evaluation Studies* (New York: Russell Sage Foundation, 1975).

2. See, for example, Robert C. Noel, *The POLIS Network: An Intercampus Consortium for Instructional Innovation in International Relations* (Santa Barbara, Calif.: University of California, Political Institutions Simulation Laboratory, March 1971).

3. Herbert A. Simon, "The Architecture of Complexity," in *General Systems,* yearbook of the Society for General Systems Research, ed. L. von Bertalanffy and Anatol Rapoport (1965), 10: 63–64. See also Todd R. La Porte, ed., *Organized Social Complexity* (Princeton: Princeton University Press, 1975), which considers the topic in some detail.

4. George A. Miller, *The Psychology of Communication* (New York: Basic Books, 1967), p. 49.

5. These and many other matters are treated at length in Ronald D. Brunner and Garry D. Brewer, *Organized Complexity* (New York: Free Press, 1971).

6. David Novick, "Mathematics: Logic, Quantity, and Method," *Review of Economics and Statistics,* 26, no. 4 (November 1954) : 357–358.

7. See Edward S. Quade and W. I. Boucher, eds., *Systems Analysis and Policy Planning* (New York: Elsevier, 1968), pp. 2, 4–5, 11, 17.

8. See J. A. Stockfisch, *Models, Data, and War: A Critique of the Study of Conventional Forces* (Santa Monica, Calif.: The Rand Corporation, R-1526-PR, March 1975).

9. Much has been said and written on this and closely related matters; Harold Orlans, "Neutrality and Advocacy in Policy Research," *Policy Sciences* 6, no. 2 (June 1975) : 107–119, summarizes the matter clearly, if somewhat polemically.

10. This paradigm of modeling has been formulated and discussed by Ralph E. Strauch in " 'Squishy' Problems and Quantitative Methods," *Policy Sciences* 6, no. 2 (June 1975) : 177.

11. The concept of lethal areas and estimates of the probability of killing a tank given a hit, which are embedded in firepower

scores and indices are an interesting illustration of this point. See Stockfisch, *Models, Data, and War,* for a detailed discussion.

12. We seem to have lost track of this point since World War II, when solid empirical work was commonplace among operations researchers; for the historical perspective, see Solly Zuckerman, *Scientists and War: The Impact of Science on Military and Civil Affairs* (London: Hamish Hamilton, 1966).

13. A follow-up survey of nonmilitary MSGs, patterned closely on the investigation described in this book, was conducted in 1974 and has been documented in Fromm et al., *Federally Supported Mathematical Models.*

14. Three preliminary versions of the questionnaire were developed and tried out on known games, with cooperative and competent respondents. The final version of the questionnaire was published in Martin Shubik and Garry D. Brewer, *Questionnaire—Models, Computer Machine Simulations, Games and Studies* (Santa Monica, Calif.: The Rand Corporation, P-4672, July 1971).

15. This figure is likely to be a very conservative estimate of the total activity. Much modeling is known to be performed by weapons developers and suppliers, and great efforts are expended to modify and refine selected existing MSGs to address specific problems. No one appears to know the full extent and cost of the business.

16. The rarity of even partial assessments of the purposes and uses of MSG is attested to by R. Coenen in "The Use of Technological Forecasts in Government Planning," *Research Policy* (April 1972) : 156–172.

17. Martin Shubik and Garry D. Brewer, *Models, Simulations, and Games—A Survey* (Santa Monica, Calif.: The Rand Corporation, R-1060-ARPA/RC, May 1972), p. 98, contains the raw information from which these estimates were derived.

18. U.S., General Accounting Office, *Computer Simulations, War Gaming, and Contract Studies* (Washington, D.C.: Government Printing Office, 1971), p. 8 (hereafter cited as GAO, *Computer Simulations*).

12. Purposes and Production

1. GAO, *Computer Simulations,* p. 8.

2. For a more detailed examination of purposes, see Shubik, *Games for Society,* chap. 1.

3. We performed this role, in cooperation with an audit team from the GAO's defense division, in the formulation and administration of the survey instrument reported in this book.

4. As noted in Gene H. Fisher, *Cost Considerations in Systems Analysis* (New York: Elsevier, 1971).

13. Operations

1. During our field interviews for this project we were told of a case in which an unusually sophisticated user requested that several sensitive input values be altered and the model rerun. The contractor declined, even though all expenses would have been covered. This tale may be apocryphal, however.

2. Gary Fromm et al., *Federally Supported Mathematical Models,* p. 246.

3. Ibid., p. 247.

4. Ibid., p. 249; the bigger the MSG, the more expensive it is to transfer; see p. 226.

5. Ibid., pp. 250–252.

6. U.S., General Accounting Office, *Improvement Needed in Documenting Computer Systems,* report no. B-115369 (Washington, D.C.: Government Printing Office, 1974).

7. Ibid., p. 7.

8. Ibid., p. 12.

9. Army Models Review Committee, *Review of Selected Army Models* (Washington, D.C.: U.S. Department of the Army, 1971), p. 8.

10. Stockfisch, *Models, Data, and War,* pp. 6–7.

11. The literature includes W. G. Cochran and G. M. Cox, *Experimental Designs* (New York: Wiley, 1957); W. J. Hill and W. G. Hunter, "Response Surface Methodology: A Literature Survey," *Technometrics* 8, no. 4 (November 1966) : 571–590; A. E. Hoerl, Jr., "Fitting Curves to Data," in *Chemical Business Handbook,* ed. J. W. Perry (New York: McGraw-Hill, 1954); K. D. Tocher, *The Art of Simulation* (Princeton: Van Nostrand, 1962). The work of George S. Fishman and Philip J. Kiviat is especially useful; see *Digital Computer Simulation: Statistical Considerations* (Santa Monica, Calif.: The Rand Corporation, RM-5387-PR, November 1967).

12. Barry W. Boehm, *Some Information Processing Implications of Air Force Space Missions: 1970–1980* (Santa Monica, Calif.: The Rand Corporation, RM-6213-PR, January 1970).

13. Donald W. Kosy, *Approaches to Improved Program Validation through Programming Language Design* (Santa Monica, Calif.: The Rand Corporation, P-4865, July 1972), is one excellent, concise treatment of the subject. Also noteworthy are Fred Gruenberger, "Program Testing and Validation," *Datamation* 14, no. 7 (July 1968) : 39–47; R. Rustin, ed., *Debugging Techniques in Large Systems* (Englewood Cliffs, N.J.: Prentice-Hall, 1971); Mark Halpren,

"Computer Programming: The Debugging Epoch Opens," *Computers and Automation* 14, no. 11 (November 1965) : 28–31.

14. The analytic case is nicely detailed in H. A. Antosiewicz, "Analytic Study of War Games," *Naval Research Logistics Quarterly 2*, no. 3 (September 1955) : 181–208; the use of sensitivity analysis in free-form, manual gaming, in Martin Shubik and Garry D. Brewer, "Methodological Advances in Gaming," *Simulation & Games*, 3, no. 3 (September 1972) : 329–348.

15. Richard L. Nolan, "Verification/Validation of Computer Simulation Models," in *Proceedings of the Summer Simulation Conference* (San Diego, 1972); Nolan notes that any modeling effort has the general purpose of capturing "important behavior" in a real system, with the behavior considered important depending on the objective of the analysis. For more on the issue of validation, see A. M. Turing, "Computing Machinery and Intelligence," in *Computers and Thought*, ed. E. D. Feigenbaum and J. Feldman (New York: McGraw-Hill, 1963), one of the original statements; Richard Van Horn, "Validation," in *The Design of Computer Experiments*, ed. Thomas H. Naylor (Durham: Duke University Press, 1969); Thomas H. Naylor and J. M. Finger, "Verification of Computer Simulation Models," *Management Science* 14, no. 2 (October 1967) : B-92–B-96; G. Arthur Mirham, "Practical Aspects of Simulation," *Operations Research Quarterly* 23, no. 1 (March 1972).

14. Benefits, Uses, and Costs

1. The same message has been repeated for nonmilitary MSGs in Fromm et al., *Federally Supported Mathematical Models*, chap. 5.

2. For the political and military exercise, see Lincoln P. Bloomfield and C. J. Gearin, "Games Foreign Policy Experts Play: The Political Exercise Comes of Age," *Orbis* 16 (Winter 1973): 1008–31.

3. Fromm et al., *Federally Supported Mathematical Models*, p. 20.

4. Adapted from Martin Shubik, *The Uses and Methods of Gaming* (New York: Elsevier, 1975), chap. 4.

5. Fromm et al., *Federally Supported Mathematical Models*, p. 20.

6. Ibid., p. 21.

7. Ibid.

15. Individual and Institutional Participants

1. See Neil Agnew and Sandra W. Pyke, "Sieves of Science," in idem, *The Science Game* (Englewood Cliffs, N.J.: Prentice-Hall, 1969), pp. 53–89.

2. The issue is not new but merely more evident and costly in recent times. See Emile Durkheim, *On the Division of Labor in So-*

ciety, trans. George Simpson (New York: Macmillan, 1933), pp. 1–31.

3. See Garry D. Brewer, "Analyses of Complex Systems," in *Organized Social Complexity*, ed. Todd R. La Porte (Princeton, N.J.: Princeton University Press, 1975), pp. 175–219.

4. Alexander L. George, "Bridging the 'Gap' between Scholarly Research and Policy-makers: The Problem of Theory and Action" (Paper presented at the Inter-University Faculty Seminar, University of Denver, May 3, 1968).

5. Max F. Millikan, "Inquiry and Policy: The Relation of Knowledge to Action," in *The Human Meaning of the Social Sciences*, ed. Daniel Lerner (New York: Meridian Books, 1959), p. 161.

6. Glenn A. Kent, "Decision-Making," *Air University Review* 22, no. 4 (May–June 1971): 62.

7. Mathematica, "Final Report: Review of TEMPER Model" (Washington, D.C.: Defense Communication Agency, Contract #DCA 100-66-C-0083, September 1966), pp. 23–24.

8. A demonstration of appraisals for other purposes is contained in Garry D. Brewer, *Politicians, Bureaucrats and the Consultant: A Critique of Urban Problem Solving* (New York: Basic Books, 1973), chaps. 2–5.

9. Millikan, "Inquiry and Policy," pp. 172–173.

10. W. Richard Scott, "Professionals in Bureaucracies: Areas of Conflict," in *Professionalization*, ed. Howard M. Vollmer and Donald M. Mills (Englewood Cliffs, N.J.: Prentice-Hall, 1966), pp. 265–275; J. A. Jackson, ed., *Professions and Professionalization* (New York: Cambridge University Press, 1970); J. Ben-David, "The Professional Role of the Physician in Bureaucratized Medicine: A Study in Role Conflict," *Human Relations* 11 (1959) : 255–274.

11. Garry D. Brewer, "Professionalism: The Need for Standards," *Interfaces* 4, no. 1 (November 1973) : 20–27. Garry D. Brewer and Owen P. Hall, Jr., "Policy Analysis by Computer Simulation: The Need for Appraisal," *Public Policy* 21, no. 3 (Summer 1973) : 343–365.

12. D. Lloyd, "The Disciplinary Powers of Professional Bodies," *Modern Law Review* 13 (1950) : 281–306.

13. The general problem is treated constructively in Robert T. Holt and John E. Turner, "The Scholar as Artisan," *Policy Sciences* 5, no. 3 (September 1974) : 257–270.

14. See his satirical treatment of this and related topics, in Amron Katz, "A Guide for the Perplexed: A Minimal/Maxim-al Handbook for Tourists in a Classified Bureaucracy," *Air Force/Space Digest* (November 1967).

15. U.S., General Accounting Office, *Improvement Needed in*

Documenting Computer Systems, report no. B-115369 (Washington, D.C.: Government Printing Office, 1974), pp. 13–15 (hereafter cited as GAO, *Improvement*).

16. Some years ago, Brownlee Haydon explored the source of information then prevalent about the number and duration of wars throughout human history—a set of facts that had gained international acceptance and received a scientific blessing. Some hard detective work revealed that these "facts" had actually been generated by a novelist and were plainly labeled as hypothetical. Through repeated use, however, the bogus data came to be accepted as gospel. See Brownlee Haydon, "The Great Statistics of War Hoax," *Air Force,* November 1964, pp. 94–96.

17. Kent, "Decision-Making," pp. 62–63.

18. Army Models Review Committee, *Review of Selected Army Models* (Washington, D.C.: U.S., Department of the Army, 1971).

16. The Decision-Making Process

1. TEMPER, a political, diplomatic, and military, all-machine MSG, described in chapter 10, provides an example of this kind of participation. In this case, the Joint War Gaming Agency (now the Studies, Analysis and Gaming Agency of the Joint Chiefs of Staff) called on Simulmatics and Mathematica, two private research firms largely made up of part-time university personnel, to try to fix a recalcitrant MSG. As it turned out, the model was beyond help.

17. Improving Standards

1. Collections of articles that, to varying degrees, address these points have been published in J. A. Jackson, ed., *Professions and Professionalization* (Cambridge: Cambridge University Press, 1970); Howard M. Vollmer and Donald M. Mills, eds., *Professionalization* (Englewood Cliffs, N.J.: Prentice-Hall, 1966).

2. J. Ben-David, "The Professional Role of the Physician in Bureaucratized Medicine: A Study in Role Conflict," *Human Relations* 11 (1958) : 225–274.

3. In different forms, all of these elements are noted in B. Barber, "Some Problems in the Sociology of the Professions," *Daedalus* 92 (1963) : 669–688.

4. See Rodney W. Nichols, "Mission-Oriented R & D," *Science* 172, no. 3978 (April 2, 1971) : 29–37.

5. The Air Force currently has approximately 12,000 active aircraft and the Navy somewhere around 500 ships; research, analysis, and managerial billets far outnumber these others, but the advancement ladder remains unchanged.

6. John K. Walker, Jr., quoted in "General Session V: Professional Ethics and Standards, Military Operations Research Symposium 27," in *Proceedings of the 27th MORS* (Arlington, Va.: Military Operations Research Society, 1971), p. 1 (hereafter cited as *Proceedings*).

7. See William Kornhauser, *Scientists in Industry: Conflict and Accommodation* (Berkeley and Los Angeles: University of California Press, 1952).

8. Warren O. Hagstrom, *The Scientific Community* (New York: Basic Books, 1965).

9. Hilbert F. Aiden, *The Influence and Development of English Gilds* (Cambridge: Cambridge University Press, 1891), places the issue in proper historical perspective; Robert T. Holt and John E. Turner, "The Scholar as Artisan," *Policy Sciences* 5, no. 3 (September 1974) : 257–270, bring us up to date.

10. D. Lloyd, "The Disciplinary Powers of Professional Bodies," *Modern Law Review* 13 (1950) : 281–306.

11. David Allison, *The R & D Game: Technical Men, Technical Managers, and Research Productivity* (Cambridge, Mass.: M.I.T. Press, 1969).

12. Bernie Rosenman, "Remembrance of Stings Past," *Phalanx* 10, no. 2 (June 1975) : 7.

13. Ibid.

14. Ibid.

15. Ibid.

16. Ibid.

17. John K. Walker makes this important recommendation in *Proceedings*, pp. 4–5.

18. A rare and forthright example of what we have in mind is contained in T. A. Brown and E. W. Paxson, *A Retrospective Look at Some Strategy and Force Evaluation Games* (Santa Monica, Calif.: The Rand Corporation, R-1619-PR, September 1975).

19. The concept of expanded and affected publics is treated in Norman Storer, *The Social System of Science* (New York: Holt, Rinehart, and Winston, 1966). See also Joseph Haberer, *Politics and the Community in Science* (New York: Van Nostrand, 1969).

20. Martin Shubik, Garry D. Brewer, and E. Savage, *The Literature of Gaming, Simulation, and Model-Building: Index and Critical Abstracts* (Santa Monica, Calif.: The Rand Corporation, R-620-ARPA, June 1972).

21. Harold D. Lasswell, "Towards a Continuing Appraisal of the Impact of Law on Society," *Rutgers Law Review* 21, no. 4 (Summer 1967) : 645.

22. National Academy of Sciences, *Technology: Processes of As-*

sessment and Choice (Washington, D.C.: Government Printing Office, 1969), pp. 26–28.

23. In "Freedom and Tyranny in a Technological Society," mimeographed (La Jolla: University of California, Department of Sociology, n.d.), Jack D. Douglas states that "this conspiratorial silence of experts can literally go on for decades before men not captured by the expert category reopen the whole issue and point out what should have been obvious" (p. 35).

24. Robert P. Bush and Frederick Mosteller, "A Comparison of Eight Models," in Readings in Mathematical Social Science, ed. Paul Lazarsfeld and Neil W. Henry (Chicago: Science Research Associates, 1966), p. 335.

25. Harold D. Lasswell, "The Political Science of Science," American Political Science Review 50, no. 4 (December 1956) : 978.

26. Robert A. Dahl and Charles E. Lindblom, Politics, Economics, and Welfare (New York: Harper, 1953), pp. 77–78.

27. The phrase was coined by Max F. Millikan in "Inquiry and Policy: The Relation of Knowledge to Action," in The Human Meaning of the Social Sciences, ed. Daniel Lerner (New York: Meridian Books, 1959), pp. 172–173.

28. Robert K. Merton, "The Role of Applied Social Science in the Formation of Policy: A Research Memorandum," Philosophy of Science 16 (July 1949) : 161.

29. This point of view is well argued in J. P. Mayberry, "Principles for Assessment of Simulation Model Validity," in Symposium on Computer Simulation as Related to Manpower and Personnel Planning, ed. A. I. Siegel (Washington, D.C.. U.S. Naval Personnel Research & Development Laboratory, July 1971), pp. 157–165.

30. See, for example, Ida R. Hoos, Systems Analysis in Public Policy (Berkeley and Los Angeles: University of California Press, 1972).

31. See Garry D. Brewer, "On Innovation, Social Change and Reality," Technological Forecasting and Social Change 5, no. 1 (1973) : 19–24.

32. Operations Research 19 (September 1971) : 1127–31; Proceedings.

33. U.S., General Accounting Office, Case Studies of Auditing in a Computer-Based Systems Environment (Washington, D.C.: Government Printing Office, 1971), p. i (hereafter cited as GAO, Case Studies).

34. Idem, Advantages and Limitations of Computer Simulation in Decisionmaking (Washington, D.C.: Government Printing Office, 1973), p. 3 (hereafter cited as GAO, Advantages and Limitations).

35. Ibid.

36. Idem, *Improvement*, p. 13.

37. Gary Fromm et al., *Federally Supported Mathematical Models*, p. 24.

38. U.S., General Accounting Office, *Ways to Improve Management of Federally Funded Computerized Models* (Washington, D.C.: Government Printing Office, 1976), pp. i–ii.

39. Idem, *Advantages and Limitations*, p. 43.

18. Improving Stewardship

1. See William Alonso, "The Quality of Data and the Choice and Design of Predictive Models," in *Urban Development Models*, ed. G. C. Hemmens, special report no. 197 (Washington, D.C.: Highway Research Board, 1968), pp. 178–192.

2. See Mayberry, "Principles," pp. 157–165.

3. Discussions between George Rathjens and Albert Wohlstetter on the proposed Safeguard antiballistic-missile system before the United States Senate illustrate the benefits that result when both sides of a question are technically competent and informed with comparable data. The entire issue of *Operations Research* 19 (September 1971) is devoted to their intelligent debate.

4. The problem is not new. During World War II, considerable effort and vast resources were expended on the basis of untested presumptions about the relative effectiveness of various types of conventional ordnance. Until Sir Solly Zuckerman took on the task, no one bothered to communicate the need for basic information to those most likely either to know or to be able to find it out. See Solly Zuckerman, "Judgment and Control in Modern Warfare," *Foreign Affairs* 40, no. 2 (January 1962) : 196–212. The problem persists; see Tyrus G. Fain, in collaboration with Katharine C. Plant and Ross Milloy, eds., *The Intelligence Community: History, Organization, and Issues* (New York: Bowker, 1977), pp. 321–322.

5. Pertinent comments on this and closely related issues are found in Alice Robbin, "Managing Information Access through Documentation of the Data Bases," *SIGSOC Bulletin* 6 (1974) : 56–68, 74–75.

6. See GAO, *Case Studies*, p. i; idem, *Improvement*, p. 13.

7. Gary Fromm et al., *Federally Supported Mathematical Models*, p. 24; "excellence" is defined here as occurring when "the documentation can be understood and the model used with a minimum of long-distance telephone calls."

8. Thinking about what might constitute a full-scale documentation effort is still in a preliminary and primitive state. See Garry D. Brewer, "Documentation: An Overview and Design Strategy," *Simulation & Games* 7, no. 3 (September 1976) : 261–280, for some initial thoughts on the matter.

9. There may be some exceptions, such as highly confidential studies, but their lack of documentation needs to be defended on an ad hoc basis by the authors.

10. J. A. Stockfisch contributed this idea in an unpublished, internal Rand Corporation memorandum in 1977.

11. This issue is discussed at length in Garry D. Brewer, *Politicians, Bureaucrats and the Consultant: A Critique of Urban Problem-Solving* (New York: Basic Books, 1973), chaps. 6, 11, 12.

19. Improving Performance

1. John R. Aker and John W. Anderson, "Operations Research in the Warsaw Pact Accord Forces," *Proceedings, Thirteenth Annual U.S. Army Operations Research Symposium* (Ft. Lee, Va: U.S. Army Logistics Group, 1974), pp. 68–72; Wade B. Holland, ed., *Soviet Cybernetic Review* (Santa Monica, Calif.: The Rand Corporation, R-700/1–R-700/7, February 1971–May 1972).

2. For example, in a much publicized account found in a prestigious journal, key findings of the analysis are found to depend entirely on the operation of a computer model; however, nothing whatsoever is offered the reader about the model, the data, the procedures used, or much else that would help him assess the validity of the strong policy claims being made; see Paul Nitze, "Assuring Strategic Stability in an Era of Detente," *Foreign Affairs* 54, no. 4 (July 1976) : 207–232. "Trust me because I know best" is a totally insufficient justification for this kind of work.

3. Both Stockfisch, *Models, Data and War,* and idem, *Incentives and Information Quality in Defense Management* (Santa Monica, Calif.: The Rand Corporation, R-1827-ARPA, 1976), qualify as essential reading for anyone concerned about these general issues.

4. Dr. John Koehler, Assistant Director for National Security and International Affairs, Congressional Budget Office, interview, February 23, 1977.

5. Army Models Review Committee, *Review of Selected Army Models.*

6. Indeed, two pioneering attempts by the Department of Housing and Urban Development have been appraised and found wanting in many of the same ways as the MSGs discussed here; the problems are apparently common. See Brewer, *Politicians, Bureaucrats.*

7. This is not to say that the sums involved are inconsequential. See Gary Fromm et al., *Federally Supported Mathematical Models.*

8. GAO, *Case Studies;* idem, *High Turnover of Managers Directing Major Research and Development Projects* (Washington, D.C.: Government Printing Office, 1970). Some progress has been made by the General Accounting Office in selecting and promoting

auditors with more than just accounting and legal skills and competencies; however, the gap in technical skills between auditors and model builders is still formidable.

9. This is not a self-evidently simple task, as R. L. Chapman stresses in "Congress and Science Policy: The Organizational Dilemma," *Bulletin of Atomic Scientists* 25, no. 3 (March 1969) : 4–7, 28.

10. The entire issue of *The Public Interest* 41 (Fall 1975) is devoted to this topic. Of particular relevance to our discussion is Daniel P. Moynihan, "The American Experiment"; Moynihan writes, "Neither liberty nor democracy would seem to be prospering—or in any event, neither would seem to have a future nearly as auspicious as their past" (p. 5). The idea of including citizens in policy decisions is contained in Richard C. Snyder, Charles F. Hermann, and Harold D. Lasswell, *A Global Monitoring System: Appraisal of the Effects of Government on Human Dignity* (Columbus, Ohio: The Mershon Center, Informal Publication Series, 1976); a parallel proposal was recently formulated in Boris Pregel, Harold D. Lasswell, and John McHale, *Environment and Society in Transition: World Priorities* (New York: World Academy of Art and Science, 1975).

11. Too long left in ignorance, the public appears to have become distrustful of technological developments over which it has little or no control. See Todd R. La Porte and Daniel Metlay, *They Watch and Wonder: Public Attitudes toward Advanced Technology* (Berkeley, Calif.: University of California, Institute of Governmental Studies, 1975); Thomas Parke Hughes, *Changing Attitudes toward American Technology* (New York: Harper & Row, 1975). Sir Geoffrey Vickers goes directly to the heart of the matter and traces out the implications of the costs of ignoring citizen views in making policy in *Freedom in a Rocking Boat: Changing Values in an Unstable Society* (New York: Basic Books, 1971).

12. Proponents of this idea include James Carroll, "Participatory Technology," *Science* 171, no. 3972 (February 1971) : 647–653; Frank von Hippel and Joel Primack, *Science, Advocacy in Technology Assessment,* staff paper no. 209 (Washington, D.C.: George Washington University, Program of Policy Studies in Science and Technology, n.d.). See also Chandler Stevens, "Citizen Feedback and Societal Systems," *Technology Review* 73, no. 3 (January 1971) : 38–45; T. B. Sheridan, "Citizen Feedback: New Technology for Social Change," ibid., pp. 46–51. Ominous predictions of what might happen if information continues to be withheld from the public have been formulated by Jack D. Douglas, ed., *The Technological Threat* (Englewood Cliffs, N.J.: Prentice-Hall, 1971); Eugene S. Schwartz, *Overskill: The Decline of Technology in Modern Civilization* (Chicago: Quadrangle, 1971).

Appendix A. The Evaluation of Models, Simulations, and Games

1. Army Models Review Committee, *Review of Selected Army Models.*

Appendix B. The Questionnaire

1. Gary Fromm et al., *Federally Supported Mathematical Models.*

2. Martin Shubik and Garry D. Brewer, *Models, Simulations and Games—A Survey* (Santa Monica, Calif.: The Rand Corporation, R-1060-ARPA/RC, May 1972).

Glossary

ABM. Air Battle Model, one of the first strategic inter-action models, created at The Rand Corporation and later transferred to the United States Air Force's Air Battle Division; also, antiballistic missile.

ACDA. United States Arms Control and Disarmament Agency, a division of the United States Department of State.

ACWS. Alternative Central War Strategy, a topic considered beginning in 1961, using MSGs to determine different offensive and defensive strategies and forces in the European land mass.

AGGREGATION. A technical term used by model builders and analysts to describe the degree of refinement in an abstract representation of a complex real-world situation. Highly aggregated models consider primarily the main interactions of weapons systems and their relationships to the surrounding environment, without concern for details; highly disaggregated models consider the operating characteristics of military units as a function of the behavior of constituent parts.

ANALOG MODEL. A physical device that reproduces, in three dimensions, the relevant aspects of the actual system under investigation.

ANALYTIC GAME. A rigid-form, highly abstract, usually mathematical representation of a structure or process. Analytic games have an advantage in terms of parsimony, logic, and rigor over other types, such as man-machine and free-form or manual games.

ARPA.   Advanced Research Projects Agency of the Defense Department, responsible for a variety of defense-related problems and issues, including computer technology, information processing, weapons research, and social and behavioral research; now officially known as Defense Advanced Research Projects Agency.

ARPA/COIN.   Advanced Research Projects Agency Counterinsurgency game, used to study aspects of conflict in Vietnam and elsewhere.

BALFRAM.   Balanced   Force   Requirements   Analysis   Model.

BASELOGS.   A base logistics management game, designed at The Rand Corporation to examine the complex issues of maintaining air force bases throughout the world.

BOARD GAME.   One of the oldest game forms, in which a situation of opposition is represented on a board or map and all rules of play are either known beforehand or discovered in the course of play. Tokens of movement are frequently employed to represent resources or players.

BRANCHING GAME.   A free-form or man-machine game in which players' decisions, the reasons for them, and the consequences of alternative choices are studied.

BREAKING POINT.   The time at which sustained combat action ends or significant changes occur in the game situation.

BRIEFING.   Instructions given to participants, before a game begins, to familiarize them with its purposes, rules, and procedures; a summary presentation, often to higher-level officials, of key results and findings generated by a game or model.

CARMONETTE.   Computerized Monte Carlo Simulation of Ground Combat Operations, a series of land-combat models built at Research Analysis Corporation in 1958–1978.

CASCADE.   An air-operations simulation used by the United States Army's Strategy, Tactics and Analysis Group.

CBM. Corps Battle Model, developed by Research Analysis Corporation.

CLUG. Community Land Use Game, a board game designed at Cornell University and used in higher education to demonstrate the complexity of social and political factors in planning practice.

CNA. Center for Naval Analyses.

COMPUTER GAME. A game conducted totally within a computer program into which all structural elements and most assumptions have been built ahead of time; sometimes called computer simulation or machine simulation.

CONEX. Conflict Control Exercise, a series of games conducted at the Massachusetts Institute of Technology in 1969–1971.

COUNTER-AIR OPERATION. A military action undertaken against all of an enemy's air force resources.

CURRICULUM GAME. An educational game played at the United States Naval War College and used to train officers and others in tactics and strategy.

DATA VALIDATION. The use of procedures to ensure the appropriateness of raw empirical information used in an MSG.

DEBRIEFING. A postgame recapitulation of events and discoveries in a manual or man-machine game.

DELPHI. A forecasting technique that involves pooling group or expert opinions about future events and includes repeated polls to enhance convergence of opinion; developed at The Rand Corporation.

DETERMINISTIC MODEL. An MSG that does not directly treat random elements. Once the initial conditions are assigned, the model produces a unique output (contrasted with a probabilistic model, in which random elements are treated explicitly).

DIVOPS. Division Operations model, part of a family of land-combat models, devised at Research Analysis Corporation, in use since the mid-1950s.

DOCTRINAL EVALUATION. An assessment of the ability of any configuration of armed forces to support established military policy.

DOCTRINE. A set of rules and procedures that constitute an overall military policy.

DOCUMENTATION. The maintenance of MSG records, including project histories, cost and use data, technical processes and procedures used to construct and operate the model, and other necessary information.

FAST-VAL. Forward Air Strike Evaluation model, used to measure air-ground effects in a limited or tactical war; devised at The Rand Corporation.

FLEET GAME. A training and operational MSG used primarily by the United States Navy to test naval operations before full-scale fleet exercises.

FORCE-MIX COST MODEL. An MSG designed to determine the likely performance and outcome of differing numbers and configurations of armed forces and to find the most efficient and effective combination of forces before resources are committed to actual systems.

FRAM. Force Requirements Analysis Model.

FREE-FORM GAME. A scenario-based game in which opposing teams of human participants are confronted with a generally realistic situation or problem and work out responses both to the situation and to moves made by their opponents.

GAME THEORY. A mathematical theory devoted to the topics of conflict and cooperation. Game-theory models involve two or more players; gains and losses to each are specified, as in constant-sum games, zero-sum games, and non-zero-sum games.

GAO. United States General Accounting Office, the watchdog auditing and assessing arm of the United States Congress.

ICBM. Intercontinental ballistic missile.

JOSS. JOHNNIAC Open-Shop System, one of the first time-shared computer systems in the world, designed by John von Neumann and built at The Rand Corporation in 1950–1954.

JWGA. Joint War Gaming Agency, the official gaming agency of the United States Joint Chiefs of Staff, created in 1961; superseded in early 1970s by Studies, Analysis and Gaming Agency.

KRIEGSSPIEL. Literally, "war game" in German. The term reflects the origins of many modern games in eighteenth- and nineteenth-century Prussian practice.

LANCHESTER'S EQUATIONS. An abstract method of calculating losses, casualties, and winners in conflict situations by means of differential equations; devised by Frederick Lanchester, a turn-of-the-century English mathematician.

LEVEL OF RESOLUTION. A measure of the degree of detail considered within a model, usually expressed in temporal and spatial terms; may range from highly abstract to very fine-grained and from microseconds to periods in excess of years.

LEVIATHAN. A large-scale man-machine model developed at System Development Corporation in the 1960s and used for research and some operational purposes.

LSL. Logistics Systems Laboratory, a man-machine environment used at The Rand Corporation in the 1950s and 1960s to study problems of air force supply, maintenance, and transportation.

MAN-MACHINE GAME. A hybrid game employing a computer and human participants, the latter either as an integral component of the game or as an object of study.

MECH-WAR '77. A board game designed and sold by Simulation Publications, Inc., which incorporates many advances in modern weapons technology.

METRO. Michigan Effectuation Training, Research, and Operations urban-planning game, devised at the University of Michigan.

MISSLOGS. A game of missile logistics designed by The Rand Corporation to determine the support systems required for intercontinental ballistic-missile systems.

MODEL. A representation of an object or structure; an explanation or description of a system, process, or series of events.

MONOPOLOGS. A relatively simple, board-based game designed to explore the gross problems of a logistics-support system for modern weapons; the term is derived from *Monopoly* and *logistics*.

MONTE CARLO. Treating probabilistic or random elements within a model or game. The model is run many times from start to finish, but each time different values are introduced. The procedure helps to explain the effects of key random elements in actual situations.

MORS. Military Operations Research Society, a specialized professional association of military analysts, including builders and users of MSGs.

MSG. A label of convenience standing for model, simulation, or game.

MSP. Master Simulation Program, the basis of the Warfare Analysis and Research System used at the gaming facility of the United States Naval War College.

MULTISTAGE GAME. A game in which the solution is reached by steps, and results of previous game interactions help structure and determine later ones.

NBS. National Bureau of Standards, United States Department of Commerce.

NEWS. Navy Electronic Warfare Simulator, housed at the United States Naval War College and used for fleet and curriculum games.

NONCONSTANT-SUM GAME. A game-theory model in which total gains and losses may vary and society as a whole may gain or lose as a function of the outcome for individual players.

OMB. Office of Management and Budget, the budgetary arm of the executive branch of the United States government.

ON-LINE COMPUTER. A computer that is readily accessible, usually through a terminal or other remote device that allows the analyst to interact directly with models and data.

ONR. Office of Naval Research, the primary research arm of the United States Navy.

OPERATIONS RESEARCH. A profession with its practical and intellectual roots in the analysis of military problems, especially during World War II; now includes the study and analysis, usually quantitative, of a wide range of problems, both military and nonmilitary.

ORSA. The Operations Research Society of America, the largest and most general professional association the members of which are actively involved in the production of MSGs.

OTA. Office of Technology Assessment, the agency of the United States Congress responsible for forecasting and appraising technological developments.

PARAMETER. A fixed value or constraint that is estimated or assigned for a given MSG and then held constant for the whole run of the model or play of the game; may be varied from run to run to determine a range of possible outcomes (a procedure followed systematically in conducting a sensitivity analysis).

POLEX. Political-Military Exercise, a manual political, military, and diplomatic game, used for training and research purposes; conducted at the Massachusetts Institute of Technology in 1956–1974.

POSTURE. The size and composition of forces.

PRISONER'S DILEMMA GAME. A two-person game-theory representation in which the payoff for teams that pursue apparently individually rational courses is worse than expected; emphasizes the need for communication and cooperation in many social settings.

PROGRAM MANAGER. An official responsible for a group of

related projects, usually associated with a major weapons system.

PROJECT MANAGER. An official responsible for a specific program element in a defense system; subordinate to a program manager.

RAC. Research Analysis Corporation.

REDWOOD. A series of map-based gaming exercises developed at The Rand Corporation to study the effects of limited war, derived from the early SIERRA series; the name is a play on its predecessor.

RICHARDSON EQUATIONS. A set of mathematical equations used to represent the dynamics of escalation, as in arms races; devised by Lewis Richardson, an English mathematician.

SAFE. Strategy and Force Evaluation game, operated in 1961–1962 at The Rand Corporation.

SAGA. Studies, Analysis and Gaming Agency of the Joint Chiefs of Staff, United States Department of Defense, a major developer and user of all varieties of MSG.

SCENARIO. An account, usually written, of a context or situation created for use in a war game, a political and military exercise, or the analysis of a weapons system, strategy, or problem in a specific setting. The term is appropriated from the film industry.

SDC. System Development Corporation.

SEARCH PROBLEM. A topic explored by mathematical models related to game theory; concerns the optimal allocation of resources in order to find and overcome an enemy force; often related to submarine and air operations.

SENSITIVITY ANALYSIS. A technique by which a model's structure is held constant while its parameters or input are systematically varied to test its performance and determine the range of its possible outcomes.

SIERRA. A series of map-based exercises conducted at The Rand Corporation to study aspects of limited war; labeled according to the letter S in the military phonetic alphabet.

SINAI. A board game developed and sold by Simulation Publications, Inc.; based to a large extent on actual combat operations in the 1967 war between Egypt and Israel.

SRL. Systems Research Laboratory, a man-machine environment built at The Rand Corporation in the 1950s to study human factors and other questions; used to study human factors by System Development Corporation in the early and mid-1960s.

STAG. Strategy, Tactics and Analysis Group, United States Army.

STOCHASTIC MODEL. A model in which chance is directly represented in terms of probabilistic functions and relied on in the play itself. Repetition of a stochastic game produces a distribution of possible outcomes, which may themselves become the object of more intense investigation.

STRAP. Strategic Actions Planner, a model devised at The Rand Corporation and intended to explore high-level interactions and options in nuclear war.

STRATEGIC GAME. A game used to examine a full range of military and social issues with respect to a nation's overall military policy.

STRIP. Strategic Intermediate Planner model, one of a family of related models of large-scale nuclear warfare devised at The Rand Corporation.

STROP. Strategic Optimizing Routine, one of family of related models of strategic nuclear conflict, including potential action options, devised at The Rand Corporation.

SUBDUEL. A submarine tactical-simulation model used by the Center for Naval Analyses and others to determine the likely effects and outcome of submarine interaction.

SUBMODEL. A constituent part of a model or game or computer program, usually with reasonably well defined purposes; may be reused, depending on the processing of the main model, many times in the play of a game or run of a simulation.

SWAP. Strategic War Planning game, devised and used at The Rand Corporation.

TACTICAL GAME. A game meant to help players understand and test the maneuvering of forces in battle; often emphasizes performance characteristics of individual units or elements of a military force.

TAFCOM. Tactical Fighter Combat Operation, a model devised at The Rand Corporation to study the interaction of air and ground forces in several different conflict settings.

TAGS. Tactical Air-Ground Study, a map-based game designed to explore the use of air forces in land warfare.

TBM-68. Theater Battle Model (1968), a land-combat model used at Research Analysis Corporation.

TEMPER. Technological, Economic, Military, and Political Evaluation Routine, created at the Raytheon Corporation for the Joint War Gaming Agency to determine causes and consequences of strategic warfare throughout the world.

TIMS. The Institute of Management Sciences, a professional association concerned with setting and maintaining standards, certification, and sanctions.

TIN SOLDIER. One of the original land-combat models devised by Research Analysis Corporation.

TOTEM. Theater Operations Tactical Evaluation Model, developed by The Rand Corporation to study the operations of air and ground forces in a range of European conflict settings.

TRANSFERABILITY. The ability of a model or game to be used by others than those directly responsible for its initial development, operation, and use.

UTILITY ANALYSIS. Assessment of the uses made of a model or game; concerned with questions such as how many times the model was used, by whom, at what cost, and with what results.

VALIDATION. The use of accepted scientific standards to assess the faithfulness, utility, and rigor of a game or model, usually by cross-checks with independently derived empirical information; also, the various technical tests of a model.

VECTOR. A series of MSGs constructed by Vector Research, Inc., to study land combat for the United States Army.

WARS. Warfare Analysis and Research System, a large-scale, computer-based naval-gaming system housed at the United States Naval War College.

WEAPONS PLATFORM. A term used to describe a vehicle, vessel, or aircraft, including all of its associated weapon systems.

XRAY. A force-planning and cost model developed at The Rand Corporation; uses a man-machine and time-shared computer-support system in which players from many different locations interact simultaneously.

ZERO-SUM GAME. A game-theory game in which the losses of one side are directly computed as the gains for the other.

Index